Rule of Law in India

Rule of Law in India

A Quest for Reason

Harish Narasappa

OXFORD

UNIVERSITY PRESS

OXFORD
UNIVERSITY PRESS

Oxford University Press is a department of the University of Oxford.
It furthers the University's objective of excellence in research, scholarship,
and education by publishing worldwide. Oxford is a registered trademark of
Oxford University Press in the UK and in certain other countries.

Published in India by
Oxford University Press
2/11 Ground Floor, Ansari Road, Daryaganj, New Delhi 110 002, India

ISBN-13 (print edition): 978-0-19-948466-9
ISBN-10 (print edition): 0-19-948466-X

ISBN-13 (eBook): 978-0-19-909205-5
ISBN-10 (eBook): 0-19-909205-2

Typeset in Arno Pro 11/13
by Tranistics Data Technologies, New Delhi 110 044
Printed in India by Replika Press Pvt. Ltd

To

Gowramma and Narasappa

For setting me on the quest for reason

CONTENTS

TABLES AND FIGURES

TABLES

FIGURES

STATUTES

A. CONSTITUTIONAL AMENDMENTS

1. Constitution (First Amendment) Act, 1951
2. Constitution (Forty-second Amendment) Act, 1976
3. Constitution (Forty-fourth Amendment) Act, 1978
4. Constitution (Fifty-second Amendment) Act, 1985
5. Constitution (Seventy-third Amendment) Act, 1992
6. Constitution (Seventy-fourth Amendment) Act, 1992
7. Constitution (Seventy-seventh Amendment) Act, 1995
8. Constitution (Eighty-first Amendment) Act, 2000
9. Constitution (Eighty-third Amendment) Act, 2000
10. Constitution (Eighty-fourth Amendment) Act, 2002
11. Constitution (Eighty-fifth Amendment) Act, 2001
12. Constitution (Eighty-sixth Amendment) Act, 2002
13. Constitution (Ninety-third Amendment) Act, 2005
14. Constitution (Ninety-fifth Amendment) Act, 2009
15. Constitution (Ninety-ninth Amendment) Act, 2014

B. ACTS

1. Andhra Pradesh Preventive Detention Act, 1970 (Act No. 1 of 1970)
2. Andhra Pradesh Suppression of Disturbances Act, 1967 (Act No. 3 of 1948)
3. Armed Forces (Special Powers) Act, 1958 (Act No. 28 of 1958)
4. Code of Civil Procedure, 1908 (Act No. 5 of 1908)

CASES

ACKNOWLEDGEMENTS

The thoughts and arguments presented in this book have developed over the years and, inevitably, many people have contributed to their germination, growth, and strengthening. Teachers, friends, and students at the National Law School of India University, where I spent time as a student and as a visiting teacher, have played an important role in the journey of these ideas. V. Vijayakumar (also my guide for the PhD thesis which was converted into this book with few modifications), T. Devidas, M.P. Padmanabha Pillai, S.V. Joga Rao, N.S. Gopalakrishnan, V.S. Mallar, and N.R. Madhava Menon have all greatly contributed to the development of my understanding of the law and the reasoning behind it. The arguments and discussions in the classroom during my undergraduate years, and later when I taught a few seminar courses, have enabled the development of many arguments in this book and I am thankful to my teachers, classmates, and students.

My friends from Oxford—Ritin Rai, Lavanya Rajamani, Gaurav Pachnanda, Kamakshya Trivedi, and Harold Brunink—will find that many of our dinner discussions have found their way into this book.

Teachers, colleagues, and friends in the practice of law—Raju Ramachandran, S.S. Naganand, Patrick Mitchell, M.V. Sundararaman, S. Sriranga, Poornima Hatti, and Vineetha M.G.—have all contributed to my understanding of the legal system in action. Colleagues and friends from civil society organizations and movements, particularly those who have worked and interacted with DAKSH, have had an invaluable impact on my understanding of the rule of law and the problems it faces from a citizen's perspective. In particular, Kishore Mandyam, Ashwin Mahesh, A.R. Vasavi, C.V. Madhukar, and Trilochan Sastry have enriched my understanding and operation of the rule of law.

Many friends have supported my activities with words of encouragement and support over the years that this book has developed. V.S. Elizabeth, the teacher who engaged with me as a friend; Ashish Ahuja; L. Viswanathan; Jigar Shah; Late Vikram Singh; Tejal Patil; Prashanth Sabeshan; R.V. Anuradha; Roopa Prasad Doraswamy; S.A. Karthik; N.S. Nigam; Ravitej Rao; Rajan Subberwal; Siddharth Raja; M.V. Rajeev Gowda; Jayanta Ray; Bhaswar and Bipasha Chatterjee; and Chandan Gowda have all liberally spared time to discuss, encourage and support different decisions that have ultimately contributed to this book.

Shruti Vidyasagar, my partner in life, not only constantly checked on the book's progress but was also kind enough to read a complete draft of the book and suggest changes. M. Ganganna, my grandfather, and K. Narasanna, my uncle, continue to be bundles of energy and have inspired me to be productive each day.

Kavya Murthy read the first draft and made many useful suggestions. Two anonymous reviewers spared time to read and give critical pointers that improved the book. Priyadarshini S., provided word processing assistance in preparing the manuscript. The team at Oxford University Press made several suggestions which improved the book.

ABBREVIATIONS

ADR	Association for Democratic Reforms
AFSPA	Armed Forces (Special Powers) Act, 1958
DRSCs	Department Related Standing Committees
FEMA	Foreign Exchange Management Act, 1999
MP	Member of Parliament
NDPSA	Narcotic Drugs and Psychotropic Substances Act, 1985
PRS	Parliamentary Research Service
POTA	Prevention of Terrorism Act, 2002
RBI	Reserve Bank of India
RTI	Right to Information Act, 2005
TADA	Terrorist and Disruptive Activities (Prevention) Act, 1985
WJP	World Justice Project

INTRODUCTION

The adoption of the Constitution on 26 November 1949 and the establishment of the Republic on 26 January 1950 marked a break from the nearly 200 years of colonial rule for Indians. Independence was achieved in 1947 and it had taken another two years for the Constituent Assembly to finalize the text of the Constitution. The adoption of the Constitution and the consequent formation of the Republic is the most disruptive event in Indian history. Four revolutionary factors determine this conclusion: First, India became a democratic country with universal adult suffrage. Second, equality, irrespective of caste, religion, and origin was guaranteed for all Indians. Third, a bouquet of fundamental rights was adopted as part of the Constitution. Fourth, the rule of law was to prevail in the country.[1]

Never before in India's history had its people enjoyed such rights. These rights and values enshrined in the Constitution were to form the basis of India's independent journey towards an egalitarian society with great speed and wipe out the inequalities perpetrated for centuries. The difficulties faced by the state in implementing the constitutional values were immense and appeared to be insurmountable at the time of adoption of the Constitution, prompting many to predict that

---

[1] A reading of the Constitution clearly reveals these four factors. The preamble to the Constitution, Chapter II of Part V, Chapter III of Part VI, Part IX, and Part IX-A are the significant provisions relating to democracy. The preamble and Part III of the Constitution contain the right to equality and other fundamental rights. The rule of law while not explicitly mentioned in the text of the Constitution is the spirit that runs through the text of the Constitution. These factors are discussed in greater detail in Chapter 2 of this volume.

the independent democratic experiment in India, together with its Constitution, was doomed to fail fairly quickly. However, India has survived as a country without appearing, on the surface, to have compromised too many of its fundamental constitutional values.[2]

CHALLENGES TO CONSTITUTIONAL VALUES

A brief analysis of the status of the four revolutionary factors since 1950 will give us an indication of the various challenges to the Constitution and constitutionalism in independent India.

Democracy

Except for a brief interlude during the internal emergency declared by Indira Gandhi in 1975, India has remained a democratic country. Elections are held regularly, a fairly healthy percentage of people continue to vote in elections, people from nearly all backgrounds contest in elections, there has been a peaceful transfer of power after each election, and there is really no obvious threat to the democratic mode of government itself. However, there are serious problems in the functioning of elected bodies across the country. The efficacy of the legislature in making law and policy and in holding the executive accountable has diminished over time. The legislature has been reduced to an appendage of a powerful political executive. This ineffectiveness of the legislature challenges the requirement of participation and consensus in lawmaking by people and their representatives. More worryingly, political parties, who constitute the primary mechanism through which people participate in democracy, function on the assumption that they are above the law, thereby posing a fundamental threat to the idea of rule of law. For example, political parties have consistently refused to make their functioning and financing transparent.[3]

[2] R. Guha, *India after Gandhi: The History of the World's Largest Democracy* (London: Picador, 2007), pp. xvi–xvii.

[3] The Association for Democratic Reforms has carried out a detailed analysis of political party funding and expenditure. The reports are available at http://adrindia.org/research-and-report/political-party-watch (accessed 26 March 2015).

Equality

The declaration of equality of all people in the Constitution was only the beginning of a promised revolution for most people in the country. Both the theoretical discourse on equality in India and the debates (political, social, and judicial) around its implementation reflect that it is not only a widely accepted right but an equally contested one. The contest primarily relates to the distribution of economic and social resources by the state to different groups, based on religion and caste. While there has been no real challenge to equality as a desirable value which has to be sustained, the contest is about its content and who is more unequal and therefore needs a 'more' equal treatment by the state. Consequently, much importance is given by political and social actors to the 'backwardness' of different groups based on caste, and religious and economic considerations. Demands for declaring certain groups as backward are made on a frequent basis and form the bedrock of many electoral battles. In particular, reservations in jobs and in the admission process to educational institutions for religious minorities and backward classes have generated much political debate and inevitably, persistent legal challenges have been mounted. Despite many rulings by the Supreme Court,[4] the issue of reservations continues to be a contested one, both politically and legally, indirectly raising questions about equality itself.

The reading of the requirement by the judiciary, that all state action has to be reasonable to satisfy the equality promise, has meant that there is regular challenge to various actions of state functionaries, small and big, on the ground of arbitrariness. This however has not reduced the feeling that the state acts with impunity, more akin to an oligarchy rather than an elected government merely exercising administrative powers on behalf of the people.

Fundamental Rights

On paper, fundamental rights have been respected by the state. The judiciary has generally protected fundamental rights, except during

---

[4] The issue of reservations has been dealt with by the Court in many cases starting from *State of Madras* v *Champakam Dorairajan* AIR 1951 SC 226. The latest in the line of many judgments by the Supreme Court are *Indra Sawhney* v *Union of India* (1992) Supp. (3) SCC 217 and *Ashok Kumar Thakur* v *Union of India* (2008) 6 SCC 1.

the internal emergency when it refused to come to the aid of the citizens whose civil and political liberties were suspended by the state. However, the gulf between the rights enshrined in the Constitution and their implementation, particularly political and civil liberties, is immense and has today assumed proportions that cannot be bridged without serious effort. The state, particularly the executive, has failed to internalize respect for such liberties, partly because of a tendency to abuse power vested in it, and partly motivated by a paternalistic attitude arising from the primary role it plays in society even today. Despite the judiciary having repeatedly declared the content of political and civil liberties, the executive, particularly the political executive and the police, regularly violates these liberties and justifies its actions, inter alia, on the basis of an imagined public interest or morality. Redressal of these violations is difficult because of an oppressively slow judicial process and the reluctance of the judiciary in ensuring compliance with its orders. An example that shocks our conscience is the continued incarceration of undertrials in many jails across the country despite orders by the Supreme Court.[5]

Rule of Law

The status of the rule of law in India is a befuddling conundrum. It is important to understand that the efficacy or otherwise of the rule of law affects, and is affected by, the other three revolutionary factors that we discussed earlier. The rule of law in India is a unique concept for many reasons. The Constitution expressly includes certain substantive social and economic goals and mandates the state to achieve those goals, giving the state a primary role in society. It also envisages equality not as an empty positivist attribute, but as a substantive concept that includes social and economic equality. Upendra Baxi observes, 'The Indian ROL

---

[5] In 2013, a study showed that more than 75 per cent of the prisoners in India are undertrials. A. Behar, Y. Kumar, and J. Samuel (eds), *Citizens' Report on Governance and Development, 2013* (National Social Watch, 2013), p. 102, available at http://socialwatchindia.net/images/documents/498/CRGD-2013_Full-Report.pdf (accessed 10 April 2015). Given that the conviction rate in India is very low the long incarceration of undertrials is in itself a violation of their rights.

[rule of law] stands here normatively conceived not just as a *sword* against State domination and violation and historic civil society norms and practices but also as a *shield* empowering an encyclopaedic regime of "progressive" state intervention in the life of civil society.[6]

This dual nature makes it impossible to categorize the Indian rule of law into the straitjacket of Western theoretical expositions. However, apart from the limited and isolated efforts of Baxi, no serious effort has been made by Indian academia to understand and provide a theoretical basis to the rule of law.[7]

Despite the lack of theoretical backing, the usefulness or acceptance of the rule of law has never been contested. A review of judgments by various courts and the processes that India's other governing institutions follow will lead us into believing that the law reigns supreme in the country. It is however in the implementation of the rule of law that the lacunae are revealed. An analysis of the functioning of the institutions that deal with the making and implementation of law reveals predominantly a 'rule by law', and at times a 'rule by whim', attitude and approach across all institutions of governance. Three scholarly works reveal this serious flaw in the rule of law apparatus. Upendra Baxi's classic *The Crisis of the Indian Legal System* provides an insight into the mechanics of the legal system's functioning and leaves us in no doubt that there is a serious threat to the rule of law.[8] If Baxi's work is a classical dissection of the functioning of the legal system, Kannabiran's *The Wages of Impunity* systematically analyses the pathologies of the legal system and points out a near total lack of rule of law across the legal system.[9] Granville Austin's *Working a Democratic Constitution* is a more benign work than

---

[6] U. Baxi, 'Rule of Law in India', *Sur, Revista Internacional de Direitos Humanos*, vol. 4, no. 6 (2007), available at http://hcraj.nic.in/joc2014/6.pdf (accessed 11 February 2015).

[7] A few lecture series and symposia have taken place where the rule of law in India has been discussed without much theoretical basis. One of the better lecture series that has been published is N.R.M. Menon (ed.), *Rule of Law in a Free Society* (New Delhi: Oxford University Press, 2008).

[8] U. Baxi, *The Crisis of the Indian Legal System* (New Delhi: Vikas Publishing, 1982).

[9] K.G. Kannabiran, *The Wages of Impunity* (Hyderabad: Orient Longman, 2004).

that of Baxi or Kannabiran, but still highlights the failure to implement constitutional values and the institutional drawbacks that underpin such failure.[10] Apart from these three classical works, many historians, political scientists, and sociologists have carried out empirical research which reveals that the rule of law is not a quality that characterizes the functioning of the state and its machinery.[11]

It is these contradictions that not only necessitate an examination of the rule of law in India, but also make it challenging and exciting. A study of the rule of law is not only a study of the country's legal and political system, but also a study about society as a whole. Ronald Dworkin insightfully observes, '[W]e take an interest in law not only because we use it for our own purposes, selfish or noble, but because law is our most structured and revealing social institution. If we understand the nature of our legal argument better, we know what kind of people we are.'[12]

This book makes an attempt to study how India is socially, politically, and legally organized; its governing institutions; and the behaviour of its people in their social and political interactions.

A PERMANENT DICHOTOMY

Since the adoption of the Constitution, India has been in a state of a near permanent dichotomy. On the one hand, institutions and laws required for the proper functioning of the country in accordance with the rule of law exist on paper, more or less in accordance with the constitutional mandate. On the other hand, most of these governing institutions do not function properly and lack the processes, systems, values, and people to function efficiently, and more importantly, in accordance with law.

This dichotomy indicates severe problems at the very core of India's governance superstructure:

[10] G. Austin, *Working a Democratic Constitution: The Indian Experience* (New Delhi: Oxford University Press, 1999).

[11] Two important works in this context are A. Shourie, *Courts and Their Judgments* (New Delhi: Rupa, 2001) and S.K. Mitra, *The Puzzle of India's Governance: Culture, Context and Comparative Theory* (Oxford: Routledge, 2006).

[12] R. Dworkin, *Law's Empire* (London: Fontana Press, 1991), p. 11.

1. in its principal democratic institutions—Parliament and legislatures—along with the political parties;
2. in its commitment to its constitutional values and the objectives driving those values;
3. in its resolve to ensure effective performance of the institutions that support and protect democratic and constitutional values, mainly the judiciary; and
4. in the social and political acceptance of the law.

While the problems are numerous, diverse, and often related to the quality of people responsible for the functioning of the institutions, there is also a common underlying reason—a fundamental failure to adhere to agreed norms of functioning, that is, the law. This failure challenges the rule of law, which has been declared to be part of the basic structure of the Constitution by the Supreme Court.[13] Interestingly, as discussed earlier, the rule of law appears to be universally accepted in Indian society as a good value.[14] Judges, politicians (both in power and outside), bureaucrats, businessmen (domestic and foreign), lawyers, and citizens all quote the rule of law regularly and extol its virtues. There is, in fact, no dissenting voice in India on the need to follow the rule of law. Often, people opposing each other rely on the rule of law to justify their actions and decry the actions of the opposing group.[15]

Despite being used in political and legal discourse regularly, there has been no effort by anyone in India to identify the meaning and contours of the rule of law. Indeed, there has been no meaningful debate about the rule of law by academics or practitioners. No scholar or practitioner has undertaken a serious study of the rule of law in India. The little scholarship that is available is in the form of short articles or lectures,

---

[13] *Kesavananda Bharati* v *State of Kerala* AIR 1973 SC 1461; *Sub-Committee on Judicial Accountability* v *Union of India* (1991) 4 SCC 699; *Indira Gandhi* v *Raj Narain* (1975) Supp. SCC 1.

[14] It is probably more accurate to say that nobody has questioned the relevance of the rule of law or its desirability.

[15] The use of the concept by opposing parties is not surprising given the amorphous nature of the rule of law. This contradiction in practice is one of the critical challenges even to theoretical discussions of the rule of law. A more detailed discussion is set out in Chapter 1.

which, by their very nature, do not provide a deep and meaningful analysis or a theoretical construct of the rule of law in India. There is no critical examination of the relevance of Western thought—which is vast, contradictory, and focused on the prevalent governance structures in that part of the world. The judiciary has used the rule of law as a convenient theoretical construct to provide justification for various reasons and conclusions in different judgments. It is clear, however, from various judgments that there is an unquestioned acceptance of the rule of law as a value that underpins many other precepts and values of the Constitution, without completely delineating the contours of the rule of law.

THEORETICAL FOUNDATIONS OF THE RULE OF LAW

Theoretically, the rule of law is an elusive concept, deeply contested by philosophers, political scientists, economists, judges, and lawyers. At no point of time have the meaning and contours of the rule of law been agreed upon, even by people who swear by its goodness. While the rule of law has been propagated in some form or the other from the times of Aristotle and Plato, it has not had a continuous and uncontested run. Nearly all rule of law postulations have originated in some form of political theory, making the rule of law primarily a political concept rather than a legal one. The meaning and content of the rule of law is also fiercely debated. Some view the rule of law as a concept that is only different from that of the 'rule of men', others debate between the rule of law and the 'rule by law'. Some strongly believe that the rule of law should not influence or make any comment about the content of the law and is only concerned about compliance with the law; others believe the content of the law is very important for the rule of law.

Among those who agree that the content of the law is indeed important for the rule of law, some feel it should only contain negative human rights, while others feel the law should deal with social, economic, cultural and educational conditions under which a man can fully realize his aspirations. Many believe the process of making the law is also important to the rule of law and therefore insist that democracy is an important component, while others believe democracy is irrelevant and the rule of law can healthily thrive even in an authoritarian state.

Tamanaha has summarized the history, evolution, theoretical foundations, and the current status of the rule of law.[16] The most common form of classifying the rule of law theories is to divide them into thin and thick theories. Thin or formalist theories do not concern themselves with the content of the law, instead they are focused on the procedural attributes that a legal system must have to comply with the rule of law. The most important of these procedural attributes are: (i) the law must be declared in advance; (ii) all laws must apply only prospectively; and (iii) the laws must be certain and apply to everyone generally and equally. Thick or substantive theories go beyond the thin theories and insist that the laws should contain certain substantive rights, aspects of political morality, and forms of government in order to comply with the rule of law, as without these rights the rule of law would be meaningless. Thick theories differ from each other based on the nature and extent of substantive rights they wish to include.

Thin and thick theories are merely a classificatory tool to understand the crowded theoretical space. Following the thin and thick theory classification is not necessarily useful to build a theoretical foundation of the rule of law in India. It is more important to understand the political and philosophical basis of the rule of law by examining the theories of Aristotle, Montesquieu, Locke, Dicey, Hayek, Unger, Raz, and others. Judith Shklar has rightly pointed out that a rule of law formulation is dependent on the political objectives it seeks to achieve.[17] It is therefore necessary to study the political objectives of the Constitution to meaningfully develop a theoretical basis of the rule of law in India.

A survey of the major works and debates on the rule of law shows that the difficult questions in relation to the rule of law operate at two distinct levels. First at a political philosophy level, where the debates are focused on: (i) the role of the state and its powers, responsibilities, and relationship with the people who establish the state and are also administered by it, (ii) the political, social, economic, and moral values, rights, and choices that are to be left outside the realm of law and those

---

[16] B.Z. Tamanaha, *On the Rule of Law: History, Politics & Theory* (Cambridge: Cambridge University Press, 2004).

[17] J.N. Shklar, 'Political Theory and the Rule of Law', in S. Hoffman (ed.), *Political Thought and Political Thinkers* (Chicago: University of Chicago Press, 1998), pp. 21–37.

that ought to be included in the realm of law, and (iii) the need for meaningful participation of people in the process of making of the laws in the form of democracy or otherwise.

Second the debates operate at a legal jurisprudence level, focusing on two primary issues: (i) The content of the law itself—whether the inclusion of substantive rights in the law undermines the concepts of stability, predictability, certainty, and equality in enforcement which are essential features of the rule of law. The main argument is that substantive rights are not capable of being determined and enforced in a uniform predictable manner that the rule of law mandates, and therefore, to keep the rule of law intact, substantive rights should be outside the law; (ii) The increasing unpredictability in judicial decision-making due to the political, social, and moral choices involved in such decisions and its negative impact on the rule of law. This revolves around the objection to the use of purposive reasoning by judges and the inchoateness of legal provisions.

THEORY VERSUS PRACTICE

Developments over the last 25 years also indicate a divergence between practitioners and theorists, primarily in Western countries. Practitioners—politicians, lawyers, judges, and bureaucrats, inter alia, appear to believe that the rule of law is a desirable good and therefore needs to be encouraged in all countries. Most international conferences mention it as a desirable quality in every country, although there is never a detailing of the contents of the rule of law accompanying such expression of desire. Certain initiatives like the World Justice Project (WJP), promoted by the American Bar Association and others, have tried to identify a set of common factors and processes that form the rule of law. The adherence to these factors by the legal systems of different countries is then measured by a combination of qualitative and quantitative parameters to arrive at a rule of law index which ranks the different countries. Interestingly, the WJP does not differentiate between thin and the thick theories—it merely identifies and lists factors in the belief that they are important and necessary in every country, irrespective of the nature of its government or ideology. The group identifies four primary 'universal' factors as comprising the rule of law:

1. The government and its officials and agents as well as individuals and private entities are accountable under the law.
2. The laws are clear, publicized, stable, and just; are applied evenly; and protect fundamental rights, including the security of persons and property.
3. The process by which the laws are enacted, administered, and enforced is accessible, fair, and efficient.
4. Justice is delivered timely by competent, ethical, and independent representatives and neutrals who are of sufficient number, have adequate resources, and reflect the makeup of the communities they serve.[18]

A plain reading of these factors indicates that they are not constrained by the limitations of the thin theories and contain many features that form part of the thick theories. India is consistently ranked in the bottom half of the list.[19]

Theorists on the other hand appear to believe that the rule of law is in perpetual decline and it has become an empty phrase bereft of all meaning. Three primary reasons are identified for this decline. First, the indiscriminate use of the phrase rule of law, arising from a lack of clear understanding, has made it mean different things to different people, or everything to everyone, thereby making it useless unless it is reconstructed properly.[20] Second, the advent of the social democratic state, where the state provides many social and economic welfare measures, has meant the decline or death of the rule of law. Dicey claims that the rule of law declined severely in the twentieth century and points to the

[18] The WJP is an initiative of the American Bar Association that aims to promote the rule of law across the world. Among other things, it brings out a comparative rule of law index every year. See https://worldjusticeproject. org (accessed 2 February 2017). There are a number of other such indicators developed by various global institutions including the World Bank. The WJP is the most comprehensive of the indices and has therefore been studied in detail.

[19] See https://worldjusticeproject.org/sites/default/files/roli_2015_0. pdf (accessed 10 November 2015) and https://worldjusticeproject.org/sites/ default/files/media/wjp_rule_of_law_index_2016.pdf (accessed 2 February 2017).

[20] See Shklar, 'Political Theory and the Rule of Law'.

late eighteenth- and nineteenth-century Western civilizations as the era in which the rule of law flourished, attributing this decline mainly to the introduction of various welfare measures by the state.[21] Third, the influence of political and social values, together with the use of purposive reasoning in the determination of disputes by the judiciary has made the law nothing but a contest of political and social choices, challenging the fundamental features of the rule of law. Interestingly, there is near unanimity on the last point among theorists even when they belong to different schools.

OVERVIEW OF THE BOOK[22]

The primary goal of this book is to understand and explain the obvious dichotomy that exists in India's rule of law. While it is exciting to attempt an indigenous theory of the rule of law based on the choices made in the Constitution, it is not the primary task of this work. However, the book tries to identify the broad contours of an Indian theory of the rule of law.

Chapter 1, 'Meaning of Rule of Law: A Critical Analysis', studies the theoretical and practical meaning of the rule of law. The crowded theoretical space makes it impossible to critically analyse every theoretical explanation of the rule of law. For the sake of a meaningful and convenient analysis, the tools developed by scholars such as Shklar and Tamanaha for categorizing the various theories are useful. In particular, Shklar's categorization of the theories into the Aristotelian and Montesquieu archetypes on the basis of political objectives and the organization of the state is extremely insightful and relevant for

---

[21] A.V. Dicey, *An Introduction to the Study of Law of the Constitution* (New Delhi: Universal Law Publishing, 10th edn, 2012), pp. 64–5.

[22] The text for this book was finalized in early 2016, with some minor updates in early 2017. Since then there have many developments that are relevant to the arguments made in the book regarding the dichotomy at the heart of India's rule of law. However, none of the recent developments undermine the arguments made in the book; to the contrary they indicate that the fault lines in the rule of law edifice identified in the book have become more prominent. They serve as mere examples in India's complex journey as a society striving for the rule of law. The author hopes to discuss such developments on another occasion.

developing a theoretical explanation for the Indian rule of law. Apart from Aristotle and Montesquieu, the classical works of Dicey, Hayek, Unger, and Raz are discussed in detail to properly understand the differing approaches to the rule of law.

The distinction between the thin and thick theories is discussed to explain the various components that comprise the rule of law according to various theories. The relationship between such components and various political, social, and economic choices is examined to lay the ground for understanding the choices made in the Constitution and their impact on the rule of law. An attempt is made to provide a theoretical explanation based on such choices. This attempt forms the basis of developing an indigenous explanation for the rule of law in India.

To explain and analyse the practical approaches to the rule of law, the primary focus of the chapter is on understanding the various components of the rule of law identified by various groups. As the WJP's approach is the most comprehensive approach currently available, the factors identified by them are explained in considerable detail.

Chapter 2, 'India's Rule of Law: A Theoretical Analysis', attempts to understand the rule of law in India using a theoretical framework. The provisions of the Constitution, mainly the Preamble and Parts III and IV are examined and analysed to evaluate if they go beyond formalism. Focusing on equality, fraternity, and liberty as revolutionary concepts that were introduced by the Constitution, it seeks to answer the question whether the Constitution heralds a complete break from India's past. The Constituent Assembly debates and the works of Ambedkar, Baxi, Austin, Khilnani, Mehta, and Kothari are reviewed and analysed to understand the values and choices made in the Constitution and whether they were a mere continuation of existing values and choices or if they were a completely new set of values and choices. A brief study of the legal structures in British colonial period and the periods prior to that, particularly in reference to the meaning and relevance of the concept of dharma, is carried out to examine the veracity of the Constitution as a revolutionary document. The important contributions by Jois, Jain, Tharoor, and Menon have been reviewed in this context.

An extremely important factor that needs to be studied in the Indian context is the central role attributed to the state in the fulfilment of political, social, and economic goals. This has a significant impact on our understanding of rule of law, as most dominant Western theories attribute a limited role to the state when compared to that envisaged in the Constitution. This issue is examined in detail by studying the provisions of the Constitution and the works of Baxi, Krishna Iyer, Austin, Kannabiran, and Mehta.

Chapter 3, 'Rule of Law in Practice: Judicial and Political Understanding', has two parts. In the first part, the interpretation and application of the rule of law by Indian courts, primarily the constitutional bench of the Supreme Court of India, are analysed. Going beyond merely reviewing cases where the rule of law has been expressly used, the judgments of the Court are examined in relation to the broad constitutional themes. A review of the major principles laid down by the Supreme Court in relation to equality and liberty is followed by a critical examination of the innovative jurisprudence developed by the Court while interpreting Article 21. The relationship between Parts III and IV of the Constitution, which is critical to understanding the rule of law in India, is also discussed in detail. An effort is made to understand if the judiciary has followed a broad cohesive approach in respect of the rule of law.

In the second part of Chapter 3, the political understanding of the rule of law is examined, particularly focusing on Nehru's comment that the rule of law should follow the 'rule of life' and its meaning and continued impact on lawmaking. The chapter concludes by identifying four broad themes of the rule of law in India. These four themes form the basis, in this researcher's view, of developing a theoretical basis for the rule of law in India.

In Chapters 4 and 5, I examine the practical status of the rule of law in the country. In Chapter 4, 'Rule of Law and Lawmaking', the focus is on the process of law making in India, both legislative law making and delegated legislation, based on specific examples. For the rule of law to be effective, it is important that the democratic process of law making works properly as envisaged by the Constitution. A dysfunctional legislature and a powerful executive weakens the rule of law severely. Lawmaking should not become an exercise of power by the majority but instead strictly adhere to the legal process for lawmaking which includes dialogue, reasoning and open debate. If this process is weakened, the rule of law will be dealt a death blow. By examining the functioning of Parliament and state legislatures over the years, the adherence, or otherwise, to the established process in the making of law is critically analysed.

The nature of the modern state, particularly a state that has a primary role in the social and economic life of society, has meant a regular exercise of the power of delegated legislation. Unfortunately, delegated legislation is accompanied by the threat of an arbitrary exercise of power as well as the influence of irrelevant considerations in decision-making. An increase in delegated legislation is, by itself, viewed as a threat to the rule of law by Dicey and Hayek. Using specific examples, the chapter examines whether the use of delegated legislation in India has been a threat to the rule of law.

Chapter 5, 'Enforcement of Rights and Laws', focuses on the implementation of rights and laws, both by the executive and the judiciary, particularly focusing on the distinction between rights and entitlements. The true test to determine if a society is governed by the rule of law lies in the enforcement of its laws and the ability to protect the rights of citizens. The proper performance of the executive and judiciary is key to achieve such a society. The primary reason attributed to the permanent dichotomy of the rule of law in India is improper implementation of laws and the lacunae in enforcement of rights. The chapter tries to identify and analyse the various reasons for improper implementation of the laws and the inability of citizens to enforce their rights. It also examines whether the crippling judicial delay is a significant contributor to the defects in enforcement.

Chapter 6, 'Quest for Reason: A Failing Endeavour?', comprises the conclusions derived from the analysis in the previous chapters. The major conclusions, relating to (i) the theoretical foundations of the rule of law in India and (ii) the reasons for the permanent dichotomy regarding the status of the rule of law, are discussed.

NOT JUST THEORY OR LAW

As discussed earlier, the rule of law is a political concept. There is no law, either statutory or otherwise, that clearly identifies the various components of the rule of law and establishes the manner in which the components, individually or collectively, are to be followed. Consequently, the status of the rule of law in a society cannot be studied as a purely theoretical exercise. Instead, it requires a study of the laws of the country, the institutions set up for the making and implementation of laws, the procedures established and followed by those institutions and whether such institutions are successfully following these procedures to achieve the implementation of the laws. Due to this dual character, there are two distinct aspects to this work. The first involves a study of the theoretical expositions of the rule of law and the second a study of the rule of law in practice. The first part comprises studying, understanding, and critically analysing the relevant and important theories of the rule of law. Such a study is multidisciplinary in nature and encompasses political science, philosophy, sociology, economics, and law.

The section on the rule of law in practice contains various components. The first involves a normative and critical study of the text of the Constitution of India and its interpretation by theorists and the courts. This required identifying, understanding, and analysing various primary and secondary materials. Primary materials consist of the text of the Constitution and various judgments. Secondary materials consist of various commentaries. The second feature involved the study of certain statutes and delegated legislation, the process by which these statutes and legislation are made and the manner in which they are implemented. For this aspect, reliance was placed on primary materials (the text of the statutes and the delegated legislation) and commentaries. The book critically analyses these statutes and delegated legislation and their implementation processes from a practitioner's perspective, as distinct from a theoretical approach.

An academic generally looks at the intent of the legislature, the substantive goal and how it is sought to be achieved in the text, the statute's compliance with the Constitution, its place in the overall philosophy and objective of governance, whether the law could have been better, and whether the authorities are implementing the statute in the right spirit to achieve its objective. A practitioner looks at a statute differently: She examines whether the statute clearly spells out the various steps to be followed by the people whose actions are regulated by the statute, and, if there is no clarity, where and how this clarity can be obtained. She also analyses who the authorities responsible for administering the statute are, and if they have (if the statute has not already done so) established the procedures necessary to implement the statute, and if these procedures have been notified for public consumption. Does any officer have unregulated discretion to determine certain action points? Are there clear remedies against official action, and do the statutes provide a clear framework to plan future action with certainty? Will the statute and its implementation mechanism protect the person who has suffered the consequences of any breach? How long will it take to benefit from such protection and at what expense? It is the answers to the legal practitioner's questions that will throw light on the rule of law in practice. The practitioner's approach requires analysis of real cases, collection of quantitative data and a logical and critical analysis of the provisions and decisions, executive and judicial, which interpret such provisions. Following this approach is critically important when analysing the rule of law in practice and the book attempts to do so.

The rule of law in practice also involves studying the functioning of the institutions responsible for the implementation of the law. For this purpose, the book relies on quantitative data, both primary and secondary. The primary data is mainly gathered from the information released by the institutions themselves or data collated by various civil society organizations, while the secondary data is from various scholarly works.

Upendra Baxi insightfully observes, '[I]t is very difficult to measure the impact of the rule of law, positive or negative, on individual citizens. It is only literature that gives us an understanding of the impact on individuals.'[23] Baxi is right, as only literature delves deep into the emotions of individual citizens affected by the law. However, it is not possible to rely on works of fiction to arrive at logical and critical conclusions. The last decade has seen many non-fictional documentary studies that throw light on the impact of the rule of law, or lack of it. These studies are qualitative in nature and rely on personal experiences of individuals, both who are involved in the implementation of the law and those who are affected by it. To get a deeper insight into the rule of law in practice at an individual level, this book has relied on these works. They have not been used to arrive at any conclusions, but only to gain further understanding into the pathologies of the impact, positive or negative, of the rule of law.

[23] U. Baxi, 'The Rule of Law in India: Theory and Practice', in R. Peerenboom (ed.), *Asian Discourses of Rule of Law: Theories and Implementation of Rule of Law in Twelve Asian Countries, France and the U.S.* (London: Routledge Curzon, 2004), pp. 324–45 at p. 336.

1

MEANING OF RULE OF LAW

A CRITICAL ANALYSIS

In its simplest form, the rule of law is contrasted with the rule of men and the rule by law. It essentially means that the 'law' should rule, rather than 'men'. While this description is generally accepted, the precise components of the rule of law are elusive. This has led to the concept being used to mean different things by different people, causing enormous confusion as to its meaning. The eminent political scientist Judith Shklar points out that, 'the phrase "the Rule of Law" has become meaningless thanks to ideological abuse and general over-use'.[1] Shklar is right about the abuse and overuse—as the contemporary theoretical landscape is populated with diverse and contradictory formulations of the rule of law. For a layman, or indeed a scholar, beginning a fresh investigation, it is difficult to decide where to begin and how to proceed in understanding the meaning of the rule of law.

---

[1] J.N. Shklar, 'Political Theory and the Rule of Law', in S. Hoffman (ed.), *Political Thought and Political Thinkers* (Chicago: University of Chicago Press, 1998). Shklar goes on to argue that the phrase rule of law is nothing but ruling class chatter and one should not waste time discussing it. She further argues that it is relevant only from a historical perspective, as the rule of law once had an important place in political theory and it would be useful to compare its current and historical status. Shklar's main argument is based on the fact that the rule of law ideal had political objectives when it was first conceived, but contemporary theories have failed to restate older, or develop newer, political objectives.

Nearly all the theoretical formulations of the rule of law originate in western Europe and the United States of America and are, therefore, predominantly 'Western' in thought and orientation. Even the late twentieth-century and early twenty-first-century attempts at theoretical expositions by Asian origin scholars rely on concepts from earlier and current Western scholars.[2] Western thought on the rule of law can be traced all the way back to the Greek philosophers, Plato and Aristotle.[3] It developed through a series of historical developments ranging from the Magna Carta, the ascendancy of parliamentary supremacy in England, the evolution of common law, the conceptualization and popularity of the social contract theories, the adoption of the American Constitution, the French revolution, and the advent of liberalism.[4] Hobbes, Locke, Rousseau, Montesquieu, the authors of the Federalist papers, and major political philosophers have had their say on the rule of law. Moreover, as it is closely identified with the legal system, every legal scholar has also said something about the rule of law. Sociologists and economists have not shied away from contributing their thoughts on this topic either, making the rule of law a popular, contested, and crowded theoretical arena. To add to the clutter, practitioners of politics, economics, and law also regularly use, opine, and comment on the rule of law without fully appreciating the phrase.

This chapter presents a snapshot of the theoretical landscape to prepare the ground for discussions on the rule of law in India. The theories of Dicey, Hayek, and Unger, which comprise the dominant modern

[2] This is because a new theoretical exposition requires a restatement of the old, or totally new, objectives. The modern rule of law is linked intrinsically to liberalism and constitutionalism that originated in liberalism. Modern Asian societies also accept some form of constitutionalism, if not liberalism, and therein lies, in this researcher's view, the inability to develop a new theory of rule of law. Differentiating the practice of the rule of law based on current political considerations does not lead to development of an alternative theory.

[3] B.Z. Tamanaha, *On the Rule of Law: History, Politics & Theory* (Cambridge: Cambridge University Press, 2004). Tamanaha points out that while the concept may be traced to the Greek philosophers, one cannot find an unbroken connection between the Greek philosophers and the later development of the rule of law, as Greek philosophy was lost to western Europe for a long time.

[4] T. Bingham, *The Rule of Law* (London: Allen Lane, 2010); Tamanaha, *On the Rule of Law*.

theories, are discussed in detail. However, because the rule of law also has a practical meaning and application, it is necessary for the modern theorist to study the practical elements that are asserted as part of the rule of law. Therefore, the chapter also examines the meaning of the rule of law in practice.

MULTITUDE OF THEORIES, BUT ONLY TWO ARCHETYPES

It is impossible for this chapter to evaluate all the innumerable theories on the rule of law, even in a cursory manner. Therefore, it mainly discusses types of theories to understand the theoretical landscape better. There are two well-known analyses of the theoretical landscape—one by Shklar and the other by Brian Tamanaha.[5] Shklar identifies two archetypes of the rule of law based on distinct meanings—the Aristotelian archetype and the Montesquieu archetype.[6] Both these archetypes treat the rule of law as a political ideal, but with differing characteristics and applicability. In the Aristotelian archetype,[7] the rule of law is linked to an entire way of life, nothing less than the rule of reason contrasted with the rule of man. This rule of law archetype has significant political, ethical, and intellectual scope and places extreme importance on the character of judges, who must rise above ordinary human passions, irrational feelings, and imperfections and deliver justice based on pure reason. It is these

---

[5] Tamanaha's classification, based on thin and thick theories of rule of law, is clearly the more popularly used classification. However, Shklar's classification is more important because it brings out the objectives of the rule of law, which get lost in contemporary discussions.

[6] Shklar, 'Political Theory and the Rule of Law'. Shklar clarifies that the classification she makes is possible only because of the interpretive licence she has exercised. However, her classification is apt and goes a long way in clearing the clutter that the rule of law theories suffer from in the 20th and 21st centuries. Shklar also clarifies that the distinction between the two archetypes is now obfuscated, as people have forgotten the political purposes and settings at the time the archetypes were propounded.

[7] Aristotle's views on the Rule of Law are primarily contained in his *Politics*. Aristotle, *Politics*, Book III in *Introduction to Aristotle*, edited by R. Mckeon (New York: The Modern Library, 1992).

rational judges who ensure that society functions properly as they apply the law in the same manner in similar circumstances.[8] In effect, Aristotle's rule of law is based on certain rational and reasonable individuals acting as judges, delivering justice without giving in to ordinary pressures and passions. This will ensure the development of a reasonable and rational system that upholds the rule of law in society. In Aristotle's words:

> And the rule of law, it is argued, is preferable to that of any individual. On the same principle, even if it be better for certain individuals to govern, they should be made only guardians and ministers of the law ... therefore, he who bids the law rule may be deemed to bid God and Reason alone rule, but he who bids man rule adds an element of the beast; for desire is a wild beast, and passion perverts the minds of rulers, even when they are the best of men. The law is reason unaffected by desire.[9]

It should, however, be noted that Aristotle's archetype does not apply to all citizens given the slave society of ancient Athens.[10] Irrespective of the political and social limitations that qualify Aristotle's statements, even today this contrast between the rule of law identified with reason and the rule of man identified with passion, is at the core of the rule of law discussions, both theoretical and practical.

The Montesquieu archetype[11] treats the rule of law as consisting of those institutional restraints that prevent governmental agents from oppressing the rest of society. Unlike Aristotle's archetype, Montesquieu's rule of law only consists of a few rules, but applies to, and benefits, everyone in society, though only in some aspects of societal life. According to Montesquieu, the rule of law must take certain types of human conduct completely out of public control because they cannot be regulated without the use of physical cruelty, arbitrariness and the creation of unremitting fear among citizens.

[8] Shklar, 'Political Theory and the Rule of Law'.

[9] Aristotle, *Politics*, p. 654.

[10] Aristotle did not think it strange that a dual society where certain citizens have no right could exist and still be a model society. This factor, by itself, however does not undermine the basic principles postulated by Aristotle.

[11] Montesquieu's views on the rule of law are contained in his *Spirit of Laws*. See Montesquieu, *Spirit of Laws*, edited by D.W. Carrithers (Berkeley: University of California Press, 1977).

According to Shklar, Montesquieu's rule of law is not the reign of reason, but the spirit of the criminal law of a free people.[12] The rule of law protects all citizens, from each other and the government, as long as they are carrying on legal activities. Citizens should only fear the law and not its administrators. Judges are essentially required only to implement criminal laws that are in place by punishing the guilty and protecting the innocent. Citizens are free to enjoy all other rights available to them. Therefore, Montesquieu's rule of law is very limited and narrow in scope compared to Aristotle's rule of law, but one should also remember that the political, societal, and 'state' settings when the two theories were put forward were radically different.[13] Montesquieu was dealing with a society where individual rights were taking root and the desire to limit the state's powers to regulate individual conduct was very high. Montesquieu also had quite a bit to say about how the state should be organized. His emphasis on 'separation of powers' between various organs of the state was a defining feature of the rule of law and has in current times become an almost inviolable requirement of the rule of law.[14]

In both these archetypes, the rule of law is an important feature of the manner and process in which societies are organized and governed. In Aristotle's archetype, the rule of law underpins society itself, as it is the embodiment of reason and its failure will inevitably lead to a societal collapse. Reason, and therefore the rule of law, is an unqualified virtue. We should remember that Aristotle lived in a society governed by direct

---

[12] Shklar, 'Political Theory and the Rule of Law'.

[13] Shklar, 'Political Theory and the Rule of Law'. See also Tamanaha *On the Rule of Law*, pp. 7–32. The inability to imagine new political goals in the context of the modern state is at the heart of Shklar's criticism of the current rule of law theories. The advent of the social democratic state and the challenges it poses to the rule of law theories of old has not been addressed in sufficient detail, although some effort has been made by Unger and the other realist thinkers. However, they do not reimagine the political objectives to rejuvenate the rule of law theory as Shklar points out. Shklar believes that Montesquieu's rule of law is rooted in a psychology and not in a theory of public efficiency or natural rights.

[14] See J. Waldron, 'The Rule of Law', in Edward N. Zalta (ed/), *The Stanford Encyclopedia of Philosophy* (Fall 2016 edn), available at https://plato.stanford.edu/archives/fall2016/entries/rule-of-law/ (accessed 4 October 2017).

democracy and it was important and necessary to avoid the tyranny of democracy through enlightened reasoning which judges would provide. In contemporary society, Aristotle's archetype appears outdated given the advent of representative democracy and the large modern state apparatus. However, the emphasis on reason as the underpinning of the rule of law and consequently, society itself, does find some followers in philosophers such as Fuller and Dworkin. Montesquieu's archetype is more familiar to modern theorists and societies as it recognizes the state apparatus and gives the task of restraining the state and its agents through the rule of law.

The political objectives of both archetypes are evident, although Montesquieu's archetype appears to have a narrower political objective when compared with Aristotle's. However, this narrower objective should be understood in the context of the unspoken rights, which the citizens have outside the construct of the state, and the rule of law debate. The significant unstated objective of both archetypes is their effort to ensure that no tyranny is unleashed by the exercise of power in its myriad forms. Indeed, the rule of law is probably one of the most imaginative concepts developed by man to regulate power, individual or collective, in a manner that is beneficial to society and individual citizens. Benefits, of course, need to be identified by the society itself and is connected to the political objectives behind each society's rule of law. This essential underlying feature should not be ignored when dealing with the multitude of contemporary theories and practices of the rule of law.

FORMAL AND SUBSTANTIVE THEORIES

Brian Tamanaha divides the existing rule of law theories into two basic categories—formal and substantive—each coming in three distinct forms.[15] These are reproduced in Table 1.1.

Formal theories are also known as thin theories and substantive theories are also known as thick theories. Broadly, formal theories emphasize the instrumental features of the rule of law, features that any

---

[15] Tamanaha, *On the Rule of Law*, p. 91. Tamanaha clarifies that his classification is only an analytical tool to understand the various theories of rule of law and that the classification is not 'substantive' in nature.

Table 1.1 Tamanaha's Rule of Law Classifications[16]

	Thinner -----------------------> ----------------------> Thicker		
Formal Versions:	1. Rule by law: Law as instrument of government	2. Formal legality: General prospective, clear, certain	3. Democracy + legality: Consent determines content of law
Substantive Versions:	4. Individual rights: Property, contract, privacy, autonomy	5. Right of dignity and/or justice	6. Social welfare and/or justice: Substantive equality, welfare, preservation of community

legal system must possess to function effectively as a system of laws, regardless of whether the legal system is part of a democratic or non-democratic society, capitalist or socialist, and liberal or theocratic.

The typical features of thin theories of rule of law are: (i) all laws must be generally applicable; (ii) the laws must be clear, stable and prospective; (iii) the laws must be enforced and fairly applied; (iv) the process of making and enforcing laws should be clear; (v) the laws must be reasonably acceptable to a majority of the populace; and (vi) the institutions making and enforcing laws should also be governed by the laws.[17] Formal theories have limited normative purposes. They include: (i) ensuring stability, and preventing anarchy and the Hobbesian war of all against all; (ii) securing governance in accordance with law by limiting arbitrariness on the part of the government; (iii) enhancing predictability, which allows people to plan their affairs and hence promotes both individual freedom and economic development; (iv) providing a fair mechanism for the resolution of disputes; and (v) bolstering the legitimacy of the government.[18]

---

[16] Tamanaha, *On the Rule of Law*, p. 91.

[17] Tamanaha, *On the Rule of Law*, pp. 91–5.

[18] Although the features of a thin rule of law are common to all rule of law systems, they will vary to some extent in the way they are interpreted and implemented depending on substantive political views and values. Accordingly, legal

Thick or substantive conceptions begin with the basic elements of a thin conception but incorporate additional elements such as: (i) forms of political morality such as particular economic arrangements (free-market capitalism, central planning, or other varieties of capitalism); (ii) forms of government (democratic, socialist, soft authoritarian); and (iii) conceptions of human rights (libertarian, classical liberal, social welfare liberal, other values, etc.).[19]

Tamanaha recognizes that while thin and thick versions of rule of law are analytically distinct, in practice, all rule of law legal systems exist within specific political, economic, social, and cultural circumstances. Tamanaha conceptualizes the relationship between a thin rule of law, particular thick conceptions of rule of law and the broader context in terms of concentric circles. The smallest circle consists of the core elements of a thin rule of law, which is embedded within a thick rule of law conception or framework. The thick conception is in turn part of a broader social and political philosophy that addresses a range of issues beyond those relating to the legal system and rule of law.[20] Figure 1.1 demonstrates this relationship.

Formal conceptions do not seek to pass judgement upon the actual content of the law itself. They are not concerned whether the law is in any sense a good law or a bad law, provided that the formal precepts of the rule of law are met. Substantive conceptions of the rule of law seek to go beyond this. They accept that the rule of law has the formal attributes mentioned above, but they wish to take the doctrine further. Certain substantive rights are said to be based on, or derived from, the rule of law. The concept is used as the foundation for these rights, which are further used to distinguish between good laws (which comply with such rights) and bad laws (which do not comply).[21] In other words, formal theories focus on the proper sources and form of legality, while substantive theories also include requirements about the content of the law (usually that it must be in consonance with justice or moral

---

systems that meet the standards of a thin rule of law will still diverge to some extent with respect to purposes, institutions, rules and outcomes due to the different contexts in which they are embedded.

[19] Tamanaha, *On the Rule of Law*, pp. 102–13.

[20] Tamanaha, *On the Rule of Law*, pp. 91–108.

[21] Tamanaha, *On the Rule of Law*, pp. 102–10.

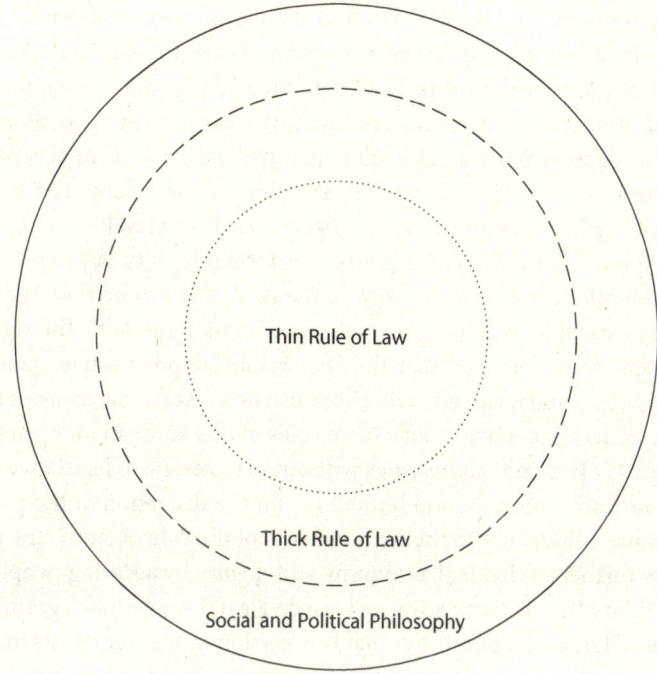

Figure 1.1 Relationship between Thin Theories, Thick Theories, and Social and Political Philosophy according to Tamanaha

principles). While this distinction is explanatory, it should not be taken as strict—the formal versions have substantive implications and the substantive versions incorporate formal requirements.

TYPES OF FORMAL VERSIONS

Formal versions range from the basic 'rule by law' theory to versions which add democracy to the purely formal principles. The commonality in the formal versions is that they do not concern themselves with the content of the law. The thinnest formal version is the rule by law concept, which means that law is the means by which the state conducts its affairs and that whatever the government does, it should do through laws. However, if the rule of law is nothing but the rule by law, then the rule of law is really an empty concept not worthy of further discussion.

Every modern state rules by law and therefore, one can conclude that the rule of law exists in every state. Some far-east Asian and Chinese scholars have tried to propagate this theory.[22] In the contemporary world, which has seen the universal acceptance of human rights, albeit in varying degrees, it is very difficult to justify the thinnest formal version.

The most popular Western formulation of the rule of law is the formal legality version, which is largely based on Hayek's rule of law principles.[23] A prominent supporter of formal legality is Joseph Raz, who identifies the basic message of the rule of law to be that 'the law must be capable of guiding the behaviour of its subjects'.[24] The rule of law, therefore, demands that the law should be prospective, general, clear, public, and relatively stable. Raz also lists several mechanisms that he considers necessary to effectuate rules of this kind: an independent judiciary, open and fair hearings without bias, review of legislative and administrative officials, and limitations on the discretion of the police to ensure conformity to the requirements of the rule of law.[25] The rule of law furthers individual autonomy and dignity by allowing people to plan their activities with advance knowledge of its potential legal implications. Tamanaha points out that this version of the rule of law makes no demand in terms of the content of the law and renders it open to a range of ends.[26] This substantively empty quality leaves it amenable to universal application, but at the same time it can also characterize societies that may be morally reprehensible. Raz himself acknowledges this point in a stark manner:

> A non-democratic legal system, based on the denial of human rights, on extensive poverty, on racial segregation, sexual inequalities, and racial

---

[22] R. Peerenboom, 'Varieties of Rule of Law: An Introduction and Provisional Conclusion', in R. Peerenboom (ed.), *Asian Discourses of Rule of Law: Theories and Implementation of Rule of Law in Twelve Asian Countries, France and the U.S.*, pp. 1–47 (London: Routledge Curzon, 2004).

[23] Hayek's principles are discussed in detail later in this chapter.

[24] J. Raz, 'The Rule of Law and Its Virtue', in J. Raz, *The Authority of Law: Essays on Law and Morality*, pp. 210–29 at p. 214 (Oxford: Oxford University Press, 1979). Raz in fact is not a complete supporter of Hayek's view of the rule of law. He is quite critical of Hayek's generalization of the rule of law principle.

[25] J. Raz, 'The Rule of Law and Its Virtue', pp. 214–18.

[26] Tamanaha, *On the Rule of Law*, pp. 93–4.

persecution may, in principle, conform to the requirements of the rule of law better than any of the legal systems of the more enlightened Western democracies ... it will be an immeasurably worse legal system, but it will excel in one respect: in its conformity to the Rule of Law. The law may ... institute slavery without violating the Rule of Law.[27]

Tamanaha further points out that the many adherents of formal legality are in substantial agreement about its requirements and its implications, except for two points: how to understand the equality requirement, and whether the rule of law itself represents a moral good.[28] The first disagreement is about the fact that various laws in the contemporary world either distinguish amongst citizens or treat everyone equally when they are actually not, thereby violating the formal equality requirement. Distinctions amongst citizens invariably bring in substantive issues and, therefore, political and moral judgements about equality. Formal legality also assumes that societies will have certain political and social conditions which enable the development of rule of law. This however, is never the case in reality, as no two countries which satisfy the formal legality requirements have similar political and social conditions. This deliberate ignorance of different political and social conditions and the political, social, and moral judgements that accompany it cannot be satisfactorily explained by supporters of formal legality.

The argument about the moral goodness of the rule of law revolves around whether rule of law is only instrumental in achieving a moral good or whether it is a moral good in itself. Lon Fuller is the main proponent of the rule of law being a moral good in itself, while Raz leads the argument for it being only instrumental.[29] Fuller argues that as the rule of law enhances individual autonomy and has an affinity with the good; it encourages all legal systems to be good.[30] Each of the requirements

---

[27] J. Raz, 'The Rule of Law and Its Virtue', p. 211.

[28] Tamanaha, *On the Rule of Law*, pp. 94–6.

[29] L. Fuller, *The Morality of Law* (New Haven: Yale University Press, 2nd edn, 1969), pp. 209–14. For Raz's views, see J. Raz, 'The Rule of Law and Its Virtue', pp. 224–5.

[30] Fuller, *The Morality of Law*, pp. 157–9. Fuller explains that societies that adhere to formal rule of law are more likely to have laws with a fair and just content. The values and principles promoted by the rule of law will make it difficult for tyrannical regimes to abide by it.

of the formal rule of law, although procedural in nature, advances the rights of citizens making the rule of law a good in itself. If the rule of law is not followed, it does not only mean that there is a bad legal system, it also means that there is nothing that can properly be called a legal system at all. This ensures that there is no reason or inducement for legal systems not to follow the rule of law. Raz, however, argues that the law is morally neutral and being morally neutral is in fact a virtue of the law as it can be put to achieve any end.[31] While there is a moral virtue in following the rule of law, it is not necessary that the rule of law is itself moral.

The third formal version of the rule of law adds democracy to formal legality.[32] Like formal legality, democracy is substantively empty; in that it says nothing about the content of the law. It is a decision-making procedure that specifies how to determine the content of the law. Jurgen Habermas says, 'The modern legal order can draw its legitimacy only from the idea of self-determination: citizens should always be able to understand themselves also as authors of the law to which they are subject to as addressees.'[33]

Roberto Unger also emphasizes that law obtains its authority from the consent of the governed.[34] Under this reasoning, formal legality and democracy are dependent on and in fact strengthen each other. Without one, the other can be undermined and lose its legitimacy. Habermas characterizes this combination (for Western countries) as the only legitimate arrangement, given contemporary beliefs and conditions, where

[31] J. Raz, 'The Rule of Law and Its Virtue', pp. 225–6. Raz uses his famous knives analogy to drive home the point. A knife is neither good nor bad in itself, but can be used either to kill a man or slice vegetables. We cannot judge the morality of a knife based on what it is used for. Waldron terms this approach as 'casual positivism'. See Waldron, 'The Rule of Law'. See also J. Waldron, 'The Concept and the Rule of Law', Public Law Research Paper No. 08-50, NYU School of Law, available at http://papers.ssrn.com/sol3/papers.cfm?abstract_id=1273005 (accessed 7 October 2017).

[32] Tamanaha, *On the Rule of Law*, p. 99.

[33] J. Habermas, *Between Facts and Norms*, translated by W. Rehg (Cambridge: MIT Press, 1997).

[34] R. Unger, *Law in a Modern Society* (New York: The Free Press, 1977), p. 178. Dicey and Hayek also require that the citizens have some sort of say in the development of law, but not necessarily in the form of a democracy.

support for natural law is declining and moral pluralism is the order of the day.[35] Of course, it is unlikely that there will ever be a consensus on the nature of democracy, direct or representative, and the nature of consent required from citizens. While direct democracy and consensus of everyone involved may be the eternal utopia, a broad acceptance of representative democracy and majority rule is the defining character-istic of nearly all modern democracies. However, democracy does not guarantee good laws or the rule of law. A democracy may still produce evil laws and also turn into a tyrannical regime without respect for the rule of law. Countries with diverse groups and sub-groups may also see the organized among such groups and sub-groups seize power, and make laws to advance particular agendas.

TYPES OF SUBSTANTIVE VERSIONS

All substantive versions of the rule of law incorporate elements of the formal rule of law and add various content specifications. The thickest substantive versions of the rule of law not only incorporate formal legality, individual rights and democracy, but add a further qualitative dimension that might be roughly categorized under the label of social welfare rights.[36] The outstanding example of this remains the International Commission of Jurists' (ICJ) Delhi Declaration in 1959:

> The rule of law is a dynamic concept for the expansion and fulfilment of which jurists are primarily responsible and which should be employed not only to safeguard and advance the civil and political rights of the individual in a free society, but also to establish social, economic, educational and cultural conditions under which his legitimate aspirations and dignity may be realized.[37]

The dynamic concept which the rule of law became in the Delhi Declaration does indeed safeguard and advance the civil and political

---

[35] Habermas, *Between Facts and Norms*, chapters 3–6.

[36] Tamanaha, *On the Rule of Law*, pp. 112–13.

[37] International Commission of Jurists, '1952–2012: Congresses and Major Conferences of the International Commission of Jurists' (2012), p. 30, available at http://icj.wpengine.netdna-cdn.com/wp-content/uploads/2012/12/CONGRESS-BOOKLET.pdf (accessed 7 October 2017).

rights of the individual in a free society, but it is also concerned with the establishment by the state of social, economic, educational, and cultural conditions under which man's legitimate aspirations and dignity may be realized. Freedom of expression may be meaningless to an illiterate, the right to vote may be perverted into an instrument of tyranny exercised by demagogues over an unenlightened electorate, and freedom from government interference must not spell freedom to starve, for the poor and destitute. It is important to remember that the ICJ's declaration was in the wake of developments such as the independence of many countries from colonial rule, adoption of the Universal Declaration of Human Rights, and concern over the lives of several indigenous people in postcolonial countries.

The inclusion of certain social and moral values in the concept of rule of law converts debates over those values into fights over the meaning of rule of law and, therefore, formal theorists argue that the rule of law should be limited to formal versions. However, that decision to limit is also a social and political choice and is no different a choice than to include certain values that are part of formal legality. Such a choice depends on the political objectives of each society rather than any requirements of a system. It is important to note that most postcolonial countries, including India, have sought to include social and economic values in their basic law. While the formal theorists may cry themselves hoarse about the undermining of the legal system because certain social values are incapable of enforcement through a closed system like the law, the fact that the rule of law is also a political value rather than a purely legal one means that it is difficult to accept that it should remain oblivious to certain social and economic values. The rule of law has to perforce make its position clear on choices that are not purely legal in character.

Ronald Dworkin is a supporter of the substantive concept of the rule of law, although for him, the rule of law is only a part of his overall theory of justice and he terms the substantive rule of law as the 'rights conception' as against the formalist version which he terms the 'rule conception'. Dworkin describes the rights conception as assuming that citizens have moral rights and duties with respect to one another, and political rights with respect to the state as a whole. Such moral and political rights have to be recognized in positive law, so that they may be enforced upon the demand of individual citizens through courts or other judicial institutions of the familiar type, so far as this is practicable.

The rule of law on this conception is the ideal of rule by an accurate public conception of individual rights and does not distinguish between formal laws and substantive justice. On the contrary, it requires, as part of the ideal of law, that the rules in the book capture and enforce moral rights. The formalist conception of the rule of law is subsumed with Dworkin's overall theory of rights.[38]

As Tamanaha rightly points out that thin and thick conceptions are analytical tools only. There is no question of one being the right way to conceive the rule of law and the other wrong. Distinguishing between thick and thin theories makes it possible to use rule of law more effectively as a benchmark for evaluating legal systems by clarifying the nature of the problem. Thin conceptions highlight certain features and purposes of a legal system. Even a limited thin rule of law has many important virtues. At a minimum, it promises some degree of predictability and some limitation on arbitrariness, and hence some protection of individual rights and freedoms. While the notion of legality may seem all too thin, a normative foundation in cases where the laws themselves are morally objectionable, even the harshest critics of the rule of law acknowledge that ensuring that government actors act in accordance with, and abide by, the laws is no small achievement. Certainly citizens rotting away in jail after being denied the right to a fair trial and other procedural protections would appreciate the importance of even a thin rule of law. Similarly, business people and average citizens alike appreciate a legal system in which laws do not change daily and are evenly applied in a fair manner by competent administrators, and judges are free from corruption. By narrowing the focus, a thin theory highlights the importance of these virtues of rule of law. Conversely, because thick theories are based on more comprehensive social and political philosophies, the rule of law loses its distinctiveness and gets swallowed up in the larger normative merits or demerits of the particular social and political philosophy.[39]

Raz observes, 'If Rule of Law is the rule of good law then to explain its nature is to propound a complete social philosophy. But if so the term

---

[38] R. Dworkin, *A Matter of Principle* (Cambridge: Harvard University Press, 1985), pp. 11–16. See also R. Dworkin, *Law's Empire* (London: Fontana Press, 1991).

[39] Tamanaha, *On the Rule of Law*, pp. 112–26.

lacks any useful function. We have no need to be converted to the Rule of Law just in order to believe that good should triumph.'[40] Certain legal systems are plagued by thin rule of law issues such as weak legal institutions and incompetent and corrupt administrative officials and judges. These kinds of problems are qualitatively different from more political and social issues such as how broad free speech or freedom of association should be, or whether historically disadvantaged and oppressed groups need various affirmative actions. Whether the rule of law should deal with these substantive issues or operate merely as an instrumental concept by ignoring such substantive issues is at the heart of the debate between thick and thin theories and is unlikely to be resolved easily.

DICEY'S RULE OF LAW PRINCIPLES

A.V. Dicey's work on the rule of law is the first major modern work on the subject. In his book,[41] he identified the rule or supremacy of law as one of the features of political institutions of England since the Norman Conquest.[42] Dicey identified three distinct conceptions as forming the rule of law:

1. No man is punishable or can be lawfully made to suffer in body or goods except for a breach of law established in the ordinary legal manner before the ordinary courts of the land, as contrasted with every system of government based on the exercise by persons in authority of wide, arbitrary or discretionary powers of constraint.
2. Not only is no man above the law, but every man, whatever be his rank or condition, is subject to the ordinary land of the realm and amenable to jurisdiction of ordinary tribunals.
3. The constitution is pervaded by the rule of law on the ground that the general principles of the constitution are a result of judicial decisions

---

[40] Raz, 'The Rule of Law and Its Virtue', p. 211.

[41] A.V. Dicey, *An Introduction to the Study of Law of the Constitution* (New Delhi: Universal Law Publishing, 10th edn, 2012).

[42] The Norman conquest of England took place in the late eleventh century. The first edition of Dicey's book was published in 1885; therefore, he is referring to a period of nearly 800 years during which the rule of law is said to have entrenched itself in England.

determining the rights of private persons in particular cases brought before the courts.[43]

Dicey's first two principles are fairly straightforward. The first principle emphasizes the supremacy or predominance of ordinary law as opposed to the influence of arbitrary power, and excludes the existence of arbitrariness, prerogative, or wide discretionary authority on the part of the government. Men can be punished only by a pre-existing law that was enacted through an established process, every man should have recourse to the ordinary courts, the laws should be clear and every man has recourse to the courts before he can be punished. Dicey also states that no decision should be made according to discretion or caprice of an individual. The second principle emphasizes that not only should no person be above the law but that the law should apply to everyone equally, irrespective of the high office that she holds. These two principles continue to form the bedrock of all rule of law formulations even today.

It is Dicey's third principle that is controversial in today's world. Dicey appears to indicate that only common law can truly be considered law. He clarifies the third principle by stating,

> [T]he dogma that a form of government is a sort of spontaneous growth so closely bound up with the life of a people that we can hardly treat it as a product of human will and energy, does, though in a loose and inaccurate fashion, bring into view the fact that some politics, and among the English constitution, have not been created at one stroke, and far from being the result of legislation, in the ordinary sense of that term, are the fruits of contests carried on in the courts on behalf of the rights of individuals.[44]

Dicey believes that the evolution of rights through resolution of disputes between ordinary citizens is superior to a mere legislative declaration of rights without organic development of remedies for breach of those rights, which in any event is not sufficient.[45]

[43] Dicey, *An Introduction to the Study of Law of the Constitution*, pp. 194–6.

[44] Dicey, *An Introduction to the Study of Law of the Constitution*, p. 196.

[45] Dicey, *An Introduction to the Study of Law of the Constitution*, pp. 203–4. Dicey's method of understanding the rule of law in practice forms the basis of many contemporary methods of evaluating a country's adherence to the rule of law. The World Justice Project's Rule of Law Index, which is discussed later in this chapter, incorporates this method to a large extent.

Commentators suggest that Dicey's third principle should be viewed in the context of various social welfare measures that were instituted in the late nineteenth century and administrative boards with wide discretion that were set up to implement such measures in England and other European countries.[46] Dicey is of a strong opinion that specific administrative measures were against the rule of law, for they introduced discretion and went against the grain of generality, equality, and certainty that the rule of law demanded. Irrespective of the context, Dicey's third principle appears to be out of place in today's world as legislative measures have been accepted as a legitimate form of making law and declaring rights and have in fact increased over the last century.

Contemporary theorists focus more on the fairness in the process of making laws and the need to obtain consent of the governed, bringing into focus the importance of democracy. Dicey's third principle does, however, lend credence to people who argue that imposing an alien system of laws on a society will never work. Its various aspects have been discussed in later chapters of this book in the context of whether the Indian Constitution is sufficiently 'Indian'.

Dicey points out that general propositions with respect to the nature of rule of law, carry us but a very little way. If one has to understand what that principle in all its different aspects and developments really mean, an effort must be made to try and trace its influence through some of the main provisions of the constitution. The best mode of doing this is to examine with care, the manner in which the law deals with the following topics—right to personal freedom, right to freedom of discussion, right of public meeting, use of martial law, the rights and duties of the army, the collection and expenditure of public revenue, and the responsibilities of ministers.[47]

HAYEK'S RULE OF LAW

F.A. Hayek is perhaps the strongest proponent of the rule of law in modern times. Hayek espouses his principles as part of his thesis on liberalism. Hayek believes that liberalism is the way forward for all

---

[46] Tamanaha, *On the Rule of Law*, pp. 64–5.

[47] Dicey, *An Introduction to the Study of Law of the Constitution*, pp. 203–4.

economic growth and the rule of law is a crucial ingredient for liberalism to succeed. For Hayek, the rule of law is a great liberal principle,[48] a mainstay of liberalism itself.

Hayek identifies certain strands of this great liberal principle as follows:

1. The government must never coerce an individual except in the enforcement of an already known rule.
2. Laws should be certain so that they can easily be followed by citizens.
3. Laws should apply generally and equally to everyone rather than specifically to certain individuals.
4. The laying down of general rules and their application to particular cases must be performed by separate persons or bodies.
5. All administrative actions should be subject to judicial review.[49]

The rule of law means that the government in all its actions is bound by rules fixed and announced beforehand, rules which make it possible to foresee with certainty how an authority will use its coercive powers in given circumstances and to plan one's affairs on the basis of that knowledge. The laws must be general, equal and certain in any rule of law system. Hayek, however, acknowledges that it is impossible for any legal system to perfectly attain these attributes, but he believed that legal systems should endeavour to achieve these attributes.

Hayek believes that the rule of law is the key for the protection of individual rights and rendering justice. It preserves the freedom to do what one pleases outside of what the law prohibits. It is not only the essence of justice but also provides greater protection to the individual than any bill of rights.[50] The rule of law will also prevent governments (including democracies) from becoming tyrannical.[51]

Like Dicey, Hayek also believes that law and discretion do not go hand in hand. Hayek goes further than Dicey and argues that the rule

---

[48] F.A. Hayek, *The Road to Serfdom* (London: Routledge, 2012), pp. 78–9.

[49] F.A. Hayek, *The Constitution of Liberty* (London: Routledge, 2012), pp. 180–92.

[50] This is a classic liberal stance. Rights are best left unsaid as the law cannot guarantee rights fully, so it is best that the law is limited and the rights are untouched by the state and its legal system.

[51] Hayek, *The Road to Serfdom*, pp. 75–90.

of law is inherently incompatible with the welfare state where the state makes a number of laws to achieve certain goals, such as substantive equality or distributive justice. Laws granting vague discretionary powers to administrative organs to achieve the goals of the welfare state will be antithetical to the rule of law. Hayek however, concedes that it is possible that regulations drawn up by administrative authorities, published in advance, and strictly adhered to may be in conformity with the rule of law. Given the nature of the welfare state and its ends, it is inevitable that governmental measures will involve arbitrary discrimination between persons and not only general enforcement of rules. The rule of law will exclude such measures involving arbitrariness and therefore the welfare state is not compatible with the rule of law.[52]

Hayek explains that a government can use coercion against citizens only when enforcing general rules and therefore, such a government has no power to achieve particular aims that require means other than those explicitly entrusted to its care and, in particular, cannot determine the material position of particular people or enforce distributive, substantive or 'social' justice. Those who favour distributive justice will in practice find themselves obstructed at every move by the rule of law. They must, from the very nature of their aim, favour discriminatory and discretionary action. However, as they are usually not aware that their aim and the rule of law are in principle incompatible, they begin by circumventing or disregarding in individual cases a principle which they often would wish to see preserved in general.[53]

According to Hayek, the rule of law is not a 'rule of the law', but a rule concerning what the law ought to be—a meta-legal doctrine or a political ideal. It will be effective only insofar that the legislator

---

[52] Hayek, *The Constitution of Liberty*, p. 199.

[53] Hayek, *The Constitution of Liberty*, pp. 202–3. Hayek believes that to achieve the aim of distributive justice, the state would have to pursue a policy which is best described by the French word 'dirigisme', that is, a policy which determines for what specific purposes particular means are to be used. This, however, is precisely what a government bound by the rule of law cannot do. If the government is to determine how particular people ought to be situated, it must be in a position to determine also the direction of individual efforts. When the opinion of the community decides what different people shall receive, the same authority must also decide what they shall do.

feels bound by it. In a democracy, this means that it will not prevail unless it forms part of the moral tradition of the community, a common ideal shared and unquestioningly accepted by a majority.[54] It is this dependency that makes so very ominous, the challenges to the principle of the rule of law. The danger is all the greater because many of the applications of the rule of law are also ideals which we can hope to approach very closely but can never fully realize. If the ideal of the rule of law is a firm element of public opinion, legislation and judicial decision-making will tend to approach it more and more closely. However, if it is represented as an impracticable, and even undesirable ideal, and people cease to strive for its realization, it will rapidly disappear. Such a society will quickly relapse into a state of arbitrary tyranny.[55] It is important to realize, Hayek stresses, that the rule of law will only restrict government in respect of its coercive activities, as against non-coercive activities.[56]

Hayek also distinguishes between true substantive laws (those that regulate relations between private persons and the state and amongst such persons) and operational regulations (diktats issued for the state apparatus) which are not really law, but which are also called law today. This distinction is important in the context of an over-regulated modern state where operational regulations are complex and manifold in character and are used to justify various actions against citizens.

Hayek argues that the goals of substantive equality and substantive (or 'distributive') justice are inherently inconsistent with the rule of law. Hayek's first objection to distributive justice is that there is no accepted system of values according to which a society can determine what is a fair distribution, so the views of some will have to prevail over others.

---

[54] Hayek, *The Constitution of Liberty*, pp. 181–2. It is believed that Hayek was inspired by various continental philosophers, including Kelsen, in respect of this specific characteristic. It is surprising, however, that Hayek does not look at constitutionalism and the limitations it imposes on lawmakers more closely and ask this question more forcefully.

[55] Hayek, *The Constitution of Liberty*, p. 182.

[56] Hayek, *The Constitution of Liberty*, p. 181. In Hayek's view, there are vast areas of government activity which do not involve coercion against citizens, for example, foreign policy.

Even in a society with a consensus on a system of values, conflicts will arise between incommensurable values, and there will inevitably be dissenters from the majority. Hayek's second objection is that any such system would by necessity be particularistic because the infinite variety of situations that arise cannot be governed by general rules established in advance. Distributive justice is therefore, inherently inconsistent with the rule of law. Substantive equality violates the rule of law for the same reason and additionally because the differential treatment it entails violates the equality requirement.

FOUR THEMES OF LIBERTY

The rule of law theories propagated by Hayek and Dicey fall into the Montesquieu archetype and are based on the assumption that societies cannot possess an unlimited power to regulate an individual's liberty.[57] In fact, most of the dominant theories of the rule of law originate in some form of liberalism. Tamanaha explains liberalism's obsession with the rule of law by pointing out that while the rule of law can survive without liberalism, liberalism cannot survive without the rule of law. He discusses four themes of liberty that are evident in liberalism's understanding of the rule of law in the modern state. Individuals are free to the extent that the laws are created democratically. Citizens have thereby, consented to, and indeed authored, the rules they are obliged to follow. The individual is at once the ruler and the ruled. Presumably under a democracy, citizens would not enact laws to oppress themselves; their power to make law is, accordingly, their own best protection. Such self-rule is 'political liberty'.[58]

The second theme entails that the individual is free to the extent that government officials are required to act in accordance with pre-existing law. Citizens are subject only to the law, not to the arbitrary will or

---

[57] Many scholars including Locke, Kant, Laski, and Rawls have explained the concept of liberty over centuries. For a concise discussion on liberty, see I. Carter, 'Positive and Negative Liberty', in Edward N. Zalta (ed.), *The Stanford Encyclopedia of Philosophy* (Spring 2012 edn), available at http://plato.stanford.edu/archives/spr2012/entries/liberty-positive-negative/ (accessed 1 November 2015).

[58] Tamanaha, *On the Rule of Law*, p. 34.

judgement of another who wields coercive governmental power. This entails that the laws be declared publicly in clear terms in advance, be applied equally, and be interpreted and applied with certainty and reliability. This is 'legal liberty'. Legal liberty is the dominant theoretical understanding of the rule of law in modern liberal democracies. The individual is free insofar that the government is restricted from infringing upon an inviolable realm of personal autonomy. These restrictions may be substantive or only procedural. This is 'personal liberty'. Freedom is enhanced when the powers of the government are divided into separate compartments (horizontal and vertical) with the application of law, entrusted to an independent judiciary. Allocating the application of law to an independent judiciary ensures that an expert legal institution is available to check the legality of government action. This is the 'institutionalized preservation of liberty'. It entails institutional structures and processes that have been devised to enhance prospects for the realization of liberty of citizens through the effective division of governmental power. This is qualitatively different from the previous three, in that it is a structural arrangement for enhancing liberty rather than a type of liberty itself.[59]

These four themes of liberty form the essence of the liberal propositions on the rule of law. This also explains why the liberals are generally adherents of the formalist theories. They wish the legal system to leave liberties alone as they believe liberty, and other rights, can be best achieved if the law does not interfere with them. In their world view, the rule of law is a negative virtue, a virtue that prevents something from happening.

UNGER AND THE CRITICAL LEGAL THEORISTS

Dicey and Hayek are leaders of conservative rights and champions of liberalism, who believe that rule of law declines if the state moves towards a welfare state, or indeed socialism. We will now examine Roberto Unger's views on the rule of law. Unger is the most important representative of the critical legal studies movement which opposed liberalism and its understanding of the rule of law and was of the firm belief that law is nothing but politics.

[59] Tamanaha, *On the Rule of Law*, pp. 34–5.

Unger agrees with Dicey and Hayek that the rule of law is one of the cornerstones of the modern liberal state. Like other theorists, Unger also believes that laws are expected to be general and address broadly defined categories of individuals and actions without personal or class favouritism. It is the generality of the legal order that establishes formal equality and shields people from the arbitrariness of the government and its officials.[60] In addition to the requirements of generality and uniformity, Unger identifies two 'contrasts', which in his view form the core of the rule of law: (i) administration must be separated from legislation to ensure generality and (ii) adjudication must be distinguished from administration to maintain uniformity.[61] This is only a loose form of the rule of law in Unger's view. A stricter version, in his view, requires that every member of the society somehow participate in the making of legislations as well. This participation will also ensure the substantive autonomy of the legal order.[62]

Unger rightly recognizes that the rule of law principle is one of the primary manifestations of society's struggle against the arbitrariness of ordinary social hierarchies.[63] Unger warns, however, that the development of the modern state and the accompanying legal order might not totally replace older systems affecting human behaviour, like customary laws and bureaucratic regulations,[64] which continue to function even in modern democracies. This coexistence means that the rule of law may

[60] Unger, *Law in a Modern Society*, pp. 53–6.

[61] Unger, *Law in a Modern Society*, pp. 53–6 and 177–8. Unger also identifies these two contrasts as the distinguishing features of the modern legal order. The other trappings of the modern legal order are its autonomy, a specialized set of professionals who interpret and apply the law and the development of its distinctive set of rules and institutions.

[62] Unger, *Law in a Modern Society*, p. 178. Unger points out that the two versions of the rule of law broadly correspond to the democratic and non-democratic variety of liberalism. They also correspond to Tamanaha's formal legality and formal legality with democracy versions.

[63] Unger, *Law in a Modern Society*, p. 176.

[64] Unger, *Law in a Modern Society*, pp. 50–1. The bureaucratic law that Unger refers to, occurs in a society with a state that is a precursor to the fully developed contemporary state with a legislature, executive, and a judiciary. Unger calls this bureaucratic law because it belongs to the 'province of centralized rulers and their specialised staff'.

never be achieved, as the legal order is at times unable to distinguish itself from the other systems, and also exists in a dominant form such that it cannot be equated with the other systems. This duality creates a tension which probably makes the achievement of the rule of law beyond reach and at the same time creates a legal and normative order that dominates the regulation of human relations. This tension brings out, simultaneously, a society's impulse to discard the rule of law ideal and the stubbornness to persist with it because of its autonomy and generality.[65] More than Dicey and Hayek, Unger recognizes the importance of understanding the development of the modern legal order, particularly in political and social contexts, if one has to fully and properly explain the rule of law in any society.

Unger points out that the reality of life in the modern liberal state is such that the fundamental assumptions of neutrality, generality, and predictability, which underpin the rule of law, are never true. The state, and consequently the legal system, is constantly caught up in the antagonism between private interests. It is almost impossible to ensure that personal preferences are kept out of administrative and judicial decision-making. Legislation can never be made in a completely autonomous and neutral manner, as the lawmaking systems themselves embody certain values and any procedure will always play a role in determining the outcome.[66]

Unger agrees with Dicey and Hayek that the advent of the social welfare state (post-liberal in Unger's view) is bringing about the dissolution of the rule of law. He elaborates on how the challenges to the rule of law identified by Dicey and Hayek go beyond the administrative context to pervasively infect the law. Two crucial changes in law are generated by the social welfare state according to Unger: First, judges are asked increasingly to apply open-ended standards like fairness, good faith, reasonableness and unconscionability. Second, courts, and not just administrative officials, are increasingly asked to engage in purposive reasoning, that is, to render decisions on best method to achieve legislatively established policy goals—a process which immerses judges in making choices from among a range of alternative means with different value implications.[67] According to Unger, these two changes are

---

[65] Unger, *Law in a Modern Society*, pp. 56–8.
[66] Unger, *Law in a Modern Society*, pp. 180–1.
[67] Unger, *Law in a Modern Society*, pp. 193–4.

inconsistent with the traditional judicial role of formal rule application, and departed from the ideal of a regime of rules with the qualities of generality, equality, and certainty:

> Purposive legal reasoning and non-formal justice also cause trouble for the ideal of generality. The policy-oriented lawyer insists that part of interpreting a rule is to choose the most efficient means to the attainment of the ends one assigns to it. But as the circumstances to which decisions are addressed change and as the decision maker's understanding of the means available to him varies, so must the way he interprets the rules. This instability of result will also increase with the fluctuations of accepted policy and with the variability of the particular problems to be resolved. Hence, the very notion of stable areas of individual entitlement and obligation, a notion separable from the Rule of Law ideal, will be eroded.[68]

If such purposive reasoning and concerns with substantive justice prevail over the strict interpretation of law, Unger believes that the style of legal discourse will be no different than that of commonplace political or economic argument.[69] The result is a system that contains an unstable oscillation between generalizing rules and ad hoc decisions.[70] This results in the decline of the rule of law. Interestingly, Unger comes to the same conclusion as Hayek, albeit for reasons entirely different from the ones Hayek and his liberalism attribute. For Unger, it is not merely social welfare measures that contribute to the decline of the rule of law; it is the pervasive failure of the legal system to stay true to its avowed principles and characteristics that causes the rule of law to decline.

Indeterminacy

Tamanaha points out that critical legal scholars have systematically critiqued two fundamental characteristics that the rule of law rests upon: conceptual formalism and rule formalism.[71] Conceptual formalism essentially means that legal concepts and principles such as property ownership have a necessary and partial substantive content within the

---

[68] Unger, *Law in a Modern Society*, p. 198.

[69] Unger, *Law in a Modern Society*, p. 199.

[70] R. Unger, *Knowledge and Politics* (New York: The Free Press, 1975), p. 99.

[71] Tamanaha, *On the Rule of Law*, pp. 75–80.

total complex of rules and concepts to form a coherent and integrated whole body of law. It is the task of the judge to discover, by identifying and formulating the principles that emerge from cases and by applying legal reasoning thereto, what these concepts and rules consist of and require. Much of the analysis is abstract, presented with an air of objectively determined conceptual necessity. Critical legal scholars argue, to the contrary, that legal concepts are malleable, filled in by implicit theories or assumptions held by judges, or determined by unacknowledged choices made by judges.

Rule formalism is the idea that rules are applied by the judges in a mechanical fashion to determine the right answer in every case, without discretion on their part and without the interjection of their values. Realists argue that there are gaps and contradictions in the law, that rules often have exceptions which allow for contrary outcomes, that there is flexibility when judges formulate the rule purportedly laid down in a previously decided case, that many rules are ambiguous, that when going from a general rule to application in a particular case there could be more than one reasonable alternative. Therefore, the interpretation of rules is often indeterminate, anything but mechanical, and open to choices and subject to influence from the values of the judge. Such interjection of choice is concealed by rule formalism. This critical analysis significantly challenges the contrast between the rule of law and rule of man.[72] Along with this indeterminacy thesis, critical legal scholars also argue that law and politics are not separate, but rather law is politics, or at the least, they are intimately intertwined, making it impossible for the application of law to be free of politics and political choices. Consequently, the rule of law cannot be independent of political and social choices.

---

[72] Tamanaha, *On the Rule of Law*, p. 79. Many critical legal theorists have put forward their views on indeterminacy and the effects it has on the legal system and the rule of law. Some prominent scholars, apart from Unger, are Joseph Singer, Andrew Altman, and Duncan Kennedy. For a concise summary of their views, see K. Kress, 'Legal Inderterminacy', *California Law Review*, vol. 77, no. 2 (1989): 283, available at http://scholarship.law.berkeley.edu/californialawreview/vol77/iss2/2 (accessed 9 February 2017). See also G. Binder, 'Critical Legal Studies', in D. Patterson (ed.), *A Companion to Philosophy of Law and Legal Theory*, (Oxford, UK: Wiley-Blackwell, 2010), pp. 267–78, available at https://ssrn.com/abstract=1932927 (accessed 7 October 2017).

From the above discussion, it is evident that there are number of questions that the theorists raise about the relevance and efficacy of the rule of law. It will be useful to examine the practical understanding of the rule of law before attempting to provide a holistic meaning of the rule of law.

RULE OF LAW IN PRACTICE

How does the rule of law work in practice? Have contemporary societies, most of which are capitalist social welfare societies in orientation, accepted some form of rule of law? Are thin theories more popular than thick ones? What are the salient features of rule of law mechanisms that societies have chosen, expressly or otherwise?

The World Justice Project (WJP), a current global initiative that seeks to promote the rule of law across the world, identifies it as a system in which the following four 'universal' principles are upheld:

1. The government, its officials and agents, as well as individuals and private entities are accountable under the law.
2. The laws are clear, publicized, stable, and just; are applied evenly; and protect fundamental rights, including the security of persons and property.
3. The process by which the laws are enacted, administered, and enforced is accessible, fair, and efficient.
4. Justice is delivered timely by competent, ethical, and independent representatives and neutrals who are of sufficient number, have adequate resources, and reflect the makeup of the communities they serve.[73]

These four universal principles are further developed into nine factors that form the basis for preparing a rule of law index every year in different countries. These are:

[73] The WJP is an initiative of the American Bar Association that aims to promote the rule of law across the world. Among other things, it brings out a comparative Rule of Law index every year. See www.worldjusticeproject.org (accessed 7 October 2017). There are a number of other such indicators developed by various global institutions including the World Bank. The author has studied the WJP in detail as it is the most comprehensive of the indices.

1. **Constraints on government powers**: Government powers should be sufficiently defined in the law and effectively limited by the legislature and judiciary. Government officials should also be subject to the law. The WJP has identified 61 variables combined to form seven sub-factors.

2. **Absence of corruption**: Government officials, in all branches, should not use their office for private gain. The WJP has identified 68 variables combined to form four sub-factors.

3. **Open government**: Official information should be accessible to the public. The laws should be stable and publicized. People should be able to participate in, and collaborate effectively with, the government. The WJP has identified 36 variables combined to form six sub-factors.

4. **Guarantee of fundamental rights**: Fundamental rights, such as equality, right to life, freedom of expression and association, freedom of religion, and labour rights, should be guaranteed effectively by the law. A system of positive law without fundamental rights can at best be called rule by law. The WJP has identified 115 variables combined to form eight sub-factors.

5. **Order and security**: The state must effectively prevent crime and violence, including political violence and vigilante justice. Assuring security of persons and property is a fundamental function of the state. The WJP has identified 17 variables combined to form three sub-factors.

6. **Regulatory enforcement**: Government regulations should be enforced properly without delay and undue influence. Due process should be followed in all government proceedings. The WJP has identified 84 variables combined to form five sub-factors.

7. **Civil justice**: Ordinary citizens should be able to resolve their disputes in a peaceful manner through formal institutions without any delay and in an effective process. Civil justice should be accessible, free of corruption, discrimination, and improper government influence, and should be effectively enforced. The WJP has identified 57 variables combined to form seven sub-factors.

8. **Criminal justice**: An effective criminal justice system is a key component of the rule of law mechanism. The criminal investigation and adjudication systems should be timely and effective. The criminal justice system should be impartial, free of government influence, and

corruption. The rights of the accused should be protected and due process followed. The WJP has identified 97 variables combined to form seven sub-factors.

9. **Informal justice**: Where informal justice mechanisms, such as community-based systems or traditional courts, exist, they should be impartial and free of improper influence. They should respect and protect fundamental rights.

Using the above principles as a touchstone, the WJP conducts qualitative and quantitative surveys across 100 countries to bring out a rule of law index every year. The index seeks to measure how the rule of law is experienced on a daily basis in different countries.[74]

The WJP principles do not fit strictly into any one theory that we have discussed. Practitioners, it appears, do not really care much for neat classifications into theories, but are more concerned with how to make things work. It is evident that the principles identified by the WJP go beyond formal legality and include a number of substantive rights in evaluating adherence to the rule of law. Except for the guarantee of fundamental rights and open government, most contemporary societies will claim adherence to the other general principles. Even societies where fundamental rights and open government are not strong points argue that such principles do, in fact, exist in their countries. The question of course, is whether, the use of the rule of law in practice has become purely rhetorical, as Shklar claims, or is there unanimity among practitioners about the meaning of the rule of law? That there is no unanimity on the meaning is very clear.[75] Whether it is mere rhetoric can only be examined by an in-depth study of each society and its systems, including the legal system, and not merely by surveys and indices.[76]

RULE OF LAW—A POLITICAL (NOT LEGAL) IDEAL

In the crowded theoretical space of the rule of law where fierce debates rage between formal theories and substantive theories, positivism and

---

[74] www.worldjusticeproject.org/rule-of-law-index (accessed 7 October 2017).

[75] Peerenboom, 'Varieties of Rule of Law'.

[76] Various scholars warn of the pitfalls in the efforts to measure the rule of law by reducing complex concepts into simple indices. See, for example, T. Ginsburg, 'Pitfalls of Measuring the Rule of Law', *Hague Journal of the Rule of Law*, vol. 3, no. 2 (2011): 269–80.

realism, inclusion or exclusion of human rights, separation of powers, judicial independence and strict legal analysis, independent of political and moral choices, very often there is a tendency to forget the fundamental purpose of the rule of law. As Shklar points out, the rule of law is first and foremost a political ideal, not a legal one.[77] Unfortunately, in the modern world it has been reduced into a debate amongst lawyers and legal theorists about the legal system alone and whether it satisfies the rule of law. Such a debate limits and renders great injustice to the rule of law and its political objectives. We need to restore the rule of law to its rightful place as a political ideal whose goals and aspirations will vary and change as societies change, perhaps because of the success or failures of the rule of law itself.

The rule of law is neither a law, nor is it only about the law and the legal system of a country. It may be primarily concerned about the legal system in contemporary times because of the growth of the state and its machineries, but it is a fallacy to consider it as being solely concerned with the legal system.[78] The rule of law is a principle about the governance of societies. It is also a socio-ethical principle about the vesting, distribution, and regulation of power in societies.[79] Through this principle, societies have sought to control tyranny in all forms. The rule of law is a part of, influences, and is influenced by, the political, economic, and social relations in a society. In the author's view, the best way to understand the relationship between the wider political, economic, social, and moral choices; the rule of law; and the legal system is to imagine them as intersecting circles with the legal system being a smaller circle within the larger rule of law circle and both of them intersecting with

[77] All the major modern philosophers, such as Hayek, Dicey, Unger, Raz, and Fuller, agree that the rule of law is a political ideal and not a legal one. However, when the characteristics of the rule of law are being debated, the debate emphasizes less on the political perspective and focuses more on the law. If one views the rule of law as a political ideal it is possible to consider its drawbacks and successes in a more dispassionate way.

[78] Raz points out that the same is true of the legal system. The legal system cannot be subjected only to the test of the rule of law as it has virtues other than the rule of law. See Raz, 'The Rule of Law and Its Virtue', p. 228.

[79] J. Stone, *Social Dimensions of Law & Justice* (New Delhi: Universal Law Publishing, 2009), pp. 619–20. Julius Stone provides a wonderful analysis of law and power in societies in Chapter 13 of his book.

the broader political, economic, social, and moral choices.[80] Figure 1.2 illustrates this relationship.

SUBSTANTIVE RIGHTS

The first major debate about the rule of law is whether it should deal only with the procedural and institutional framework of the law as the thin theorists argue, or it should also contain within it some substantive rights as the thick theorists propound. As the rule of law is a political ideal and a choice made by a society, it is acceptable, and perhaps inevitable, for each society

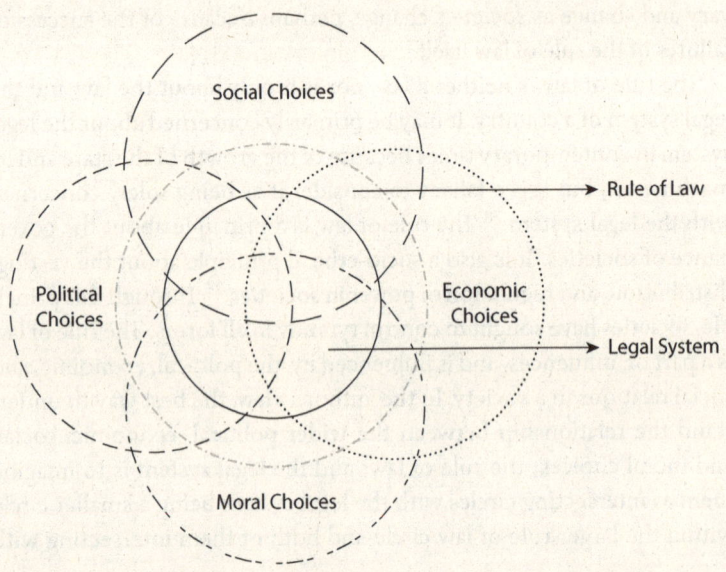

Figure 1.2 Relationship between the Rule of Law, Legal System, and Political, Social, Economic, and Moral Choices

Source: Author's own.

[80] This conclusion is supported by the arguments of Unger, Shklar, and Raz. Amongst the three it is Unger whose arguments support this conclusion the most, as he argues that while the legal system is the primary system, it competes with other systems in society to regulate human relationships. A logical extension of that is the fact these systems do not operate exclusively of each other but do interact. Tamanaha also recognizes this aspect when he argues that the theories do not adequately theorize the fringes of the rule of law.

to selectively choose what aspects of the rule of law, over and above the minimum requirements, should apply to itself. In contemporary society it is impossible to exclude certain values that could possibly be excluded a couple of centuries ago. For example, it is unthinkable to accept slavery in any form today whereas slavery continued to persist in the United States of America until as recently as 150 years ago, even after that country had attained independence and adopted the principle that all men are equal. Similarly, the situation in apartheid South Africa, where the majority of the population did not have any rights despite a legal system that would meet the requirements of a thin theory of rule of law, is simply unacceptable. With the near-universal acceptance of self-determination and human rights, a choice in relation to the rule of law necessarily involves making a choice on political, social, and moral values, such as self-determination, equality, and other human rights. While there are countries today where citizens are not entitled to these rights, those countries are viewed as outliers, rather than as exceptions. The rule of law, therefore, has to deal with political and moral choices in some form or another.

If a society chooses a rule of law that does not expressly deal with some difficult political, social, or moral issues, then that society also needs to clarify how, and in what manner, those issues will be addressed. As discussed earlier, the rule of law primarily manifests itself through the legal system and the legal system dominates all societies today by its sheer scale and reach. The legal system has arrogated to itself, to the exclusion of other systems, the role of regulating societal relations. If such a dominant system chooses to ignore certain key societal issues, it undermines the legitimacy of that system itself. The legal system and, therefore, the rule of law cannot afford to ignore certain kinds of relations; it will have to take a position even if that position is one of minimal or no interference.

It is not a question, therefore, of whether the rule of law should take a position or not, but of what kind of position it should take. The answer to this question depends on the processes through which the rule of law has developed in each society. If values such as equality, liberty, human rights, and most of the other good things that thick theories insist on, are generally accepted in a society and their violation does not occur often or if the existing institutional mechanism is strong enough to redress such violations, then the rule of law in that society can afford a position of minimal interference.[81] This cannot, however, be the case in

---

[81] Many Western countries have seen the rule of law develop over centuries accompanied by accretive political, social, and economic changes. Certain

other societies where the legal system will have to use its coercive force to effectively guarantee certain rights.[82] Of course, there will be difficulties in enforcing certain rights and these difficulties could challenge the rule of law itself, but difficulties should never come in the way of a principle. Nor should they come in the way of continuously reimagining the rule of law, as political ideals should be reimagined to address changing political, social, and moral scenarios.

SOCIAL WELFARE

The second important point of contention, and one closely linked to the first, is whether the advent of the social welfare state challenges the rule of law, as the administration of social welfare involves discretionary choices, purposive reasoning and application, which are incompatible with the rule of law. In fact, it will lead to a rule of men according to Unger and the critical legal theorists. The criticism is valid, as the enforcement of social welfare measures based on fact-specific situations derogates from the concept of general, uniform, and equal application of legal provisions. However, this is a criticism of the manner in which the legal system operates rather than the rule of law itself. If the legal system has imperfect processes in its functioning, that should not make the political aspiration of substantive justice invalid. The need of the hour is to reimagine the functioning of the legal and administrative system to reduce discretionary powers and purposive reasoning.[83]

---

substantive rights are accepted in these societies as a part of their common law, without the need for defining them in any statute or constitution. This does not mean that these rights are not part of their political ideal or the rule of law; it only reflects that their legal system does not have to coercively enforce these rights.

[82] Most postcolonial societies have drafted constitutions incorporating many substantive rights. Their evolution into independent countries with new aspirations demands that various substantive rights need to be enforced to give meaning to their independence. If the thin theorists are right, then most of these societies will not be rule of law societies at their very inception.

[83] It is important to remember that purposive reasoning is adopted by judges while interpreting the law generally and not just in the context of substantive justice. Purposive reasoning is by no means a taboo for judges across the world. Merely because purposive reasoning is involved, it does not mean that the rule of law should give up the goal of substantive justice.

As Raz points out, the rule of law can never eliminate the participation of men in decision-making and be only about the law; it will always be the rule of law and men.[84] The onerous task is to lay down the principles that limit open-ended discretion of the judges and officials interpreting and implementing the law by providing sufficient guidelines in advance to determine the outcome of individual cases addressed. As long as these guidelines and processes help people in planning their lives, the objection against discretion in social welfare measures should be discounted. It is only when uncertainty is created by administrative functioning that the discretionary use of power challenge assumes significance.

GROWTH OF THE REGULATORY STATE

Closely linked to, but distinct from, the debate on social welfare measures is the impact of growth of the contemporary regulatory state, with specific situation-based administrative processes, on the rule of law. Tamanaha points out that in addition to traditional parliamentary lawmaking, situation-specific administrative decrees are the order of the day. Various specialist regulatory authorities are increasingly being set up across the world and these regulatory organizations respond to situations on a case-by-case and need basis rather than always following the principle of declaring applicable law in advance.[85] These regulatory authorities are expected to respond quickly to changing situations in society and do not always follow traditionally accepted methods of making law or regulations.[86] However, as Raz stresses, the key is to ensure that there are adequate guidelines to address the particular decision-making processes.[87] The development of regulatory organizations and their circumstance based orders does not render the rule of

[84] Raz, 'The Rule of Law and Its Virtue', p. 212.

[85] Tamanaha, *On the Rule of Law*, pp. 96–8.

[86] One of the biggest challenges for regulatory organizations has been the rapid advancement of technology which contributes to activities not contemplated by existing laws and regulations. Authorities scramble to regulate new technology and in their eagerness to regulate, very often ignore basic and accepted principles of lawmaking. An example is the recent controversy surrounding regulation of internet-based taxi aggregators in India and other countries. This is addressed in detail in Chapter 4 of this book.

[87] Raz, 'The Rule of Law and Its Virtue', p. 216.

law into mere rhetoric. It certainly poses challenges but those can be addressed by ensuring that the regulatory organizations function within a framework of general laws.

INDETERMINACY

The last of the serious threats to the rule of law is the indeterminacy problem that the critical legal theorists highlight. Their argument is that every law has gaps that judges and administrators must fill in during interpretation and implementation in specific fact scenarios. The law is almost never completely clear and determinate, and when judges and administrators interpret and implement that law, they are influenced by their personal choices, making the rule of law merely the rule of men. This criticism, while it appears grave, has been tackled in theory and practice. As Aristotle pointed out thousands of years ago, judges need to use reason to ensure that their personal choices do not come in the way of correct decision-making. The modern legal system makes an effort to reduce the impact of these personal choices through various procedural safeguards such as public hearings, requirement of written and rea-soned orders, and the need to follow principles of natural justice. While the influence of personal choices can never be ruled out completely, the requirement of applying legal reasoning and certain procedures does reduce the possibility of personal prejudices significantly. As discussed earlier, the rule of law can never rule out the involvement of men; by its very nature, it is the rule of law and men. One needs to reduce the influ-ence of passion and promote reason in all decision-making. The rule of law only demands that society is not subject to tyranny because of the arbitrary personal choices of men. As long as systems claiming to com-ply with the rule of law implement measures to reduce this arbitrary exercise of power, the indeterminacy issue can be tackled, although it is unlikely to ever be eliminated.

Law has its limits, and so does the rule of law—conceptually, norma-tively, and practically. However, that does not mean one should aban-don the rule of law. Efforts should be made to iron out the deficiencies without being seduced by the magic surrounding the phrase 'rule of law'. Rule of law may not be an answer to all the social ills of modern societies, but it is a minimal requirement for any society.

2

INDIA'S RULE OF LAW

A THEORETICAL ANALYSIS

A constitution framed after a liberation struggle or a struggle for independence is, like poetry, emotion recollected in tranquillity. It is a severance from the past, a termination of imposed suzerainty and the setting up of a political sovereignty of one's own people. It rests on the proclamation of legal discontinuity, the transition of a people from the status of subjects to that of citizens, of a nation whose sovereignty is located in the people. This announcement of discontinuity we find in the Declaration preceding the Preamble to the Indian Constitution. We resolved to constitute India into a sovereign democratic socialist republic and thereafter set out the goals which this republic had to achieve. We moulded our struggle on liberal values and the rule of law. We rejected imperial domination but not the parliamentary system, which animated the politics and history of Britain and the British people's struggles against absolute monarchy.[1]

The Constitution was adopted on 26 November 1949[2] and India became a republic on 26 January 1950. The rule of law runs like a golden thread through our Constitution.[3] A study of the rule of law in

[1] K.G. Kannabiran, *The Wages of Impunity* (Hyderabad: Orient Longman, 2004).

[2] 26 November 1950 is celebrated as 'Law Day' by the legal fraternity in India, indicating the close link between the Constitution and rule of law.

[3] S. Sorabjee, 'Rule of Law: An Unruly Horse? Some Reflections on Its Application in India', *The Round Table: The Commonwealth Journal of*

India has to therefore begin with its Constitution.[4] The Preamble sets out the peoples' aspirations, hopes, ideals and the results they desire. It declares that India has been constituted by its people into a sovereign socialist secular democratic republic.[5] It further states that the people have resolved to secure for all of India's citizens, (i) social, economic and political justice; (ii) liberty of thought, expression, belief, faith and worship; (iii) equality of status and of opportunity, and to promote among them all; and (iv) fraternity, assuring the dignity of the individual, and the unity and integrity[6] of the nation.[7] These words marked a revolutionary change for the people of India. Never before in their history had Indians been promised these goals and rights in such an explicit manner.

A reading of the Preamble itself leaves us in no doubt that the Constitution embodies a thick version of the rule of law, as it does not talk generally about justice, liberty, equality, and fraternity, but specific ideas under each of those terms.[8] Various substantive provisions in the text of the Constitution seek to give meaning to the aspirations and

---

International Affairs, vol. 101, no. 4 (2012): 331, available at http://www.tandfonline.com/doi/full/10.1080/00358533.2012.707514?scroll=top&neededAccess=true (accessed 13 February 2017). Of course, the rule of law in any country is not limited to its constitution, and constitutions rarely claim explicit adherence to any political ideal including the rule of law.

[4] S. Sorabjee, 'Rule of Law: Its Ambit and Dimension', in N.R.M. Menon (ed.), *Rule of Law in a Free Society* (New Delhi: Oxford University Press, 2008), pp. 3–9. See also, S. Deva, 'Rule of Law in India: An Overview', in Matthias Koetter and Gunnar Folke Schuppert (eds), *Understandings of the Rule of Law in Various Legal Orders of The World*, Rule of Law Working Paper Series No. 10, Berlin (2010), available at http://wikis.fuberlin.de/download/attachments/22347870/Deva+India.pdf (accessed 15 February 2017).

[5] The words 'socialist secular' were added with effect from 3 January 1977 by way of the Constitution (Forty-second Amendment) Act, 1976.

[6] The word 'integrity' was added with effect from 3 January 1977 by way of the Constitution (Forty-second Amendment) Act, 1976.

[7] Seervai points out that the objectives set out in the preamble are themselves ambiguous and cannot throw any light on the provisions of the Constitution. H.M. Seervai, *Constitutional Law of India*, Vol. 1 (New Delhi: Universal Book Traders, 4th edn, 2002), pp. 280–2.

[8] The Preamble is a part of the Constitution according to many Supreme Court decisions. In the initial years after the Constitution was adopted, there

ideals set out in the Preamble, although only social, economic, and political justice is directly mentioned in the Constitution—in Articles 38 and 39. For the concepts of equality, liberty, and fraternity, one needs to review the substantive provisions. This chapter briefly reviews some of these provisions to get a better understanding of the social, economic, and political choices made by the Indian Constitution.

FUNDAMENTAL RIGHTS

Part III of the Constitution contains the fundamental rights of the people. No law made in India can take away or abridge the rights conferred by Part III and if it does so, it is void to the extent of the contravention.[9] Law is defined to include not only rules, orders, regulations, bylaws, and notifications made by the state, but also custom or usage having the force of law. The inclusion of custom and usage is significant, as it indicates that Part III rights will trump any custom or usage that may not strictly be part of the legal system.[10]

EQUALITY

Article 14 provides that the state shall not deny to any person equality before the law or equal protection of the laws within the territory of India. Article 15(1) prohibits the state from discriminating against any citizen on the grounds of only religion, race, caste, sex, place of birth, or any of them. Article 15(2) widens the principle by providing that no citizen shall, on grounds only of religion, race, caste, sex, place of birth, or any of them, be subject to any disability, liability, restriction, or condition with regard to (i) access to shops, public restaurants, hotels, and places of public entertainment, or (ii) the use of wells, tanks,

---

was a doubt as to whether the preamble was part of the Constitution. See Seervai, *Constitutional Law of India*, pp. 278–9.

[9] Article 13(2) of the Constitution. Article 13(1) includes a similar provision for laws made before the commencement of the Constitution.

[10] The judiciary has taken divergent views on personal laws and customs. While personal laws have been found to be outside the purview of Part III, customs must yield to Part III. See *Madhu Kishwar* v *State of Bihar* (1996) 5 SCC 125 and *Ahmedabad Women Action Group* v *Union of India* (1997) 3 SCC 573.

bathing ghats, roads and places of public resort maintained wholly or partly out of state funds or dedicated to the use of the general public. Articles 15(3), 15(4), and 15(5) empower the state to make special provisions for women, children, socially and educationally backward classes or citizens, and scheduled castes and tribes, including in admissions to educational institutions. Article 15(4) was included by way of the Constitution (First Amendment) Act, 1951 and Article 15(5) was included by way of the Constitution (Ninety-third Amendment) Act, 2005, with effect from 2006.

Article 16(1) provides that there shall be equality of opportunity for all citizens in matters relating to employment or appointment to any office under the state. Article 16(2) provides that no citizen shall, on grounds of only religion, race, caste, sex, descent, place of birth, residence, or any of them, be ineligible for, or discriminated against in respect of, any employment or office under the state. Article 16(3) empowers the state to make provisions relating to residency requirements in connection with employment. Articles 16(4), 16(4A), and 16(4B) empower the state to make reservations in respect of certain posts in favour of backward classes of citizens and scheduled castes and tribes, which, in the opinion of the state, are not adequately represented in the services of the state. Article 16(5) protects existing requirements to belong to certain religions or denominations to hold office in connection with the affairs of such religions or denominations. Articles 16(4A) and 16(4B) were included by way of the Constitution (Seventy-seventh Amendment) Act, 1995, the Constitution (Eighty-first Amendment) Act, 2000 and the Constitution (Eighty-fifth Amendment) Act, 2001.[11]

Article 17 abolishes untouchability and makes its practice an offence punishable by law. Article 18 abolishes all titles except military or academic distinctions conferred by the state.

LIBERTY

Article 19(1) provides that all citizens shall have the right to (i) freedom of speech and expression; (ii) practise any profession, or carry on any

---

[11] The Constitution (Eighty-Fifth Amendment) Act, 2001 was given effect retrospectively from 1995. It inserted an additional phrase into Article 16(4A). Retrospective application of law itself is a challenge to the rule of law.

occupation, trade, or business; (iii) move freely or reside and settle in any part of India; (iv) form associations or unions; and (v) assemble peaceably and without arms. The right to acquire, hold, and dispose of property was deleted by the Constitution (Forty-fourth Amendment) Act, 1978. Articles 19(2) to 19(6) empower the state to pass laws imposing reasonable restrictions on the rights guaranteed by Article 19(1), with a view to protecting certain specific interests set out in those clauses.

Article 21 provides that no person shall be deprived of his life or personal liberty except according to procedure established by law. Article 21A, introduced by the Constitution (Eighty-sixth Amendment) Act, 2002, obligates the state to provide free and compulsory education to all children of the ages of 6–14 years in such manner as the state may by law, determine. Article 25 provides that all persons are equally entitled to freedom of conscience and the right to freely profess, practise, and propagate religion.

Article 20 provides that no person shall be convicted of, or punished for, any offence except for the violation of law already in force. No person can be prosecuted or punished for the same offence more than once. Article 22 contains various protections against arrest and detention of persons and also prescribes limitations on laws providing for preventive detention.

RIGHT AGAINST EXPLOITATION

Article 23 prohibits forced labour and trafficking in human beings. Article 24 prohibits the employment of children below 14 years in any mine, factory, or hazardous employment.

CULTURAL AND EDUCATIONAL RIGHTS

Article 29(1) protects the rights of any section of citizens having a distinct language, script, or culture to conserve the same. Article 29(2) provides that no citizen shall be denied admission into any educational institution maintained by the state or receiving aid out of state funds on the grounds of only religion, race, caste, language, or any of them. Article 30(1) empowers religious or linguistic minorities to establish and administer educational institutions of their choice. Article 30(2) prohibits the state from discriminating against any educational institution on the ground that it is under the management of a religious or linguistic minority in granting aid.

RIGHT TO CONSTITUTIONAL REMEDIES

Article 32(1) guarantees the right to move the Supreme Court of India to enforce any of the other fundamental rights in Part III of the Constitution. Article 32(2) empowers the Supreme Court to issue appropriate directions, orders, or writs for the enforcement of any of the Part III rights. Article 32(4) provides that the rights guaranteed by Article 32 shall not be suspended except as otherwise provided in the Constitution itself.

FUNDAMENTAL RIGHTS: BEYOND FORMALISM

A literal interpretation of the Part III rights leaves us in no doubt that the Constitution includes rights that go beyond generality and formal equality and seeks to achieve substantive equality. While Article 14 deals with the general principle of formal equality,[12] Articles 15 and 16 address fact-specific situations to achieve substantive equality. They recognize the pluralism, widespread discrimination, and social and economic backwardness of certain classes that were prevalent in Indian society at the time of independence. Articles 15(4) and 16(4) empower the state to provide for special measures, including reservations for certain classes of the society, thereby creating an exception to the formal equality and generality principle. This is clearly a substantive and situation-specific principle aimed at improving the social and economic status of certain classes of the society. That this is sought to be achieved by a specific provision in the Constitution rather than through a legislative or a discretionary administrative measure indicates that there was a conscious political choice made to address these inequalities.

Article 17 is another example of a substantive right. If the Constitution had adopted only formal equality, there was no need for Article 17, as the equality provision of Article 14 would have sufficed.

---

[12]   The Supreme Court has read in some elements of substantive equality by permitting classification of people when formal equality is applied. The result is that any provision that differentiates between those who are not 'equal' will not fall foul of Article 14. This principle is discussed in greater detail in Chapter 3.

The specific prohibition in Article 17 clearly shows that the Constituent Assembly was conscious of the widespread practice of untouchability in India at that time and that the formal equality in Article 14 would have no meaning if untouchability was practised in some form or another. Articles 23 and 24 are of a similar substantive nature.

The Constituent Assembly and the leaders of the Congress, the dominant political force at the time, were determined that the discriminatory practices that had been in vogue in Indian society for several centuries should be done away with in independent India. They were very clear that the goal of independent India should be to ensure that all its people enjoy the rights and fruits of development that they expected India to achieve.[13]

At first glance, Article 21 appears to be a very formal right to ensure that there is no arbitrary deprivation of rights and liberties of citizens. In the rule of law parlance, it ensures that without the force of law no person's life or personal liberty is deprived. However, owing to judicial interpretation, Article 21 has been converted into a fount of various substantive rights ranging from one's right to livelihood to environmental rights.[14] Article 21 has essentially become the vehicle for the judiciary to read in various substantive principles of social and economic good as well as some of the principles of Part IV.

Articles 29 and 30 seek to ensure that India's pluralism, both linguistic and religious, is protected by recognizing the rights of minorities to maintain their identity through various means. This was a very important matter for the Constituent Assembly and the leaders of the independence movement. Accompanying independence was also the partition of the country into India and Pakistan on religious grounds, which was followed by a massive genocide in both territories. This background made the leadership determined to ensure that the rights of minorities were specifically protected in the Constitution. The linguistic minority rights recognized that India was home to many languages and that all of them need to be protected and preserved. Of course, the

---

[13] G. Austin, *The Indian Constitution: Cornerstone of a Nation* (New Delhi: Oxford University Press, 1999), pp. 26–112.

[14] L. Rajamani and A. Sengupta, 'The Supreme Court', in N.G. Jayal and P.B. Mehta (eds), *The Oxford Companion to Politics in India* (New Delhi: Oxford University Press, 2010), pp. 80–97.

representatives of south India were also worried that in the absence of linguistic rights, their languages, which were spoken in smaller territories compared to Hindi, would suffer from discrimination.

It was not only the goal of substantive equality that the Constituent Assembly had in mind when writing Articles 15, 16, 17, 29, and 30 into the Constitution—they also had the goal of fraternity and unity of the country in consideration. For too long, India was divided on the grounds of religion, caste, and language and the Constituent Assembly wanted to protect the country from further division on these grounds. Expressly guaranteeing equality amongst the diverse peoples of India would keep the country united; at least, that was the Constituent Assembly's hope and vision for India.[15]

DIRECTIVE PRINCIPLES OF STATE POLICY

Part IV of the Constitution contains certain principles which are not enforceable in any court, but are nevertheless fundamental in the governance of the country and which the state is obligated to apply in making laws.[16] Article 38 provides that the state shall strive to promote the welfare of people by securing and protecting, as effectively as it may, a social order in which social, economic, and political justice shall be the hallmark of all institutions of national life. In particular, the state is obligated to strive for the minimization of inequalities in income and must endeavour to eliminate inequalities in status, facilities, and opportunities, not only amongst individuals but also amongst groups of people residing in different areas or engaged in different vocations.[17] Article 39 lists certain principles of policy to be followed by the state to secure for all citizens an adequate means of livelihood. Principal among them are that the ownership and control of the material resources of the community is to be so distributed as best to subserve the common good and that the economic system operates in such a manner that it does not result in the concentration of wealth and means of production to the common detriment. Articles 39A to 51 include many other social, economic and political goals. Of particular significance are

[15] Austin, *The Indian Constitution*, pp. 26–75.
[16] Article 37 of the Constitution.
[17] Article 38(2) of the Constitution.

Article 44, which requires the state to endeavour to secure a uniform civil code; Article 46, which requires the state to promote with special care the educational and economic interests of the weaker sections of society, and, in particular the scheduled castes and scheduled tribes, and protect them from social injustice and all forms of exploitation; and Article 50, which requires the state to take steps to separate the judiciary from the executive.

THE JUSTICE DELIVERY SYSTEM

The Constitution envisages a separate and independent judicial system to protect and preserve fundamental rights.[18] Chapter IV of Part V provides for the establishment, and specifies the powers, of the Supreme Court of India. Chapter V of Part VI provides for the establishment, and specifies the powers, of the high courts in each state. Chapter VI of Part VI provides for the manner of appointment of the subordinate judiciary in each state.

Apart from dealing with resolution of disputes between private individuals or between governments, the judiciary has wide powers in redressing government actions that violate the rights of private individuals. While Article 32, which guarantees a remedy before the Supreme Court for violation of fundamental rights, is itself a fundamental right, Article 226(1) empowers the high courts in each state to issue directions, orders or writs for the enforcement of rights in Part III of the Constitution and for any other purpose. The words 'for any other purpose' have been construed widely and the high courts essentially exercise jurisdiction in all matters involving exercise of power

---

[18] The independence of the judiciary has been the subject matter of many cases before the Supreme Court. The Supreme Court has over the years zealously guarded the judiciary's independence, aided by the principle of 'separation of powers' being made part of the basic structure of the Constitution. The Court has essentially established the right of the judiciary to appoint, manage, and regulate itself. This position has become secure with the declaration that the Constitution (Ninety-ninth) Amendment Act, 2014, which sought to reclaim the power to appoint judges to the higher judiciary from the collegium, violates the basic structure doctrine and is therefore unconstitutional. See *Supreme Court Advocates-on-Record Assn. v. Union of India* (2016) 6 SCC 1.

by the government and organizations supported or controlled by the government.[19] Article 142(1) provides that the Supreme Court may in exercise of its jurisdiction pass such decree or make such order as is necessary for doing complete justice in any cause or matter pending before it. Article 141 provides that the law declared by the Supreme Court shall be binding on all courts within the territory of India. Article 144 mandates that all authorities, civil and judicial, in the territory of India shall act in aid of the Supreme Court.

DEMOCRACY

The Constitution chooses direct elections on the basis of adult suffrage to elect representatives to both the Lok Sabha (referred to as the House the People in the text of the Constitution) and the state legislative assemblies.[20] Article 326 provides that elections to the Lok Sabha and the legislative assembly of every state shall be on the basis of adult suffrage, that is to say, every person who is a citizen of India and not less than 18 years of age shall be entitled to be registered as a voter at any such election. Universal adult suffrage was a revolutionary step in India's history as it was the first time that every citizen was entitled to vote and choose the government in the state and the country.

Article 330 reserves certain seats in the Lok Sabha for the scheduled castes and scheduled tribes. Article 332 makes a similar reservation in the legislative assemblies of states. These reservations are to be made in the same ratio as that of the population of scheduled castes and tribes to the general population in each state. Articles 331 and 333 provide

[19] The jurisdiction under Article 226 is extremely wide and virtually any and every government action can be reviewed by a high court through the exercise of its powers. Government has been deemed to include even private organizations that may receive substantial funding from the state as well as those organizations that are controlled by the state due to its power to appoint their governing bodies or the majority of them. As a result of this construction, a major portion of the litigation in the high courts is against government action. This issue is addressed in greater detail in Chapters 4 and 5.

[20] Article 81(1) deals with direct elections to the Lok Sabha and Article 170(1) deals with direct elections to the legislative assembly of each state. The electoral constituencies are to be divided such that the number of people, as far as practicable, are the same in each constituency.

for nomination of members belonging to the Anglo-Indian community (if the community is not adequately represented) in the Lok Sabha or the legislative assembly, respectively. According to Article 334, the reservations under Articles 330 to 333 were to be in force for 10 years from the date of commencement of the Constitution. This has been extended regularly by successive periods of 10 years and is currently in force until 2020.[21]

THE CONSTITUTION—A DOCUMENT FOR SOCIAL REVOLUTION?

The fundamental rights go beyond generality and equality and seek to address specific social inequalities. Articles 15, 16, and 17 are the personification of the attempt to go beyond formal equality and achieve substantive equality for all citizens. It is unusual for a constitution to identify specific social inequalities and seek to redress them. However, this identification and inclusion was certainly intentional in India's Constitution. Further, the directive principles make the country's policy ideals and objectives apparent. The Constituent Assembly clearly wanted the new republic to focus on achieving meaningful substantive equality. The Constitution is therefore not just a legal and political document but also a social and economic promise. Granville Austin terms the Constitution a document for social revolution. He observes,

> The Indian Constitution is first and foremost a social document. The majority of its provisions are either directly aimed at furthering the goals of the social revolution or attempt to foster this revolution by establishing the conditions necessary for its achievement. Yet despite the permeation of the entire Constitution by the aim of national renascence, the core of the commitment to the social revolution lies in Parts III and IV, in the Fundamental Rights and in the Directive Principles of State Policy. These are the conscience of the Constitution.[22]

That the Constitution hoped to bring about a social revolution is now universally accepted. Upendra Baxi goes further than Austin and claims that the Indian Constitution marks a historic break with

---

[21] The Constitution (Ninety-fifth Amendment) Act, 2009 provides for the latest extension.

[22] Austin, *The Indian Constitution*, p. 50.

modern constitutionalism and that its normative discontinuities are, astonishingly inaugural.[23] Baxi states, 'No previous constitutional model envisaged such an explicit and comprehensive transformation of a "traditional" society and installed a description of a constitutionally desired social order and good life, and ways of deep contention regarding these.'[24]

Justice Krishna Iyer concurs with Baxi and Austin and observes, 'The Constitution is more than legal parchment. It is a socio-economic instrument with a revolutionary thrust.... Justice Vivian Bose once said that the Constitution was meant for the butcher, the baker and the candle-stick maker; May I add, the bonded labourer, the weaker gender, the dalit sector, the tortured prisoner and the marginalised dissenter?'[25]

How did the Constituent Assembly decide that the Constitution was to be a document promising social revolution? Was Indian society ready, politically, socially, and economically for these rights, adult suffrage, and a society primarily led by the state in all respects? These are some of the questions that have agitated political, social, and legal commentators since 1950.

The Constitution was drafted and adopted just after India achieved independence from more than 150 years of British colonial rule. The freedom movement lasted for nearly 100 years. The longish freedom struggle meant that Indians did not only seek political independence from the British, but also wanted a new paradigm of governance and development for their society.[26] The search for a new paradigm—embodying freedom from existing discriminatory social structures,

[23] U. Baxi, 'The (Im)possibility of Constitutional Justice', in Z. Hasan, E. Sridharan and R. Sudarshan (eds), *India's Living Constitution: Ideas, Practices, Controversies* (New Delhi: Permanent Black, 2006), pp. 31–63 at p. 55.

[24] Baxi, 'The (Im)possibility of Constitutional Justice'.

[25] V.R. Krishna Iyer, *Human Rights: A Judge's Miscellany* (New Delhi: B.R. Publishing, 1995), p. 30.

[26] S. Saberwal, 'Introduction: Civilisation, Constitution, Democracy', in Z. Hasan, E. Sridharan and R. Sudarshan (eds), *India's Living Constitution: Ideas, Practices, Controversies* (New Delhi: Permanent Black, 2006), pp. 1–30, Rajani Kothari also makes the point that the longish freedom struggle coupled with the introduction of Western literature and law to India brought about a new consciousness among Indians to reform their society. Kothari's views are discussed later on in this chapter.

respect for multiple cultures, recognition of individual rights and aspirations, and desire for a united country in order to help India develop and reach new heights as a society—led to the rights and governance structure set out in the Constitution.[27] Austin points out that nearly every shade of opinion in the country was represented in one form or another in the Constituent Assembly.[28] The consultation process outside the Constituent Assembly reached an even larger set of people. This ensured that the Constitution was generally accepted by all the people in the country, although a few argued that the text resembled the music of an English band, while people wanted the notes of a veena.[29]

A Collage of Borrowed Ideas?

Sunil Khilnani argues that is difficult to accept the view that the Constitution was the capstone of a long story of constitutional and democratic development based on the slow entrenchment of a democratic ethos and principles among Indians. Khilnani further argues that India did not have the liberal climate to support the goals and aspirations of the Constitution. The Constitution essentially imposed a political equality in a society of great economic and social inequality.[30] Khilnani's views on equality echo Ambedkar's observations:

> We must begin by acknowledging the fact that there is complete absence of two things in Indian society. One of them is equality. On the social plane, we have in India a society based on the principle of graded inequality which means elevation for some and degradation for others. On the economic plane, we have a society in which there are some who have immense wealth

[27] Austin points out that the Constituent Assembly considered different routes to achieve this paradigm. The first route was to follow the 'village panchayat' model advocated by Mahatma Gandhi and others, where the village was to be centre of the republic. The second was the route finally adopted. Austin, *The Indian Constitution*, pp. 26–46.

[28] Austin, *The Indian Constitution*, pp. 8–25.

[29] G. Austin, *Working a Democratic Constitution: The Indian Experience* (New Delhi: Oxford University Press, 1999), p. 6.

[30] S. Khilnani, 'The Indian Constitution and Democracy', in Z. Hasan, E. Sridharan and R. Sudarshan (eds), *India's Living Constitution: Ideas, Practices, Controversies* (New Delhi: Permanent Black, 2006), pp. 64–82.

as against many who live in abject poverty. On the 26th of January, 1950 we are going to enter a life of contradictions.[31]

Ambedkar and Khilnani are right in pointing out that Indian society was neither liberal nor egalitarian at the time the Constitution was written. But there is absolutely no doubt about the goals, ideals, and aspirations that were written into the Constitution. Khilnani does great injustice to the Constitution by comparing the rights in the Constitution to those in a liberal regime as the Part III rights are qualitatively different from those of a liberal typography with their conscious focus on the achievement of substantive equality led by the state. The answer to the question of whether the Constitution is a document for social revolution is clearly yes, and the views of Khilnani and Ambedkar actually support this assertion as the Constitution does not seek to push the then-existing societal inequality under the carpet. Instead, it makes an effort to tackle these inequalities head on.

Khilnani's views do however raise the question of whether the constitutional principles were merely imported from the liberal West. The answer may not matter much for the current discussion as we are examining what the Constitution contains and the political choices involved in writing the Constitution. Whether these principles were home grown or borrowed should not make a difference if it was the conscious choice of a people rather than the act of a blind follower. There is no denying the influence of Western liberal philosophy, socialism, the British parliamentary system, and other concepts on the leaders of the freedom movement and the Constituent Assembly. Ramachandra Guha asserts that the concepts were not completely alien and explains that the longish freedom struggle meant that there was familiarity with these concepts in the Constituent Assembly and amongst the leaders of the Congress, the dominant party.[32]

A Vision for the Future Only

Uday Mehta has an interesting and different perspective on this issue. He broadly agrees with Baxi that the Constitution was burdened with the

[31] Constitutional Assembly Debates, Volume 11, pp. 972–81.

[32] R. Guha, *India after Gandhi: The History of the World's Largest Democracy* (London: Picador, 2007), pp. 103–27.

challenge of bringing an age to an end and drawing a curtain on the past. However, he points out that it was equally a search for the future and the vision in the Constitution is associated only with the future, as the future was the sole temporal register in which India could be spoken of at the time of independence.[33] Mehta believes that the Constitution did not have a choice but to include the broad concern of political power with the social issues of the day, as it (i) reflected the reality of the issues facing India and (ii) gave legitimacy to the Constitution itself. Not including social issues would have seriously challenged the 'We, the People' phrase in the Preamble of the Constitution. Mehta believes that the inclusion of the commitment to social justice constitutes the grounds of sovereignty for India and also further articulates the revolutionary agenda of the Constitution. Mehta adds, 'The Indian Constitution, along with the conception of the political that it puts in place, does not so much emerge from history as it emerges in opposition to history and with a firm view of the future ... one might say that in India, following the Constitution, the political became power absolved from history.'[34]

Mehta notes that in addition to the revolutionary agenda, focus on national unity, again a feature important because of the circumstances in which India became independent, ensured that the state was given the primary role and other forms of power and authority were rendered secondary. More than any liberal character, Mehta believes that this feature gives the Constitution a Hobbesian touch. Mehta adds,

> The Indian Constitution authorizes a conception of power that articulates a vision that is, in fact, revolutionary, precisely because of the way it conceptualizes the question of national unity and its relationship with extant forms of social order. Its deep concern with the social is part of a piece with an equally deep worry regarding the diversity of the social order and its viability as an alternative nexus of power and authority- an alternative, that is, to the purely political vision, which the Constitution attempted to inscribe.[35]

---

[33] U.S. Mehta, 'Constitutionalism', in N.G. Jayal and P.B. Mehta (eds), *The Oxford Companion to Politics in India* (New Delhi: Oxford University Press, 2010), pp. 15–27 at p. 16.

[34] Mehta, 'Constitutionalism', p. 22.

[35] Mehta, 'Constitutionalism', pp. 18–19. The Hobbesian reference is an interesting one and has not been explored much by scholars. Given the centrality of the state in India, comparing the constitution's political schema to the

In this paragraph, Mehta highlights the issues that continue to trouble the state and influence the country's political and social discourse after Independence and pose a serious challenge to the constitutional vision and the rule of law regularly.

The political scientist Rajani Kothari, supports Mehta by arguing that the Indian system, which came into place following the adoption of the Constitution, was a combination of three factors. The first is Hinduism, which according to Kothari, is the solid bedrock and unifying framework of Indian society. The second is the concept of a centralized rational-legal authority that was introduced by the British, which, while mainly operating in the legal and administrative spheres, also affected fundamental political beliefs and relationships. The third is the reconstructive nationalism of the pre-independence era that developed as a means to political independence and social reform in the context of an expanding democratic framework.[36]

There are two conclusions from the above discussion that are important. First, the Constitution was a culmination of a political and social choice that Indians had made.[37] It was not imposed on them by any external power. The Constituent Assembly functioned as a sovereign entity[38] and the Constitution was a conscious choice setting out clearly

---

one propounded by Hobbes, where the state has enormous power, may not be wrong at all. However, such a comparison does not sit well as Hobbes did not envisage the modern state in all its diversity, particularly the acceptance of separation of powers making the modern state, even in India, a less unified force than the one Hobbes had in mind.

[36] R. Kothari, *Politics in India* (Hyderabad: Orient Blackswan, 2nd edn, 2012), pp. 21–2. Kothari, in the author's opinion, does not really justify the Hinduism argument very well, but it is an interesting viewpoint that is relevant in the context of the influence that the concept of *Dharma* may have on the rule of law in India. This issue is discussed later in this chapter. Other scholars see more of a Buddhist rather than a Hindu influence. See, M. Ganesh, 'The Indian Constitution and Nationalism', a Constitution Day Lecture organized by Daksh delivered on 26 November 2016. A summary of the lecture is available at http://dakshindia.org/inclusivity-time-nationalism/ (accessed 27 February 2017).

[37] Kothari, *Politics in India*, pp. 103–5.

[38] Both Austin and Seervai point out that while the Assembly was initially created with the blessing of the British and agreement with the Muslim League, because of partition and independence in 1947, the fact that it was

the political, social, and economic ideals that the country had chosen. The text of the Constitution was debated threadbare for a long time and went through numerous drafts and iterations. There cannot be any doubt about the choices, and the reasons for those choices, as they form a matter of record.[39] There was indeed a conscious borrowing of concepts and ideas from others but that borrowing was to better themselves, rather than merely an eagerness to imitate through ignorance.

Second, the rule of law was an important part of the political and social choice. The principle that all people in the territory are equal runs through the Constitution. In combination with the other Part III rights such as the right to life, an independent judiciary with the power to enforce the law against everyone including the government, universal adult suffrage, and the supremacy of the Constitution itself, it is very clear that the rule of law was one of the political ideals that the Constitution sought to achieve. The rule of law ideal in the Constitution has certain unique choices made with a hope and concern for the country's situation as we have already discussed. Together with the idea of a social revolution led by the state, the rule of law in India acquires an even greater interesting dimension.

RULE OF LAW—A REVOLUTIONARY DOCTRINE IN INDIA

The revolutionary nature of the Constitution naturally raises the question whether there was a rule of law in India prior to 1950. Clearly, there was a semblance of the rule of law during British colonial rule. The British established an administrative and judicial order that formed the substratum on which the post-Independence administrative and judicial system has been built. The British were the first to introduce

---

elected and the Assembly passed a resolution saying that it could not be dissolved unless two-thirds of the members agreed, had the effect of converting it into a sovereign assembly deriving power from the people of India. Curiously, there is not too much serious objection to this assertion. See Austin, *The Indian Constitution*, pp. 3–8; Seervai, *Constitutional Law of India*, p. 155.

[39] The proceedings of the Constituent Assembly were printed in eleven bulky volumes. For a summary, see B.S. Rao, *The Framing of India's Constitution: Select Documents*, Vols 1–4, edited by S.C. Kashyap (New Delhi: Universal Law Publishing, 2nd edn, 2004).

a rudimentary independent judicial system that had the power to review executive action with the formation of the Supreme Court at Calcutta (now Kolkata) in 1774.[40] This led to the establishment of a judicial system based on the English judicial system in the presidency towns which, however, mainly catered to British citizens living in those towns. In the areas outside the presidency towns under British control, elementary *adalat* (court) systems were introduced to administer justice to Indians. These adalat systems administered indigenous laws and were manned by civil servants who also doubled up as judges. This dual system continued until 1862, when high courts were established in Calcutta, Madras (now Chennai), and Bombay (now Mumbai), which can be said to be the precursor of the modern judicial system we see in independent India.

The British also introduced positivist legal traditions in India by codifying laws. They passed various statutes for the territories controlled by them some of which are in force even today.[41] All these statutes and codes were based on English law of the day and not many local customs were included in the statutes. This codification exercise was perhaps the first example of centralized and systematic lawmaking by the sovereign in India. The British also introduced elections to the legislative assemblies in British India,[42] which however had limited powers and were subject to the directions of the British sovereign and his/her representatives in India.

---

[40] M.P. Jain, *Outlines of Indian Legal & Constitutional History* (Nagpur: Wadhwa and Company, 6th edn, 2006), pp. 1–3. This ability to review administrative action was soon curtailed in 1781 and thereafter courts were really only relevant for settling disputes between private individuals.

[41] Some important statutes that are still in force are the Indian Penal Code, 1860, the Indian Contract Act, 1862, the Transfer of Property Act, 1882, the Indian Evidence Act, 1872 and the Code of Civil Procedure, 1908. It is the continued existence of these laws even after nearly 70 years of independence that is the basis for many to argue that the Constitution did nothing to encourage serious legal reform in many important areas.

[42] The developments in British India also encouraged certain princely states to introduce similar measures in their territories, which influenced developments in independent India. A significant example is the princely state of Mysore. Mysore initiated perhaps the first steps for substantive equality through affirmative action for certain classes of society, which was the precursor to Articles 15(4) and 16(4).

All this gives the impression of an established rule of law, which is true to some extent, as the laws were implemented and enforced. However, the British rule was primarily concerned with the maintenance of law and order and the collection of revenue and did not guarantee any fundamental rights to citizens, particularly Indians, who were the subjects of the colonial rule.[43] It was a legal system set up by a ruler who wanted to keep the natives in check through the instrument of law. It must be admitted however that the introduction of the English legal system played a role in influencing the leaders of the independence movement for nearly 100 years, which resulted in some of the choices made in the Constitution.[44] Many legal scholars point out the similarities between the Constitution and the Government of India Act, 1935, particularly in respect of the federalist approach, the organization of executive and legislative powers, the overriding power of the Union of India in certain cases and the emphasis on territorial unity and integrity.[45] They also point out that the Indian National Congress was involved in drafting the 1935 Act.[46] However, it is only by stretching one's fertile imagination that one can assert that the Constitution was a continuance of the 1935 Act. The character and nature of the Constitution are fundamentally different from that of the 1935 Act. Part III and Part IV are the clearest examples of this fundamental difference.

Shashi Tharoor argues that claims that the British introduced rule of law into India are incorrect as the rule of law that the British sought to introduce was 'intended to perpetuate the British hold over India, it was designed as instrument of imperial rule'.[47] Tharoor makes the following two compelling points to argue that there was no rule of law during British rule:

[43] Jain, *Outlines of Indian Legal & Constitutional History*, pp. 209–17, where Jain points out the rampant racial discrimination in the judicial system.

[44] Jain finds that the origin of many developments in law in independent India can be traced back to the British colonial period. Jain, *Outlines of Indian Legal & Constitutional History*.

[45] For example, see H.K. Saharay (ed.), *C.L. Anand's Constitutional Law and the History of Government of India* (New Delhi: Universal Law Publishing, 8th edn, 2008), pp. 19–71.

[46] Saharay (ed.), *C.L. Anand's Constitutional Law and the History of Government of India*.

[47] S. Tharoor, *An Era of Darkness: The British Empire in India* (New Delhi: Aleph Book Company, 2016), p. 111.

1. The imperial system of law was created by a foreign race and imposed upon a conquered people who had never been consulted in its creation. It was, pure and simple, an instrument of colonial control. The British used the law to criminalize all types of political dissent.

2. The British legal system was discriminatory, racist, and partial. Indians were victimized whereas the British in India got away lightly with any breach of law. The system was manipulated to operate against Indians at all times. Sentences handed down by British judges were never equal for Indians and Europeans. In Calcutta, Indian prisoners' sentences exceeded those for Europeans by a factor of 10 for the same crimes.[48]

BEFORE THE BRITISH: DHARMA

Prior to the British rule, it is difficult to find evidence to suggest that the rule of law, as we understand it today, existed. India certainly could not be called a lawless society, as edicts of various kings, and religious and moral laws were in vogue and an effective adjudication system, albeit rudimentary compared to modern standards, was in place.[49] The legal scholar M.P. Jain notes, 'The present judicial system is what the British created, and hardly has any correlation, continuity or integral relationship with the pre-British institutions. In the field of law and justice, as in many other fields, the British period constituted a fundamental break from our traditions of the hoary past.'[50]

It is therefore not very relevant for the purpose of this book to examine in detail if there was any kind of rule of law in the pre-British

---

[48] Tharoor, *An Era of Darkness*, pp. 105–18. Tharoor cites many examples of lawmaking, racist trials, and biased sentencing to buttress his arguments. See also, A.G. Noorani, *Indian Political Trials: 1775–1947* (New Delhi: Oxford University Press, 2005), which contains narratives of trials during colonial rule that the British manipulated to punish Indians using the legal system in order to maximize commercial and political success for the British.

[49] A good historical record of the legal and constitutional history of India going back all the way to ancient India can be found in Justice Rama Jois' two-volume work. See M.R. Jois, *Legal and Constitutional History of India*, Vols I and II (New Delhi: Universal Law Publishing, 1984).

[50] Jain, *Outlines of Indian Legal & Constitutional History*, p. 2.

times. It is useful to however examine briefly the claim linking the Hindu concept of dharma to the rule of law.

Madhava Menon argues that as Indian culture is shaped in the philosophy of dharma, rule of law is not an alien concept but is innate in the Indian ethos and tradition. According to Menon, the spiritual content of dharma and the rule of law both rest in universal values of justice and tolerance:

> tolerance of people who differ from you, tolerance of systems, beliefs and practices which are at variance from yours, tolerance with a view to coexist peacefully in a diverse world respecting the rights of others in equal measure as you claim for yourself. It is too simple a proposition to need an explanation for people with common sense. The Rule of Law involves a sense of human equality and respect for basic human rights of all people irrespective of their status in society.... The Rule of Law rests in an attitude of the mind, which accommodates differences, respects all human beings alike, and submits to the collective wisdom expressed in the form of law in case conflicts arise.[51]

Dharma is the ultimate normative but elusive concept, more elusive than the rule of law. It is universal in the true sense of the world as it applies to all human affairs but escapes strict meaning. Consequently, dharma has only been explained by many but not defined. It is said to be the foundation of all affairs of the world, embracing all righteous conduct, covering every aspect of life essential for the sustenance and welfare of the individual and society, and includes rules which guide and enable those who believe in God and heaven to attain moksha. Dharma sometimes means the supreme law as even kings are subordinate to it, but it is also something that governs ordinary human conduct in private affairs as well.[52] It also means justice (*nyaya*) or what is right in a given circumstance.

If dharma is followed by all there is no need for a state and we could live in a stateless society. Since everyone does not necessarily follow dharma voluntarily, the state is established. The duty of the state or

---

[51] N.R.M. Menon, 'Constitutional Institutions and the Maintenance of Rule of Law', in N.R.M. Menon (ed.), *Rule of Law in a Free Society* (New Delhi: Oxford University Press, 2008), pp. 41–56 at p. 43.

[52] M.R. Jois, *Legal and Constitutional History of India: Ancient Legal, Judicial and Constitutional System* (New Delhi: Universal Law Publishing, 1984), pp. 1–12.

rajdharma is the pursuit of dharma itself. In any state, dharma is the supreme power and above the king who is only the instrument to realize the goal of dharma.[53] Justice Jois quotes from Manu, 'Dharma protects those who protect it. Those who destroy dharma get destroyed. Therefore, dharma should not be destroyed so that we may not be destroyed as a consequence thereof.'[54] Justice Jois believes that this short verse incorporates within it the entire concept of the rule of law, as it conveys that an orderly society would be in existence if everyone followed his dharma.

According to Justice Jois, rules of dharma regulate individual conduct by restricting the individual's rights in the interest of other individuals and society.[55] Although dharma is a pervasive concept enveloping life itself, it lends itself to precise meaning depending on the context in which it is used and is capable of being applied to specific circumstances. It does not have a universal prescription or an absolute ethic and its meaning has to be extracted and understood according to circumstances.[56] Jois adds that dharma in the context of the state only means law and *dharmarajya* means rule of law.[57] The logical question is where do we find the principles of dharma? All the major Hindu texts—vedas, smritis, the epics, Mahabharata and Ramayana—contain some description of what dharma is, in given circumstances. Every major ancient Indian saint, starting from Manu, to every advisor to the kings, such as Kautilya, has had a say on what dharma and/or rajdharma means.

Dharma certainly introduces a concept of moral duty and righteous conduct in all human affairs—political, social, and religious. It is not characterized by positive law and legality as in western traditions.[58] However, because of its malleable nature and abuse it has also at times become a rhetorical word, bereft of meaning, in common parlance.

---

[53] Jois, *Legal and Constitutional History of India*, pp. 575–8.

[54] Jois, *Legal and Constitutional History of India*, p. 8.

[55] Jois, *Legal and Constitutional History of India*, p. 8.

[56] Kothari, *Politics in India*, p. 27.

[57] Jois, *Legal and Constitutional History of India*, p. 9.

[58] A.K. Giri, 'Rule of Law and Indian Society: From Colonialism to Post-Colonialism', in P. Costa and D. Zola (eds), *The Rule of Law: History, Theory & Criticism* (Springer Netherlands, 2007), pp. 587–614, at p. 587.

Ambedkar rightly points out that dharma certainly did not prevent the origin and persistence of an unequal society where certain groups and castes were permanently abused and discriminated against. In fact, the very texts that are supposed to convey the meaning of dharma do not prohibit inequality and have been interpreted to support continuous discrimination.[59]

The existence and practice of the concept of dharma does not by itself prove that the rule of law as we know today was in vogue in ancient India. There were certainly no formal institutions of law or justice. The existence of a king's advisors and ministers and forums for seeking justice does not mean that there was rule of law.[60] In any event, there was certainly no unbroken and continued practice of dharma by rulers that culminated in the rule of law in the Constitution. However, the real impact of the ancient Hindu order on the rule of law is in the development of traditions and values that have had a lasting effect on all subsequent periods, as Kothari and Menon point out. Jawaharlal Nehru, the first prime minister of India, held a similar opinion and pointed out that the 'whole background of our ancient law' recognizes individual rights and the rule of law.[61]

The Constitution heralded not just a social revolution but also a rule of law revolution. The principles of generality and equality, supremacy of the law, independent judiciary, and participation of the people in law-making, albeit indirectly, brought into force a new regime of governance that India and its people had not experienced before. The existence of some continuity in the institutions and governance apparatus from the

---

[59] B.R. Ambedkar, *The Annihilation of Caste*, edited by S. Anand (New Delhi: Navayana, 2014).

[60] P. Chidambaram, 'The Citizen and the Rule of Law', in N.R.M. Menon (ed.), *Rule of Law in a Free Society* (New Delhi: Oxford University Press, 2008), pp. 10–21 at p. 11.

[61] See Nehru's inaugural speech at the International Congress of Jurists in Delhi in 1959, available at http://icj.wpengine.netdna-cdn.com/wp-content/uploads/2012/12/CONGRESS-BOOKLET.pdf, pp. 31–3, (accessed 3 March 2015). Many scholars however point out that individual rights were never recognised by Indian traditional law and that dharma did not promote an egalitarian society. Indian traditional society was a sui generis model without emphasis on individual rights. See Giri, 'Rule of Law and Indian Society'; Ambedkar, *The Annihilation of Caste*.

British colonial era and some amount of historical consciousness of righteous conduct in private and public affairs does not take away the fundamental revolutionary nature of the rule of law after 1950.

WHAT KIND OF RULE OF LAW?

Upendra Baxi rightly points out that the Indian rule of law is not just a sword against state domination but also a shield empowering state intervention in the life of society.[62] In Baxi's view, the distinctiveness of the Indian rule of law lies in the space it provides for a continuing conversation among four core notions—rights, development, governance, and justice.[63] This conversation offers a revision of the liberal Western conception of the rule of law and indeed, the concept of rights. Baxi goes further, saying that the Indian rule of law model offers a template to the global south.[64]

Baxi's views on the rule of law are an accurate summary of the political ideals set out in the Constitution. The choices made in the Constitution make it difficult to squarely fit the Indian rule of law into any of the classifications that Western theorists have identified. The emphasis on substantive rights, justice, and equitable development leaves us in no doubt that India has chosen a thick or substantive conception (see Tamanaha's classification of various rule of law formulations in Chapter 1) of the rule of law. Some choices go against the accepted thinking of mainstream Western theories. The choice of substantive

---

[62] U. Baxi, 'Rule of Law in India', *Sur, Revista Internacional de Direitos Humanos,* vol. 4, no. 6 (2007), available at http://hcraj.nic.in/joc2014/6.pdf (accessed 11 February 2015). A similar article by the same author is also available in R. Peerenboom (ed.), *Asian Discourses of Rule of Law: Theories and Implementation of Rule of Law in Twelve Asian Countries, France and the U.S.* (London: Routledge Curzon, 2004). See also Sorabjee, 'Rule of Law: An Unruly Horse? Some Reflections on Its Application in India'.

[63] Baxi, 'Rule of Law in India', p. 7. See also S. Deva, 'The Rule of Law in India: The Chasm between Paper and Practice', in Guiguo Wang and Fan Yang (eds), *The Rule of Law: A Comparative Perspective* (Hong Kong: City University of Hong Kong Press, 2013), pp. 27–45.

[64] Baxi, 'Rule of Law in India'. Baxi adds that this is in contrast to the hegemonic Western concepts that are forced upon everyone as a 'universal' conception of the rule of law.

equality as against formal equality, the imposition of a positive duty (albeit non-justiciable) on the state to achieve social justice and attributing a primary role to the state in the realm of social justice and development go against the prescriptions and warnings of Dicey, Hayek, Raz, and even Unger. The state and its organs have an enormous amount of discretion in making laws, and taking decisions under those laws, in the pursuit of these goals. While this assumption of a primary role by the state and the need for discretion to play that role meaningfully can be explained by historical circumstances, the continued leadership of the state in India even after more than 67 years indicates that historical choices are being reaffirmed continuously.[65]

The state, although circumscribed by the constitution, is the primary arbiter in society—it continues to make political, economic, and social choices in fact-specific circumstances and to exercise discretion in the implementation of those choices. The primary role of the state does not mean that people accept all the choices it makes. In reality, the state is constantly questioned for not exercising its power in a reasoned and fair manner, primarily on the basis of the equality and reasonableness principles, and courts regularly pass orders on the fairness of those decisions.[66] However, there has been no serious challenge to the state playing such a role. In fact, it appears that most people in society look to the state to continue playing the role of primary arbiter in almost every area of human interaction. This is probably because of two factors: First, in a truly diverse society, the state forms one of the few institutions that elicits participation from everyone in society. Second is the lack of a true Indian liberal narrative in the Western sense of a minimal state and maximum individual

[65] Even the economic liberalization policies followed by different governments during the 1990s and after did not herald a small and limited state that only regulated actions rather than prescribing and implementing policies. The current government of India, led by Prime Minister Narendra Modi, although led by a party (Bharatiya Janata Party) claiming to adhere to free market policies, has not really announced any measures to dismantle the primary role of the state.

[66] The writ jurisdiction under Article 226 is invoked on a daily basis to question such actions. As an example, more than 69,000 writ petitions were filed in 2014 in the Karnataka High Court alone, challenging various forms of government action.

liberty. Indian liberalism is instead associated with modernity, pluralism, secularism, and multiculturalism as opposed to religious dogma and identification of India with Hinduism alone. The Indian liberal has generally accepted, and in fact, supported state intervention from 1950 and no serious mainstream effort has been made to change this approach.

The primary role of the state and its officers and the obligation on them to act reasonably and fairly to achieve substantive societal goals are more in the nature of the Aristotelian rule of law archetype than the Montesquieu archetype. Aristotle's archetype involves a set of people, mainly judges, acting reasonably and against the influence of personal passions, taking the primary responsibility of upholding civilizational values. Montesquieu's archetype has a limited state, intervening only in certain areas of human conduct with freedom for individuals in other areas. Along with fitting in to the Aristotelian archetype, we could also argue that the Indian rule of law is part of the dream of equality and justice that the Constitution embodies, making it similar to Dworkin's argument that the rule of law is part of a larger theory of justice.

The Indian rule of law is heavily dependent on the personal and institutional reasonableness of the lawmakers, bureaucracy, and judges in pursuing the substantive goals set out in the Constitution. However, this reasonableness is tempered by the principles in law and not by untrammelled discretion as feared by Unger, at least in the constitutional scheme. The paraphernalia of the modern state indicates that the Indian rule of law also adheres to the Montesquieu archetype like most other modern states, but its quest for substantive justice based on equality and reason makes it more a follower of Aristotle. This argument gathers additional support if we accept the views of Kothari and Menon who believe that the Indian system has absorbed aspects of Hinduism such as righteous conduct for the betterment of society as a whole.

3

RULE OF LAW IN PRACTICE

JUDICIAL AND POLITICAL UNDERSTANDING

This chapter examines the judicial and political understanding of the rule of law in India and how this understanding has shaped its practical application. The judiciary's views on the rule of law are critical for infusing practical meaning and strength into the rule of law principle, as the judiciary is vested with the responsibility of protecting the rights of citizens and ensuring that the other organs of the state comply with the law. In a democracy, the actions of the political leadership determine the success or failure of the rule of law, as the political leadership has the responsibility to translate societal aspirations into policy and implement it successfully.

JUDICIAL INTERPRETATION OF THE RULE OF LAW

There are 2,004 decisions of the Supreme Court that use the phrase rule of law, out of which 144 have been rendered by constitution benches.[1] Among the high courts, there are 17,593 decisions that make

---

[1] A bench of five judges or more. The number of decisions or orders by various courts that used the phrase rule of law was found by carrying out a search for the phrase 'rule of law' in the SCC online database of Supreme Court

reference to the phrase.[2] However, very few of these decisions have tried to identify the contours of the rule of law as understood by the courts. This chapter first examines the few constitution bench decisions of the Supreme Court that endeavour to throw some light on the concept of the rule of law. The declarations by constitution benches essentially form the broad guiding principles that are followed by the smaller benches and lower courts. Later, the chapter studies the rule of law in practice by reviewing the Court's views on the various principles constituting the rule of law rather than the concept itself. The focus of this review is to elicit the Court's approach in implementing the rule of law and not to understand intricate details of the Court's discussions and proclamations on various other principles of law.

In *Kesavananda Bharati* v *State of Kerala*,[3] the Supreme Court is 'said' to have declared that the rule of law is part of the basic structure[4] of the Constitution. This conclusion was arrived at by a subsequent decision of the Supreme Court in *Indira Nehru Gandhi* v *Raj Narain*.[5] In the *Kesavananda* judgment itself, the summary points of the majority do not contain this declaration. So, any reference to the rule of law made by the individual judges has to be extracted by reading the separate judgments authored by the judges. Unfortunately, only some of the 13 judges expressly refer to the rule of law and that too in passing.[6] The Court did

---

decisions on 12 February 2015. A similar search on the Westlaw India database on 16 February 2017 yielded 2,202 results with 243 decisions by constitution benches.

[2] The number of decisions or orders by various courts that used the phrase rule of law was found by carrying out a search for the phrase 'rule of law' in the SCC online database of high court decisions on 12 February 2015.

[3] (1973) 4 SCC 225.

[4] Very briefly, the basic structure doctrine prevents the Parliament from making any amendments to the Constitution that violate certain principles that form part of the core of the Constitution. There is no exhaustive list of the basic structure features. The Supreme Court has from time to time identified various principles that form part of the basic structure. The Court has the final word on whether a principle forms part of the basic structure or not.

[5] 1975 Supp SCC 1.

[6] *Kesavananda* judgment. The references to the rule of law are by way of the following: (i) Article 14 contains the English principle of the rule of law;

not find the need to define the principle, nor identify the components of rule of law that forms part of the basic structure. The Court also did not go into any detailed analysis of the relationship between the rule of law and constitutionalism. Therefore, if litigants are able to convince the judges of the Supreme Court that certain principles are indeed part of the rule of law, then the Parliament cannot amend the Constitution in a manner that infringes those principles.

In *Indira Gandhi*, Mathew J. wrote perhaps the first exhaustive analysis of the concept of rule of law in any Supreme Court judgment. After quoting both Dicey and Hayek and terming their theories 'extravagant versions or ideals' of rule of law which may never be achieved in the world of action, the learned judge noted,

> There is a genuine concept of rule of law and that concept implies equality before the law or equal subjection of all classes before the ordinary law. But, if rule of law is to be a basic structure of the Constitution, one must find specific provisions in the Constitution embodying the constituent elements of the concept. I cannot conceive of rule of law as a twinkling star up above the Constitution. To be a basic structure, it must be a terrestrial concept having its habitat within the four corners of the Constitution. The provisions of the Constitution were enacted with a view to ensure the rule of law. Even if I assume that rule of law is a basic structure, it seems to me that the meaning and the constituent elements of the concept must be gathered from the enacting provisions of the Constitution. The equality aspect of the rule of law and of democratic republicanism is provided for in Article 14.[7]

Mathew J. made two significant points: (i) the rule of law has to be found within the Constitution for it to have a legal bearing and (ii) the theories of rule of law do not have a place in the interpretation or determination of the basic structure.

(ii) the rule of law is equivalent to *dharma* and *rita* (means cosmic balance or moral law of the world); (iii) judicial subjectivism undermines the rule of law; (iv) fundamental rights are vital to the rule of law; (v) the rule of law implies supremacy of the Constitution and the laws as opposed to arbitrariness; (vi) the rule of law reigns supreme in our country; and (vii) the rule of law has been ensured by providing for judicial review which cannot be excluded by any constitutional amendment.

[7] 1975 Supp SCC 1 at 336–7.

Justice Mathew's views contradict Justice Shah's observations in *Madhava Rao Jivaji Rao Scindia* v *Union of India*: '[T]he foundation of our Constitution is firmly laid in the rule of law and no instrumentality, not even the President as the head of the executive is invested with arbitrary authority.'[8] The Court further held that the rule of law is the bedrock of our Constitution. The question that arises is whether the rule of law is part of the Constitution or vice versa.

Radhakrishnan J., speaking for the constitution bench in *KT Plantation (P) Ltd* v *State of Karnataka*,[9] gave a slightly different analysis. Assuming that the rule of law is part of the basic structure, the judge ruled that the statutes that violate the rule of law can be found to be unconstitutional. The learned judge observed that the origin of the rule of law can be traced to Aristotle and philosophers like Hobbes, Locke, Rousseau, Montesquieu, and Dicey. After discussing the concept in its many shades and colors, he declared,

> Rule of law as a concept finds no place in our Constitution, but has been characterised as a basic feature of our Constitution which cannot be abrogated or destroyed even by the Parliament and in fact binds the Parliament.... Rule of law affirms parliamentary supremacy while at the same time denying it sovereignty over the Constitution.... Rule of law as a principle contains no explicit substantive component like eminent domain but has many shades and colours. Violation of principle of natural justice may undermine rule of law so also at times arbitrariness, proportionality, unreasonableness, etc., but such violations may not undermine rule of law so as to invalidate a statute. Violation must be of such a serious nature which undermines the very basic structure of our Constitution and our democratic principles. But once the Court finds, a Statute, undermines the rule of law which has the status of a constitutional principle like the basic structure, the above grounds are also available and not vice versa. Any law which, in the opinion of the Court, is not just, fair and reasonable, is not a ground to strike down a Statute because such an approach would always be subjective, not the will of the people, because there is always a presumption of constitutionality for a statute. Rule of law as a principle, it may be mentioned, is not an absolute means of achieving the equality, human rights, justice, freedom and even democracy and it all depends upon the nature of the legislation and the seriousness of the violation. Rule of law as an over-

---

[8] (1971) 1 SCC 85, 146.
[9] (2011) 9 SCC 1.

arching principle can be applied by the constitutional courts, in the rarest of rare cases, in situations, we have referred to earlier and can undo laws which are tyrannical, violate the basic structure of our Constitution, and our cherished norms of law and justice.[10]

This paragraph is indicative of the reigning confusion about the status and practical use of the rule of law principle in the constitutional framework. Justice Matthew's efforts to provide clarity are not only ignored but a different and vague approach adopted.

Krishna Iyer J. in *State of Karnataka* v *Ranganatha Reddy* gave a very wide meaning to the rule of law by observing,

> Our emphasis is on abandoning formal legalistics or sterile logomachy in assessing the vires of statutes regulating vital economic areas, and adopting instead a dynamic, goal based approach to problems of constitutionality. It is right that the rule of law enshrined in our Constitution must and does reckon with the roaring current of change which shifts our social values and shrivels our feudal roots, invades our lives and fashions our destiny.[11]

With this opinion, Justice Iyer understood the rule of law as a principle that must address the various inequalities and problems in our society. In one statement the learned judge elevated the rule of law to a moral obligation and a good in itself. As interpreted by Justice Iyer, the rule of law in India goes beyond even the broadest of substantive theories and appears to surpass even the Aristotelian archetype that equates the rule of law with the rule of reason.

In a similar, albeit narrower, vein Bhagwati J. in *Bachan Singh* v *State of Punjab*, observed,

> Now if we look at the various Constitutional provisions including the Chapters on Fundamental Rights and Directive Principles of State Policy, it is clear that the rule of law permeates the entire fabric of the Constitution and indeed forms one of its basic features. The rule of law excludes arbitrariness; its postulate is 'intelligence without passion' and 'reason freed from desire'. Where we find arbitrariness or unreasonableness there is denial of the rule of law. That is why Aristotle preferred a government of laws rather than of men. 'Law' in the context of the rule of law, does not mean any law enacted by the legislative authority, howsoever arbitrary or despotic it

---

[10] *KT Plantation (P) Ltd* v *State of Karnataka* (2011) 9 SCC 1, 60–2.
[11] (1977) 4 SCC 471, 496.

may be. Otherwise even under a dictatorship it would be possible to say that there is rule of law, because every law made by the dictator howsoever arbitrary and unreasonable has to be obeyed and every action has to be taken in conformity with such law. In such a case too even where the political set up is dictatorial, it is law that governs the relationship between men and men and between men and the State. But still it is not rule of law as understood in modern jurisprudence, because in jurisprudential terms, the law itself in such a case being an emanation from the absolute will of the dictator it is in effect and substance the rule of man and not of law which prevails in such a situation. What is necessary element of the rule of law is that the law must not be arbitrary or irrational and it must satisfy the test of reason and the democratic form of polity seeks to ensure this element by making the framers of the law accountable to the people.... There are three Fundamental Rights in the Constitution which are of prime importance and which breathe vitality in the concept of the rule of law. They are Articles 14, 19 and 21.[12]

The rule of law is enumerated as a principle which stands as a bulwark for democracy, fairness, reason, equality, liberty and life. In fact, the principle laid down by Justices Iyer and Bhagwati is so wide that it is possible to include any good principle within the definition.

Validating our understanding of what Justices Iyer and Bhagwati said, in *IR Coelho v State of Tamil Nadu*[13] a nine-judge bench held, 'Articles 14, 19 and 21 represent the foundational values which form the basis of the rule of law. These are the principles of constitutionality which form the basis of judicial review apart from rule of law and separation of powers.'[14] It also noted, 'Fundamentals such as secularism, separation of powers, equality and also judicial review which are the basic features of the Constitution and essential elements of rule of law.'[15] Further, 'Equality, rule of law, judicial review and separation of powers form parts of the basic structure of the Constitution. Each of these concepts are [sic] intimately connected. There can be no rule of law, if there is no equality before the law. These would be meaningless if the violation was not subject to judicial review.'[16]

---

[12] 1982 Indlaw SC 195 at paras 196–7.
[13] (2007) 2 SCC 1.
[14] *IR Coelho v State of Tamil Nadu* (2007) 2 SCC 1, 79.
[15] *IR Coelho v State of Tamil Nadu* (2007) 2 SCC 1, 105.
[16] *IR Coelho v State of Tamil Nadu* (2007) 2 SCC 1, 105.

In a similar fashion, K. Ramaswamy J. in *SR Bommai* v *Union of India*,[17] observed,

> Rule of law has been chosen as an instrument for social adjustment in the event of clash of interests. In a free society, law interacts between competing claims in a continuing process to establish order with stability. Law should not only reflect social and religious resilience but has also to provide a lead by holding forth the norms for continuity for its orderly march towards an ideal egalitarian social order envisioned in the preamble of the Constitution.

He added later, '*Democratic society realises folly of the vigour of religious practices in society. Strong religious consciousness not only narrows the vision but hampers the rule of law.*' Further, 'Rule of law has been chosen as an instrument of social adjustment and resolution of conflicting social problems to integrate diverse sections of the society professing multi-religious faiths, creed, caste or region fostering among them fraternity, transcending social, religious, linguistic or regional barriers.'[18]

In the same case, Jeevan Reddy J. observed,

> Democratic rule based on adult franchise was being introduced for the first time. Almost 1/3rd of the country, under princely rule, had never known elections. Rule of law was a novelty in those areas. The infant democracy required careful nurturing. Many a hiccup was expected in the days to come. This perhaps explains the need for a provision like the one in Article 356.[19]

In many other judgments, the Court has noted the fundamental place of the rule of law in India and has relied on it to support and validate many other diverse principles, including those which form part of the basic structure on their own. Bhagwati J. in *SP Gupta* v *Union of India* noted, 'If there is one principle which runs through the entire fabric of the Constitution, it is the rule of law and under the Constitution it is the judiciary which is entrusted with the task of keeping every organ of the State within the limits of the law and thereby making the rule of law meaningful and effective.'[20]

[17] (1994) 3 SCC 1.

[18] (1994) 3 SCC 1, 162, 163, and 206.

[19] (1994) 3 SCC 1, 214. Article 356 empowers the President to dismiss the democratically elected government of a state if the President is satisfied that a situation has arisen in which the government of the state cannot be carried on in accordance with the Constitution.

[20] AIR 1982 SC 149, 22–4.

In *Sub-Committee on Judicial Accountability* v *Union of India*, B.C. Ray J. observed, 'Rule of law is a basic feature of the Constitution which permeates the whole of the constitutional fabric and is an integral part of the constitutional structure. Independence of the judiciary is an essential attribute of rule of law.'[21]

At the same time, the Court has not hesitated to create room for maneuvering in order to address 'practical' day-to-day administrative difficulties by finding that the vesting of discretion is by itself not in violation of the rule of law. In fact, the Court has made an effort to find a median between the need for discretion and the requirement to curb arbitrariness. In *Supreme Court Advocates on Record Association* v *Union of India*, J.S. Verma J. pointed out,

> It is, therefore, realistic that there has to be room for discretionary authority within the operation of the rule of law, even though it has to be reduced to the minimum extent necessary for proper governance; and within the area of discretionary authority, the existence of proper guidelines or norms of general application excludes arbitrary exercise of discretionary authority.[22]

Similarly, Bharucha J., speaking on behalf of a nine-judge bench in the *Special Reference No 1 of 1998, Re.*, says,

> It has to be borne in mind that the principle of non-arbitrariness which is an essential attribute of the rule of law is all pervasive throughout the Constitution; and an adjunct of this principle is the absence of absolute power in one individual in any sphere of constitutional activity…. The rule of law envisages the area of discretion to be the minimum, requiring only the application of known principles or guidelines to ensure non-arbitrariness, but to that limited extent, discretion is a pragmatic need. Conferring discretion upon high functionaries and, whenever feasible, introducing an element of plurality by requiring a collective decision, are further checks against arbitrariness.[23]

LACK OF A COHESIVE APPROACH

The Supreme Court has clearly not felt the need to strictly adhere to Justice Mathew's prescription that the rule of law should be found within the text of the Constitution and not in political theories. At times

---

[21]   (1991) 4 SCC 699, 719.

[22]   (1993) 4 SCC 441, 683.

[23]   (1998) 7 SCC 739, 754.

the Court has followed Justice Mathew's approach and at other times it has conveniently used the rule of law principle(s) without referencing the Constitution at all. There is no cohesive approach to the rule of law. While the lack of a cohesive approach is not surprising, as the Court primarily operates in division benches and there is no requirement to develop a cohesive principle, it is the lack of a uniform approach even by constitution benches, and indeed among judges who are writing concurring opinions on the same bench, that is disappointing. The Court has not really made an effort to analyse if the Constitution follows any particular rule of law theory. Indeed, the Court has not found the need to neither identify one theory, nor craft a unique one to locate the principles that it has followed from time to time. On the occasions that the Court has found the need to refer to any theory, Dicey's emerges the favourite, although our analysis has shown that India's constitutional choices are not circumscribed by Dicey's theory. In fact, many judges quote Dicey and immediately go on to declare, casually, the very principles that Dicey was fully opposed to.

A reading of the various declarations by the Court shows that the rule of law in the Court's view comprises the following:

1. The rule of law is an essential part of the Constitution; indeed, it forms part of the basic structure of the Constitution and cannot be derogated from by any institution in India.
2. The rule of law is primarily embodied in the principles of equality in Part III of the Constitution.
3. No institution is above the law and the Constitution; the law is supreme.
4. Judicial review of administrative action is an important aspect of the rule of law and is part of the basic feature of the Constitution. Without judicial review, there will be no government of laws and the rule of law would become a teasing illusion and a promise of unreality.
5. The rule of law demands judicial independence and without judicial independence the rule of law could be threatened. Separation of powers is also an important aspect of the rule of law.
6. The rule of law is a dynamic concept and needs to reckon our social values. The rule of law has been chosen as an instrument of social adjustment.

7. Arbitrariness strikes at the heart of the rule of law and therefore, no government action can be arbitrary.

8. The rule of law does not rule out discretion completely; however, this discretion is tempered by distribution of power and general principles guiding the exercise of such power even in the case of high constitutional authorities.

9. The rule of law demands that all laws and governmental actions under such laws need to be fair and reasonable; otherwise they are not in accordance with the rule of law and can be struck down.

10. Strong religious consciousness hampers the rule of law. Secularism is an essential part of the rule of law.

11. The rule of law is a basic feature of democracy.[24]

12. The rule of law needs to run close to the rule of life.[25]

13. The rule of law cannot be violated even by judicial directions.[26]

There are four obvious, but important, conclusions that we can distil from these propositions. First, their range, breadth, and depth are staggering. The Supreme Court has read into our system a version of the rule of law so wide and substantive that even the thickest of theories feel like a thin theory in comparison. For the Court to state that the rule of law is dynamic and needs to reckon our social values or that secularism is an essential part of the rule of law is to lock, stock, and barrel throw the theories of Dicey, Hayek, and Raz out of the window, as none of them would countenance the Court's views. The Court's efforts at harmonizing discretion and the rule of law has the effect of rendering Unger and the legal realists' criticisms invalid. The sum of the Court's

---

[24] *Kihoto Hollohan* v *Zachilhu* 1992 Supp (2) SCC 651.

[25] This dictum has mainly been used in various judgments by Krishna Iyer J. In my view, he means various things by this statement, but the primary meaning is that the rule of law (although he never really fully explains what he means by it) has to be as close as possible to the realities of life in society. For example, see his opinion in *Bar Council of Maharashtra* v *MV Dabholkar* (1975) 2 SCC 702 at 719. While Justice Iyer does not identify any source for this statement, it appears that he may have borrowed this from Prime Minister Nehru's speech to the ICJ at the Delhi conference in 1959. Available at http://icj.wpengine. netdna-cdn.com/wp-content/uploads/2012/12/CONGRESS-BOOKLET. pdf pp. 31–3, (accessed 3 March 2015).

[26] *AR Antulay* v *RS Nayak* (1988) 2 SCC 602.

pronouncements proves that the Court's version of the rule of law is unique and distinct from any legal theory that has been enumerated.

Second, there is a lot of rhetoric and confusion in the use of the phrase rule of law. At times, it appears that Shklar's fear that the phrase rule of law has become meaningless due to rhetorical over use has come true in the hands of the Supreme Court. The confusion can be partly explained because the Court has not only used the phrase to mean the great political ideal but also to drive home the message of the existence of a rule of law rather than pure arbitrary action. This second and more common usage only indicates that there is a law, properly made, that occupies and governs the relevant field. However, equating it to the concept of rule of law, as the Court has done many times, causes confusion.[27]

Third, the Court has used the rule of law as a convenient ideal to be invoked from time to time to justify various conclusions that cannot easily be justified on the basis of substantive provisions of the Constitution or statutory law. Wherever possible, the Court has identified specific principles that comprise the rule of law, but those cases are far and few. In the majority of the cases, the Court has invoked the rule of law without specifying which of its aspects is being invoked.[28]

Fourth, the Court has equated the rule of law to reasonableness. As discussed earlier, the Court has declared, inter alia, that: (i) laws and governmental actions have to be reasonable to satisfy the rule of law, (ii) lack of reasonableness is not compatible with a democratic society, and (iii) the rule of law demands reason freed from desire and intelligence without passion. Even by the Court's own extraordinary pronouncements, this reading of reasonableness is unparalleled.

---

[27] For example in *Lalita Kumari* v *Govt of UP* (2014) 2 SCC 1, Justice Sathasivam while dealing with instances of the police failing to register first information reports equates their failure to uphold the law of criminal procedure to a failure to uphold the rule of law. While the first leads to the second, it is not correct to equate the two.

[28] For example in *Maganlal Chaganlal (P) Ltd* v *Municipal Corporation of Greater Bombay* (1974) 2 SCC 402, Justice Hegde specifically identified the certainty requirement of the rule of law to warn against regular reversal of earlier decisions by the Court. However, in many of Justice Krishna Iyer's decisions invoking the rule of law no specific principle has been identified although he relies on the rule of law to justify his conclusions. An example is *Bar Council of Maharashtra* v *MV Dabholkar* (1975) 2 SCC 702 at 719.

As these pronouncements are not isolated, we have to assume that the Court genuinely believes that the rule of law is nothing but reasonableness. Perhaps the Court does not have a choice but to read reasonableness into the rule of law, given the impossibility of controlling discretion in a predictable manner in the functional processes of an all-pervasive state. This is all the more important, as the Court has time and again recognized that the state has a primary role in realizing the revolutionary choices made in the Constitution.

The Court has identified the principles of equality, liberty, and judicial review as primarily containing or comprising (depending on whether Justice Mathew's approach is followed or not) the rule of law. The following sections examine the Court's views on these principles in greater detail.

EQUALITY

The fundamental principle of equality is contained in Article 14 of the Constitution. Article 14 has been described, inter alia, as the basic principle of republicanism[29] and a necessary corollary to the high concept of rule of law.[30] Article 14 contains two phrases, 'equality before the law' and 'equal protection of the laws'. The first phrase is a classic rule of law requirement—that everyone is equal before the law. The second phrase appears to reiterate the first requirement of equality before the law. However, scholars and judges have taken different views on the two phrases. Durga Das Basu believes that the first phrase has a negative connotation implying equal subjection of all to the law and absence of privileges. On the other hand, the second phrase has a positive content and denotes equality of treatment.[31] Seervai takes a similar position.[32] Some observations of Subba Rao J. in *State of UP v Deoman Upadhya*,[33]

---

[29] *Basheshar Nath v Commissioner of Income-Tax, Delhi & Rajasthan* AIR 1959 SC 149.

[30] *Satwant Singh Sawhney v D Ramarathnam, Assistant Passport Officer, Government of India, New Delhi* AIR 1967 SC 1836.

[31] D.D. Basu, *Commentary on the Constitution of India*, Vol. B (Calcutta: R.N. Sarkar, 7th edn, 1993), pp. 4–8.

[32] H.M. Seervai, *Constitutional Law of India*, Vol. 1 (New Delhi: Universal Book Traders, 4th edn, 2002), pp. 438–9.

[33] AIR 1960 SC 1125.

and in *Lachman Das* v *State of Punjab*,[34] give support to Basu's perspective. Jeevan Reddy J. suggests, in *Sri Sreenivasa Theatre* v *Govt. of Tamil Nadu*,[35] that the word 'law' in the expression 'equality before the law' means law in the general sense, whereas the same word in the expression 'equality before the laws' denotes specific laws. Justice Reddy adds that equality before the law is a dynamic concept having many facets: one denoting the absence of any privileged class or person who is above the law and the other denoting the obligation of the state to bring about a more equal society as envisaged in the preamble and Part IV of the Constitution.[36]

There are two distinct principles that the Court has fashioned out of Article 14: the principle of non-discrimination based on the doctrine of classification; and the principle of reasonableness. In the initial years after the Constitution came into force, the Court applied the principle of equality strictly to invalidate cases of discrimination against persons by the state. However, in the late 1970s and the early 1980s, after the case of *EP Royappa* v *State of TN*,[37] the Court has decided that Article 14 requires the state to act reasonably and any arbitrary action will violate Article 14. Both these principles are regularly applied by the Supreme Court and high courts on a daily basis, as government actions are challenged with extreme frequency, particularly on the grounds of arbitrariness.

The Court's decisions[38] on the doctrine of classification, prior to the advent and establishment of the reasonableness principle, can be summarized through the following propositions:[39]

1. All laws, both substantive and procedural laws, are subject to the guarantee of equality before the law and equal protection of the laws

---

[34]   AIR 1963 SC 222.

[35]   AIR 1992 SC 999.

[36]   AIR 1992 SC 999, 1004.

[37]   (1974) 4 SCC 3.

[38]   Some important decisions on the issue of non-discrimination and classification are *RK Dalmia* v *Justice Tendulkar* AIR 1958 SC 538 and *Re, The Special Courts Bill* (1978) 1 SCC 380.

[39]   Similar summaries have been made by many scholars based on the judgments. A good summary can be found in U.R. Rai, *Fundamental Rights and Their Enforcement* (New Delhi: PHI Learning, 2011), pp. 455–7.

contained in Article 14. Both statutes and administrative actions can be challenged for violation of Article 14.

2. Article 14 prohibits class legislation but does not prohibit reasonable classification. However, to be valid, the classification must fulfil two essential conditions: First, there must exist an intelligible differentiation between the persons or things who form part of the group being included within the ambit of the law in question and the group who are left out of the law. Second, there should exist a reasonable nexus between the law and its objectives and the basis for classification, which means the differentiation, must be relevant to the purpose of the law. The basis for classification and the object of the law are two separate and distinct things.

3. The basis for classification cannot be something prohibited by the Constitution, such as religion, language, race, or caste. Outside these prohibited areas, classification can be done on any basis whatsoever, including income, geography, and time.

4. Since the classification is done on the basis of generalization and large groups, it is possible that some people who may not strictly fit into the group are included. Similarly, some people may be excluded.

5. An individual may form a class or a group of his own if the conditions of classification as described above are met.

6. The classification may be made by the legislature itself through statute or delegated to the executive. However, the legislature has to lay down sufficient guidelines which the executive should follow in making the classification. If the legislative policy or guidelines are not clear, the law and the classification will be void. If the policy or guidelines are clear, but the classification is not made in accordance with such policy and guidelines, the classification alone will be invalid, but not necessarily the law.

7. There is a presumption of constitutionality in favour of the law and the burden of proof lies on the person who challenges its constitutional validity.

8. There is also an assumption that the legislature correctly understands and appreciates the needs of the people and that discrimination and classification is based on adequate grounds. Essentially, the judiciary will not substitute its opinion for legislative or executive judgment unless it is shown that the discrimination and classification is not valid.

In *Royappa*, Bhagwati J. observed,

Equality is a dynamic concept with many aspects and dimensions and it cannot be 'cribbed, cabined and confined' within traditional and doctrinaire limits. From a positivistic point of view, equality is antithetic to arbitrariness. In fact equality and arbitrariness are sworn enemies; one belongs to the rule of law in a republic while the other, to the whim and caprice of an absolute monarch. Where an act is arbitrary, it is implicit in it that it is unequal both according to political logic and constitutional law and is, therefore, violative of Article 14.[40]

This principle was fully developed by the Court in *Ajay Hasia* v *Khalid Mujib*, wherein Bhagwati J. speaking for a Constitution Bench observed,

It must therefore now be taken to be well settled that what Article 14 strikes at is arbitrariness because an action that is arbitrary, must necessarily involve negation of equality. The doctrine of classification which is evolved by the Courts is not [*sic*] paraphrase of Article 14 nor is it the objective and end of that article. It is merely a judicial formula for determining whether the legislative or executive action in question is arbitrary and therefore constituting denial of equality. If the classification is not reasonable and does not satisfy the two conditions referred to above (i.e. intelligible differentia and reasonable nexus between the differentia and the object sought to be achieved by the impugned government measure), the impugned legislative or executive action would plainly be arbitrary and the guarantee of equality under Article 14 would be breached.... The concept of reasonableness and non-arbitrariness pervades the entire constitutional scheme and is a golden thread which runs through the whole of the fabric of the Constitution.[41]

The decision in *Ajay Hasia* had two consequences: First, it clarified that Article 14 is not circumscribed by the classification doctrine that the Court had adopted in the initial decades after independence and actually strikes against all arbitrary action. The doctrine of classification is only a tool to identify actions violating Article 14 and is a sub-set of non-arbitrariness. Second, and equally important, it opened up a whole area of government action to judicial review. The principles declared by the Court following the new approach in *Ajay Hasia* can be summarized through the following propositions:[42]

[40] *EP Royappa* v *State of TN* (1974) 4 SCC 3, 38.

[41] (1981) 1 SCC 722, 741.

[42] A summary of the important decisions can be found in Rai, *Fundamental Rights and Their Enforcement*, pp. 545–69. See also M.P. Jain, *Indian Constitutional Law*, edited by S. Pal and R. Pal (Gurgaon: Lexis Nexis, 2014), pp. 876–910.

1. Any government action that suffers from arbitrariness violates Article 14 and is invalid. Arbitrariness is the antithesis of the rule of law and has no place in the scheme of the Constitution. This is not linked to comparative discrimination between two persons but rather to the manner of exercise of power.
2. The Courts will examine the basis for classification and the relationship between the basis of classification and the object of the law at the threshold of reasonableness. The basis of classification must be real and intelligible, not imaginary or perceived.
3. Courts will examine the substantive reasonableness of any special and differential treatment of certain classes.
4. Executive discretion cannot be absolute—it has to be tempered by setting out guidelines for the exercise of discretion, otherwise, it will not be in accordance with Article 14.
5. It is not merely executive or administrative action that can be invalidated on the grounds of being arbitrary. Statutes passed by the legislature can also be found to be arbitrary, although courts exercise extreme caution when questioning legislative motives and reasoning.
6. Non-application of mind is also equivalent to being arbitrary. Government action has to be based on reasons; not giving reasons is an example of arbitrary exercise of power.
7. Administrative decision-making must comply with rules of natural justice, such as an opportunity to be heard, etc.
8. All actions of the government must comply with the principle of reasonableness, whether the government is performing an administrative function or fulfilling a contractual obligation towards private parties. The same principle applies to distribution of welfare benefits by the state.

As is evident from the above discussion on Article 14, the Supreme Court has interpreted and applied Article 14 in a manner broadly consistent with the principles of generality and equality. While there are criticisms based on the inconsistency in interference by the judiciary in all cases—its deference to the wisdom of the executive in certain matters, substituting judicial opinion on what is reasonable for decisions made by other institutions and refusal to understand certain kinds of classifications that have resulted in discrimination[43]—the point to be noted here is that the judiciary is not shying away from regularly intervening and invalidating government action in order to uphold the principles of Article 14.

From a rule of law perspective, two principles are to be noted: (i) treating arbitrariness as an antithesis to, and equating reasonableness to, equality, and (ii) accepting the classification principle as a valid tool to achieve equality even if it goes against the generality principle of rule of law.

SOCIAL RESERVATIONS: ARTICLES 15 AND 16

Articles 15 and 16 further the equality principle in Article 14 by prohibiting discrimination on the basis of certain specified classifications such as gender, race, caste, descent, place of birth, and residence. However, as discussed earlier, Articles 15 and 16 also empower the state to make special provisions for certain classes of society—women, children, scheduled castes, scheduled tribes, and other backward classes. These provisions were important to the political leadership before and after independence because of the severe inequalities in the country. The inclusion of these special provisions has been the subject matter of many a political and judicial battle ever since the Constitution came into force, as evidenced by the number of amendments to Articles 15 and 16 and the judgments of the Supreme Court in this regard.

The special provisions have essentially taken the form of reservations of certain posts in employment and seats in educational institutions. Courts address, on an almost everyday basis, issues of reservation of posts in employment and promotions, and admissions to educational institutions. As the government, directly and indirectly, is still the largest employer in the country and has a very significant presence in education, the 'special provisions' have become a seriously contested concept. While the topic is important and interesting in itself, it is not necessary to discuss this issue in the minute detail that the Courts have addressed it. For the purpose of this book, broad legal principles have been identified and discussed their evolution.

---

[43] See Rai, *Fundamental Rights and Their Enforcement*, pp. 452 and 578–87 for a critical analysis of the use of the classification principle.

The Supreme Court has been concerned with the following issues in connection with the making of special provisions: first, identification of the beneficiaries, namely the scheduled castes and tribes and the backward classes and secondly, the nature and extent of the reservations to be made. The question of whether reservation is the right kind of 'special provision' is something that only dominates political debate and not the legal debate before the Courts. Following the decisions in *Indra Sawhney v Union of India*[44] and *Ashok Kumar Thakur v Union of India*,[45] the law appears to be settled for the moment. The principles that currently occupy the field are as follows:

1. Identification of scheduled castes and tribes, and backward classes is to be done by the government. This identification is subject to judicial review. We should note, however, that the identification of scheduled castes and tribes is directly addressed by the Constitution, whereas the identification of backward classes is not.[46] The Constitution only provides for a commission to be appointed to study the conditions of the backward classes.[47] It is the manner of identification of the backward classes that has been the subject matter of more debate than the identification of the scheduled castes and tribes.

2. Backward classes in Article 16(4) are not the same as the socially and educationally backward classes mentioned in Article 15(4) and Article 340. Backward classes may be identified by reference primarily to castes, as castes form a separate class in the country. However, sections of any caste that are affluent and prosperous should be excluded from benefitting from any reservations available. This has been termed as the 'creamy layer' exclusion. This position is a result of the *Indra Sawhney* decision and overrules earlier judgments of the Supreme Court which had provided that caste could only be one of the determining factors in the 'backwardness' of a section of people. The 'creamy layer' exclusion does not apply to reservations for scheduled castes and scheduled tribes.

---

[44] 1992 Supp. (3) SCC 217.
[45] (2008) 6 SCC 1.
[46] Articles 341 and 342, respectively.
[47] Article 340.

3. Backward classes cannot be determined solely on the basis of economic criteria. The government may identify and differentiate between backward classes and most backward classes.

4. The express specification of reservation is only an extension of the classification principle that the Court has applied in Article 14. It is possible for the government to make reservations even without the specific provisions, if the classification tests are met.

5. No reservation should generally exceed 50 per cent of the total number of available posts or seats.

6. Some relaxation, in terms of age and the qualifying marks, are also provided for, while determining the eligibility for posts or seats.

7. Reservation is not considered advisable in certain fields such as defence services and defence equipment production, technical posts in establishments engaged in research and development, atomic energy and space, technical teaching posts of the level of professors and above, super specialities in medicine, engineering, and other scientific and technical subjects.

8. While the Supreme Court has held that reservations in promotions are not advisable, the insertion of Article 16(4A) by way of a constitutional amendment has ensured that reservations in promotions, for scheduled castes and tribes, can continue.

9. After the inclusion of Article 15(5), the state can make laws requiring reservations of seats in any educational institution, whether financially or otherwise aided by the state or not, excluding minority institutions.

10. The government has the discretion to decide whether certain classes are adequately represented in the services under the state. However, such decision should be made on the basis of facts.

This apparently settled position of law has evolved over nearly 50 years of state action, constitutional amendments, and judicial decision-making. It is, however, by no means settled, as it is a deeply contentious topic in the country and affects people on a daily basis. The fact that the Constitution directly contains certain provisions and the judiciary is closely involved in the articulation of the social issues and rights involved drives home the message that there is a continued discourse on the goals and aspirations of the Constitution in a manner that both challenges the constitutional mandate and also renews it.

RIGHT TO LIFE AND PERSONAL LIBERTY

The relationship between the Part III rights and the Part IV principles has been brought out in all its dimensions, other than in Articles 15 and 16, in the judicial discourse on Article 21. As in the case of Article 14, the Supreme Court's interpretation of Article 21 has seen two distinct approaches in respect of the meaning of the words 'procedure established by law'. In the initial decades and almost until the imposition of the emergency in 1977, the Court took the view that a person can be deprived of his life or liberty if a law is passed in accordance with the Constitution.[48] It was only in the *Maneka Gandhi v Union of India*[49] case that the Supreme Court found that the words 'procedure established by law' means also that the procedure established in the law should be reasonable, fair and just. The decision in *Maneka Gandhi* and the decision on Article 14 in *Ajay Hasia* opened the floodgates for a combined reading of Article 14 and Article 21 to enable judicial review of legislation and government action on the grounds of substantive reasonableness. In addition, in the 1980s and 1990s, Article 21 also became the vehicle through which the Court read many other rights on behalf of the citizens on the basis of the Part IV principles. Through this expansive interpretation of Article 21 and encouraged by the widening of the writ jurisdiction through the means of public interest litigation, the judiciary took the lead in pushing forward the social agenda for the country.

Some of the important propositions from the wide array of principles that the Court has laid down while interpreting Article 21 are as follows:

1. The term 'personal liberty' is of the widest amplitude, covering a variety of rights that constitute the personal liberty of man. Some of these rights are specifically mentioned in the Constitution as distinct fundamental rights under Article 19.
2. The procedure established by law that takes away the life and personal liberty of any person cannot be arbitrary, unfair, or unreasonable. The procedure has to meet the criterion of reasonableness and the judiciary has the power to review any such procedure from a

---

[48] This principle was first laid down in *AK Gopalan* v *State of Madras* AIR 1950 SC 97.

[49] AIR 1978 SC 597.

reasonableness perspective. The procedure has to be right, just, and fair and not arbitrary, fanciful, or oppressive. Principles of natural justice should be adhered to.

3. The right to life includes the right to live with human dignity and all that goes along with it—the bare necessities of life, such as adequate nutrition; clothing and shelter and facilities for reading, writing, and expressing oneself in diverse forms; free movement and mixing and commingling with fellow human beings.[50]

4. The right to life has been found to include the right to privacy,[51] food, water and decent environment,[52] education,[53] livelihood,[54] and medical care.[55]

5. The Court found that sexual harassment or abuse of women at the workplace amounts to a violation of their rights under Articles 14, 15, and 21.[56] Noting that there was no law relating to sexual harassment at the workplace, the Court itself laid down certain guidelines that were to be followed until such time that a legislation was brought into force.

6. An entire jurisprudence on environmental law has been developed by the Court by reading in principles such as sustainable development, inter-generational equity and precautionary principle into Article 21, as the right to life includes the right to pollution-free water and air. The Court has gone on to order closure of industries,[57] use of clean fuel in all public vehicles[58] and issued various directions to the administration towards protecting the environment and reducing pollution.[59]

---

[50] *Francis Coralie Mullin* v *Administrator, Union Territory of Delhi* (1981) 1 SCC 608.

[51] *People's Union for Civil Liberties* v *Union of India* AIR 1997 SC 568.

[52] *Chameli Singh* v *State of UP* (1996) 2 SCC 549.

[53] *Unnikrishnan* v *State of Andhra Pradesh* (1993) 1 SCC 645.

[54] *Olga Tellis* v *Bombay Municipal Corporation* (1985) 3 SCC 545.

[55] *Paramanand Katara* v *Union of India* (1989) 4 SCC 248.

[56] *Vishaka* v *State of Rajasthan* (1997) 6 SCC 241.

[57] *MC Mehta* v *Union of India* (1987) 4 SCC 463.

[58] There are various orders in this matter from 1999 to 2002, all under the title *MC Mehta* v *Union of India*.

[59] For a detailed discussion on the various measures on ecology, see M.P. Jain, *Indian Constitutional Law*, 1173–8.

7. The Court has used Article 21 to grant interim compensation to rape victims,[60] and damages to victims of police violence.[61]

8. The Court has also used Article 21 to protect various rights of under trials and prisoners by bringing them under the scope of life and personal liberty. This has led to several reforms in the prison system and the administration of criminal justice.[62]

9. The right to legal aid has been read into Article 21 so as to ensure that the procedure taking away the personal liberty of a person is fair. Article 39A of the Part IV principles was read with Article 21 in coming to this conclusion.[63]

10. Delayed execution of a death sentence has also been found to be dehumanizing and depriving a person of his life in an unjust, unfair and unreasonable way so as to offend Article 21.[64]

11. The Court has found that Article 21 includes within it the right to a speedy trial. Quick justice is now regarded as a *sine qua non* of Article 21. Inordinately long delay may be taken as presumptive proof of prejudice. Prosecution should not be allowed to become persecution.[65]

12. A fair trial is at the heart of criminal jurisprudence and, in a way, an important facet of a democratic polity that is governed by the rule of law.[66] Failure to hear material witnesses is certainly denial of fair trial.[67]

These are just some of the rights that the Court has read into Article 21. In the post *Maneka Gandhi* era, one does not know what rights may be read into Article 21 by an activist judge. This activist role of the

---

[60] *Bodhisattwa Gautam* v *Subhra Chakraborty* (1996) 1 SCC 490.

[61] *Khatri* v *State of Bihar* (1981) 1 SCC 627.

[62] Some important cases are *Francis Coralie Mullin* v *Administrator, Union Territory of Delhi* (1981) 1 SCC 608; *Sunil Batra (II)* v *Delhi Admn* (1980) 3 SCC 488; *Prem Shankar* v *Delhi Admn* (1980) 3 SCC 526.

[63] *Hussainara Khatoon* v *State of Bihar* (1980) 1 SCC 98.

[64] *Triveniben* v *State of Gujarat* (1989) 1 SCC 678.

[65] *Anita Kushwaha & Others* v *Pushpa Sadan & Others* 2016 Indlaw SC 828; *Vakil Prasad Singh* v *State of Bihar* (2009) 3 SCC 355.

[66] *Rattiram* v *State of MP through Inspector of Police* AIR 2012 SC 1485.

[67] *Zahira Sheikh* v *State of Gujarat* (2004) 4 SCC 158.

Court expands the liberties of individuals and restricts the ability of the state to interfere whimsically in the lives of ordinary citizens. Such restriction assumes importance in the context of the centralized role of the state. However, the Court has also gone on to impose positive obligations on the state by reading in the Part IV principles into Part III rights. In some cases, the Court has itself set up committees to monitor the implementation of various rights and directly report to the Court rather than to the executive.[68] The Court's rulings have also led to the right to education being added to the Constitution by way of an amendment.[69] Various laws and regulations have been passed by the legislature to address some of the concerns raised by the Court—the most important being in preventing sexual harassment at the workplace.[70]

That the Supreme Court's decisions on Article 21 in the post *Maneka Gandhi* era, have concluded that life and personal liberty cannot be taken away merely by a procedure established by law, but only through a substantively fair and reasonable procedure, is a big victory from a rule of law perspective. It should however, be noted here that judicial inconsistency, and inability, in reacting to similar fact situations and the mere declaration of various rights as fundamental rights, read with the meaning given to procedure established by law, has not necessarily added either to the value of fundamental rights or the rule of law, given the lack of implementation of these rights. It has perhaps only increased the popularity of the judiciary.[71]

---

[68] The most obvious example is the appointment of the Supreme Court commissioners in the right to food case, *PUCL v Union of India*, Writ Petition (Civil) 196 of 2001. For the full orders and the powers of the commissioners, see www.sccommissioners.org (accessed 3 February 2015).

[69] Article 21A guaranteeing free and compulsory education to all children of the ages 6 years to 14 years was introduced by way of the Constitution (Eighty-fourth Amendment) Act 2002.

[70] Following the Court's decision in *Vishaka v State of Rajasthan* (1997) 6 SCC 241, the Parliament enacted the Sexual Harassment of Women at the Workplace (Prevention, Prohibition and Redressal) Act, 2013.

[71] See Rai, *Fundamental Rights and Their Enforcement*, 230–73 for a detailed discussion on these issues. The issue of enforcement has been discussed in greater detail in Chapter 5 of this book.

LIBERTIES UNDER ARTICLE 19

The judicial discourse on the rights under Article 19 has centered on three primary issues: (i) the meaning, scope, and extent of the rights in Article 19(1); (ii) the scope of the restrictions in Article 19, clauses (2)–(6), whether they are inclusive or exhaustive in nature and how they should be imposed; and (iii) the reasonableness or otherwise of the restrictions imposed and whether they ought to have been imposed in the first place. The deletion of the right to acquire, hold, and dispose of property by the Constitution (Forty-fourth Amendment) Act, 1978 has meant that the roaring battle between the Parliament and the judiciary in respect of land acquisition, land reforms and fair compensation has become irrelevant to Article 19. The focus is now firmly on the scope of the right to freedom of speech and expression, peaceful assembly and the right to form associations and the restrictions applicable to these rights. In this book, only the judiciary's views on the restrictions and their reasonableness has been examined.

The following propositions can be derived from the various judgments in relation to Article 19 (excluding the right to property):

1. The rights in Article 19(1) are not absolute, but subject to the restrictions in Article 19, clauses (2)–(6). The rights of each individual have to be limited so the whole can enjoy it better.
2. The Supreme Court has repeatedly held that the restrictions mentioned in Article 19, clauses (2)–(6) are exhaustive.[72] Consequently, any restriction imposed by the state has to be found in the express enumerations of Article 19, clauses (2)–(6) and cannot be implied.
3. The restrictions can be imposed only by law, either by legislation, by-laws, rules, or regulations.
4. The restrictions have to be reasonable, both substantively and procedurally, and are subject to judicial review. The Court has held that there is no general formula of reasonableness and it has to be decided on the facts in each case.[73] The relevant factors to be considered are the nature of the right infringed, the purpose of the restrictions imposed, the circumstances during which the restriction was imposed, the proportion of the restriction and the

---

[72] For example, in *Bennett Coleman & Co* v *Union of India* (1972) 2 SCC 788.
[73] *State of Madras* v *VG Row* AIR 1952 SC 196.

extent and urgency of the evil sought to be remedied, or nature of the interest sought to be protected, by the restriction.

5. There must be a direct and proximate nexus between the restriction imposed and the object sought to be achieved.[74]

6. The imposition of the restriction should not be productive of more evil than it seeks to remedy.[75] Further, the restriction should not be more than what is necessary.[76]

7. The Court will judge the effect of a restriction, and not just the subject matter, in deciding if a right has been infringed.[77]

The Court has by and large remained conservative in the enforcement of Article 19. The Court's approach has swung between a moral-paternalistic approach that demands that citizens be protected from the perverse and corrupting effects of free speech and a liberal-autonomous vision.[78] The lack of an 'activist' approach has meant that hardly a week goes by in the country without some demand for a ban on free speech in one form or another. With the Court insisting that reasonableness of the restriction must be examined in each case, and the executive not shy of imposing restrictions on the basis of imagined law and order situations, or for purely political or religious reasons, free speech is a threatened commodity. This is a surprising status given the judiciary's desire to innovate and fashion new concepts in the context of Articles 14 and 21 to favour citizens.

JUDICIAL INDEPENDENCE AND JUDICIAL REVIEW

Judicial independence has been fiercely safeguarded by the judiciary. The Supreme Court has held that judicial independence is part of the basic structure of the Constitution and cannot be abrogated even by

[74] Shreya Singhal v Union of India 2015 SCC Online SC 248; Papanasam Labour Union v Madura Coats Ltd (1995) 1 SCC 501.

[75] S Rangarajan v P Jagjeewan Ram (1989) 2 SCC 574.

[76] Chintaman Rao v State of MP AIR 1951 SC 118.

[77] Bennett Coleman & Co. v Union of India (1972) 2 SCC 788.

[78] G. Bhatia, Offend, Shock, or Disturb: Free Speech under the Indian Constitution (New Delhi: Oxford University Press, 2016), pp. 326–7. The liberal-autonomous vision is, unfortunately, not to be found very often. As Bhatia's book was published after this work was completed, the author has not had a chance to discuss his work in great detail.

way of a constitutional amendment. The supreme importance given to judicial independence has also transformed the Court's approach to judicial review of constitutional, legislative and executive action. Following the decisions in *Kesavananda, Maneka Gandhi,* and *Ajay Hasia,* it is fair to state that there is no area of constitutional, legislative or executive action which is not subject to judicial review. The Court does show some deference to executive and legislative wisdom in pure policy matters, but that has become more the exception than the rule. If there is any violation of fundamental rights or indeed, any right that the Court considers important, it exercises its jurisdiction of judicial review to test the constitutionality of such government action.

The scope of judicial review has widened and deepened substantially after the Court adopted a liberal view on the *locus standi* of a litigant and developed the concept of public or social interest litigation. This opened the floodgates for various writ actions in the interest of society both before the Supreme Court under Article 32 and the high courts under Article 226. The Court has adopted innovative measures to exercise its jurisdiction and fashion remedies in matters that have come before it.

Judicial independence has been developed to such an extent that the appointment of judges to the superior courts is also in the control of the judiciary following the decisions in the *Supreme Court Advocates on Record Association* case[79] and the *Special Reference 1 of 1998.*[80] It was only in 2014 that the Parliament passed a constitutional amendment and a statute that sought to establish a Judicial Appointments Commission and take away the exclusive power of the judiciary in the matter of appointment of judges to the Supreme Court and high courts.[81] The

---

[79] *Supreme Court Advocates on Record Association* v *Union of India* (1993) 4 SCC 441, 683.

[80] (1998) 7 SCC 739.

[81] The Constitution (Ninety-ninth) Amendment Act, 2014, introduced Article 124A that establishes the National Judicial Appointments Commission to make recommendations to the President for appointment of judges to the Supreme Court and high courts. The Commission was to consist of six members—the Chief Justice of India, the next two most senior judges of the Supreme Court, the law minister and two members from civil society to be nominated by a committee consisting of the Prime Minister, the Chief Justice of India, and the Leader of the Opposition in the Lok Sabha.

Supreme Court has in October 2015 in the *Supreme Court Advocates on Record Association v Union of India*,[82] found the amendment establishing the Judicial Appointments Commission to violate independence of the judiciary, which is part of the basic structure and therefore unconstitutional. This essentially gives the judiciary complete control over the appointment of judges to the Supreme Court and high courts.

The following propositions can be derived in connection with judicial independence and judicial review from the various decisions of the Court:

1. Independence of the judiciary is a basic feature of the Constitution and cannot be taken away even by way of a constitutional amendment. Independence of the judiciary is part of the scheme of separation of powers envisaged by the Constitution and is an essential feature of the rule of law.[83]

2. Judicial review is an integral part of the rule of law and the constitutional system.[84] Judicial review, more than any other feature of the Constitution, is basic and fundamental to the maintenance of democracy and the rule of law. The power of judicial review extends to reviewing Constitutional amendments and deciding if these amendments violate the basic structure of the Constitution.

3. It is the duty of the judiciary to ensure that fundamental rights are protected and the rule of law is upheld.

4. The powers of the Supreme Court and high courts cannot be taken away by any law even when special tribunals or courts are set up. The power to interpret the law and exercise the power of judicial review under Articles 32 and 226 are part of the inviolable basic structure of the Constitution.[85]

---

[82] (2016) 6 SCC 1.

[83] *Kesavananda Bharati v State of Kerala* (1973) 4 SCC 225.

[84] *SP Sampath Kumar v Union of India* (1987) 1 SCC 124.

[85] *L Chandrakumar v Union of India* (1997) 3 SCC 261. See also *Madras Bar Association v Union of India* (2014) 10 SCC 1, where the Court reviewed all the cases on judicial independence and review from *Kesavananda* and held that establishment of tax tribunals as a parallel to the high courts and Supreme Court is unconstitutional and violates the principle of rule of law.

5. A collegium of judges consisting of the Chief Justice of India and the four most senior judges of the Supreme Court shall have the final word on who is to be appointed to the Supreme Court and the high courts. A similar collegium functions in each high court to assist with the appointment of judges to the high courts.

6. The Court has liberalized the *locus standi* principle to design the concept of public interest litigation. The Court can hear matters brought to its attention by concerned citizens who may have not suffered a violation of their rights but are agitating the matter on behalf of others, who cannot approach the court, or the society at large. The Court also takes *suo moto* cognizance of matters. Letters written by prisoners or affected citizens have been converted into writ petitions by the Court.[86] The expansion of locus standi appears to have created a direct dialogue between the judiciary and the people through various social, legal and judicial activists.

7. The Court has been creative in fashioning remedies to redress violation of citizens' rights. It has used its powers under Article 32 in conjunction with its power to render 'complete justice' in any matter before it under Article 142. It has not only issued writs, but also, inter alia, awarded damages, framed policy guidelines, issued directions, supervised investigations, and made new law until a statute is enacted.[87]

8. The Court has pointed out that for efficacy of judicial adjudication and people's faith in the rule of law, people must have absolute faith and confidence in the honesty, integrity, impartiality, courage, and independence of the judge.[88]

The interplay of the concepts of judicial independence and judicial review have made the judiciary and particularly the Supreme Court an extremely powerful institution of governance in India. Some argue that

---

[86] There are numerous cases that have followed these principles. See Jain, *Indian Constitutional Law*, pp. 1370–5 for a concise discussion.

[87] See L. Rajamani and A. Sengupta, 'The Supreme Court', in N.G. Jayal and P.B. Mehta (eds), *The Oxford Companion to Politics in India* (New Delhi: Oxford University Press, 2010), pp. 80–97 at pp. 86–91 for a concise and critical analysis of such exercise of power.

[88] *Krishna Swami* v *Union of India* (1992) 4 SCC 605.

it may be the most powerful institution in the country and probably, the most powerful judiciary in the world.[89] Upendra Baxi observes, 'Adjudicatory power has acquired a dimension of autonomy not imminent in the Constitutional scheme and indeed transcendent of it.'[90]

However, the Supreme Court (not the high courts) did not use its great power in the people's hour of need. The Court's refusal to intervene in *ADM, Jabalpur* v *Shivakant Shukla*,[91] when fundamental rights were suspended during the internal emergency of 1975–7 is considered by many to be the lowest point of the judiciary in India. To the Court's credit, it quickly recovered ground and went on an activism spree in the late 1970s and 1980s which formed the basis for much of the Court's powers today. However, this accumulation of great power by the judiciary including the right to appoint themselves, upsets the rule of law as it gives primacy to one institution, an unaccountable one at that, over other constitutional institutions. These issues are discussed in greater detail in Chapter 5.

DIRECTIVE PRINCIPLES AND FUNDAMENTAL RIGHTS

Article 37 clearly states the provisions contained in Part IV are not enforceable in any court of law. It, however, goes on to say that the directive principles in Part IV are nevertheless fundamental in the governance

---

[89] See for example, Rajamani and Sengupta, 'The Supreme Court'. See also, R. Ramachandran, 'Judicial Supremacy and the Collegium' (2013), available at http://india-seminar.com/2013/642/642_raju_ramachandran.htm (accessed 24 February 2015).

[90] U. Baxi, 'The Avatars of Indian Judicial Activism: Explorations in the Geographies of [In]Justice', in S.K. Verma and Kusum (eds), *Fifty Years of the Supreme Court of India: Its Grasp and Reach* (Oxford University Press, New Delhi, 2003), pp. 156–209 at p. 156. A few scholars have suggested that the judiciary appears to be behaving like the traditional Indian priestly class who had the final say on interpreting the Dharmasastras, which was binding on the kings. See, A.K. Giri, 'Rule of Law and Indian Society: From Colonialism to Post-Colonialism', in P. Costa and D. Zola (eds), *The Rule Of Law: History, Theory & Criticism*, p. 587 (Springer Netherlands, 2007), p. 587; C. Fuller, 'Hinduism and Scriptural Authority in Modern Indian Law', *Comparative Studies in Society and History*, vol. 30, no. 2 (1988), pp. 246–7.

[91] AIR 1976 SC 1207.

of the country and that it shall be the duty of the state to apply these principles in making laws. We can argue that this clearly indicates the reluctance of the Constituent Assembly in bringing into the realm of rights, principles of policy. The same argument can be extended to make the case that certain 'substantive rights' are not strictly part of the rule of law conception in India. However, the relationship between Part III and Part IV has been the subject matter of much political and judicial debate.

The Supreme Court initially took the view that the Part IV principles have to conform and run as subsidiary to the Part III rights.[92] However, the Court gradually relaxed its views to state that the Part IV principles should be harmoniously read with the Part III rights[93] and that the Court can while interpreting the scope and ambit of the Part III rights, look to the Part IV principles for guidance. This approach of harmoniously reading Part III and Part IV led to the Court's decision in *Kesavananda*, upholding the validity of Article 31C, which sought to give constitutional protection to policies of the state in furtherance of the objectives in Article 39, clauses (a) and (b) even if those policies violate the fundamental rights in Articles 14 and 19. Article 39(a) provides that the state shall direct its policy towards securing that the citizens, men and women equally, have the right to an adequate means of livelihood, while Article 39(b) requires the state to secure that the ownership and control of material resources of the community are so distributed as to best serve the common good. While most of the judges in *Kesavananda* agreed with the harmonious construction approach, Mathew J. went further to state, 'In building up a just social order it is sometimes imperative that the Fundamental Rights should be subordinated to Directive Principles ... economic goals have an uncontestable claim for priority over ideological ones on the ground that excellence comes only after existence. It is only if men exist that there can be Fundamental Rights.'[94]

However, the Court in *Minerva Mills*,[95] declared unconstitutional the additional amendment to Article 31C, which sought to protect policies made to implement all the Part IV principles. The Court based

---

[92] *State of Madras* v *Champakam Dorairarajan* AIR 1951 SC 226.

[93] *Re, Kerala Education Bill* AIR 1958 SC 956.

[94] *Kesavananda Bharati* v *State of Kerala* (1973) 4 SCC 225, 879.

[95] *Minerva Mills* v *Union of India* (1980) 3 SCC 625.

its decision on the premise that the Constitution is based on the 'bedrock of balance' between the Part IV principles and the Part III rights and to give absolute primacy to one over the other would disturb this balance. The goals set out in the Part IV principles should be achieved without abrogating the Part III rights. Recently, the Court restated this principle in *IR Coelho*:

> By enacting fundamental rights and directive principles which are negative and positive obligations of the States, the Constituent Assembly made it the responsibility of the Government to adopt a middle path between individual liberty and public good. Fundamental rights and directive principles have to be balanced. That balance can be titled in favour of the public good. The balance, however, cannot be overturned by completely overriding individual liberty. This balance is an essential feature of the Constitution.[96]

The Supreme Court has also declared many times that the Part IV principles seek to introduce the concept of a welfare state in India and that the primary duty of government is to secure the welfare of the people.[97]

No discussion on the rule of law and the delicate balance between the Part III rights and the Part IV principles can be complete without understanding the history and current status of the right to property. The right to property has been the casualty of the Court's carefully constructed edifice of delicate balance between the Part IV principles and the Part III rights. The original Article 19(1)(f) contained the right to acquire, hold, and dispose of property. Article 31 ensured that the state could not compulsorily acquire a person's property except by authority of law and payment of compensation. Both Articles 19(1)(f) and 31 were deleted by the Constitution (Forty-fourth Amendment) Act, 1978. Today, Article 300A only provides that no person shall be deprived of his property save by authority of law. Articles 31A, 31B (read with the Ninth Schedule), and 31C ensure that no form of property right or the rights under Articles 14 and 19 come in the way of various policy measures implemented by the state to achieve the policies in Articles 39(a) and 39(b).

---

[96] *IR Coelho* v *State of Tamil Nadu* (2007) 2 SCC 1, 98.

[97] For example, in *Paschim Banga Khet Mazdoor Samity* v *State of West Bengal* (1996) 4 SCC 37.

The genesis of the Constitution (Forty-fourth Amendment) Act, 1978, began immediately after the Constitution was adopted. The Union government and a number of states passed a series of legislations to reform land holdings and tenures, with a view to reconstruct the agrarian economy. Similarly, in urban areas measures were initiated to provide housing to the poor and impose a ceiling on urban land ownership. The government also took steps to nationalize certain commercial undertakings. Most of these measures were challenged in courts. The courts upheld Articles 19(1)(f) and Article 31 and required the state to pay just compensation for any property rights that were lost as a result of the reform measures.[98] The legislature reacted through a series of constitutional amendments to modify Article 31 drastically, introduce Articles 31A, 31B, and 31C first, and then finally remove Articles 19(1)(f) and 31 by way of the Constitution (Forty-fourth Amendment) Act, 1978.

It is not relevant for this discussion to dwell in detail on the various judgments of the Supreme Court and every constitutional amendment. The interesting points from a rule of law perspective are the following:

1. The recognition by the Court that the Part IV principles and the Part III rights need to be harmoniously interpreted, at times with a tilt in favor of Part IV, is a curious and vague position fraught with difficulties for enforcing individual liberty. Although the Part III rights are justiciable and enforceable as hard legal rights, to say that they should make way for non-justiciable policy principles occasionally is to render the principles of certainty, generality and equality meaningless. It is also the most explicit acceptance, beyond rhetoric, of the extreme importance of social justice in the Constitution and central role of the state in deciding priorities for achieving citizens' welfare and the methods of reaching that goal.

2. The delicate balance that the Court has placed its bet on is no different from a political and social evaluation of priorities made by the legislature. There is a complete absence of legal principles that can be applied without personal, political and social preferences in the determination of this delicate balance.

3. The Court's opinion that the Part IV principles can be used to understand the width, scope and depth of the Part III rights and the reasonableness of the restrictions imposed on the Part III rights

[98] See for example, *State of Bihar* v *Kameshwar Singh* AIR 1952 SC 458.

also suffers from the same political thicket problems discussed in point 2.

4. Despite its proclamation of a delicate balance, the Court has not found it contradictory to read various Part IV principles into the Part III rights, particularly Article 21, clearly showing that even the Court believes, behind all the rhetoric, that Part III rights have a superior standing. The legislature also acknowledges this as evidenced by the incorporation of Article 21A.

5. The legislature has been extremely persistent and obstinate in pursuing the goal of land law reforms, reconstruction of the agrarian economy and nationalization of various commercial enterprises. The legislature believes that it is mandated to take these measures by the Constitution and failure to do so would result in breach of constitutional promises. The political class has also not viewed kindly the judiciary's insistence on the payment of adequate or just compensation, so much so that the judiciary appears to have admitted defeat on the issue of compensation by finally only insisting that the compensation provided not be illusory but real instead of adequate or just compensation.[99]

6. The constitutional technique of introducing the Ninth Schedule to the Constitution to protect the validity of certain laws dealing with property rights is extremely unique. However, this unique measure raises many fundamental questions from a rule of law perspective, given the lack of any substantive or procedural guidelines or principles regarding the inclusion of laws into the schedule. There is no certainty about the nature of the laws that can be included in the Ninth Schedule given the continued expansion of its contents.[100] The only conclusion that we can come to is that the Court has accepted the status quo after the Constitution (Forty-fourth Amendment) Act, 1978, in respect of the individual right to property, although it has tried to salvage the position marginally by stating that laws introduced into the Ninth Schedule after the *Kesavananda* decision could be examined on the basic structure threshold.[101]

---

[99] *Bhim Singhji* v *Union of India* (1981) 1 SCC 166. This was following the observations in *Kesavananda Bharati* v *State of Kerala* (1973) 4 SCC 225 and *State of Karnataka* v *Ranganatha Reddy* (1977) 4 SCC 471.

[100] Currently, there are 284 statutes listed in the Ninth Schedule.

[101] *Waman Rao* v *Union of India* (1981) 2 SCC 362.

7. Articles 31A and 31C go beyond the 'delicate balance' principle, which, the Court has repeatedly stated, exists between the Part IV and the Part III rights. If anything, these two Articles upset this delicate balance in favour of the Part IV principles. The Court has not explained the inconsistent approaches it has taken in *Kesavananda* and *Minerva Mills* on the validity of Article 31C.

Seervai criticizes the Court's position on the relationship between Part III and Part IV. He states that the Court's approach leads him to ask two questions:

> What would have happened if directive principles had not been enacted in our Constitution or are struck out? And, what would have happened, if fundamental rights had not been enacted or are struck out? I came to the conclusion that if directive principles had not been enacted or were struck out nothing would have happened. But if fundamental rights had not been enacted or struck out, the result would have been disaster.[102]

Seervai bases his conclusion on two reasons. First, every state works towards the welfare of its citizens and therefore, inclusion or otherwise of such principles in the Constitution makes no difference. In either case if the government of the day does not work for the welfare of the citizens it will be thrown out by the people during elections. Second, the fundamental rights are a limitation on the exercise of power by the state and cannot be read harmoniously with directive principles which are not fetters on the exercise of state power. In any event, fundamental rights also have the welfare of the citizens in mind. This is particularly the case in the Constitution, as certain specific rights like Articles 15, 16, and 17 have been included to further the welfare of citizens.[103] Seervai further points out that the Part III rights cover a much larger field than the Part IV principles. The Part III rights are in full harmony with the objectives set out in the preamble while the Part IV principles only cover few policies and are not exclusive.[104]

The relationship between the state's role in social welfare measures and the rule of law is a contentious one. The two are mutually incompatible and

---

[102] Seervai, *Constitutional Law of India*, Vol. 2, p. 1921.

[103] Seervai, *Constitutional Law of India*, Vol. 2, pp. 1921–2020.

[104] Seervai, *Constitutional Law of India*, Vol. 2, pp. 1944–5.

cannot coexist according to a near unanimous opinion amongst western theorists. The Supreme Court, on the contrary, appears to believe that the rule of law demands state action to bring about social welfare. The Court does not appear to have entertained any serious thought on the perceived incompatibility between the two concepts, although it has made it clear that the state has to act reasonably while implementing the social welfare measures and cannot be arbitrary.

POLITICAL UNDERSTANDING OF THE RULE OF LAW

I feel, however good a Constitution may be, it is sure to turn out bad because those who are called to work, happen to be a bad lot.... The working of the Constitution does not depend wholly upon the nature of the Constitution. The Constitution can provide only the organs of state such as the Legislature, the Executive and the Judiciary. The factors on which the working of those organs of the state depend are the people and the political parties they will set up as their instruments to carry out their wishes and their politics. Who can say how the people of India and their parties will behave?... If they adopt the revolutionary methods, however good the Constitution may be, it requires no prophet to say that it will fail. It is, therefore, futile to pass any judgement upon the Constitution without reference to the part which the people and their parties are likely to play.[105]

—B.R. Ambedkar, Constituent Assembly Speech

Jawaharlal Nehru, the first prime minister of the country, felt that the rule of law had to closely follow the rule of life.[106] In his inaugural address to the International Commission of Jurists at Delhi in 1959, Nehru noted that a society without the rule of law would be lawless and anarchical and that the rule of law is essential for a civilized existence. Nehru stressed on two points in his speech: First, that the law cannot be static and needs to address the problems people face in 'today's' world. While this can lead to a conflict between the fundamentals of law which are static in nature and the need for addressing current problems which

[105] Ambedkar's speech to the Constituent Assembly on 25 November 1949, available at http://parliamentofindia.nic.in/ls/debates/vol11p11.htm (accessed 20 March 2015).

[106] See http://icj.wpengine.netdna-cdn.com/wp-content/uploads/2012/12/CONGRESS-BOOKLET.pdf, pp. 31–3, (accessed 3 March 2015).

are different, there is a need to manage this conflict. Second, Nehru agreed that judicial independence is a necessary requirement for protecting rights of people. However, he went on to warn that judges are often left behind, with the statutes they interpret and administer, by developments in society of which the executive may be more aware.[107]

Nehru's comments, which were made at the time when the judiciary had invalidated a number of land reform legislations forcing the Parliament to bring about constitutional amendments, are instructive and perhaps reflect the general attitude of India's political class to the rule of law. Generally, the political class has adhered to constitutional principles at a broad level, although in their day to day functioning, they do not think twice before violating the law. All political parties accept that India is a society with a rule of law, guaranteed fundamental rights and an independent judiciary, although the National Democratic Alliance government constituted a Constitution Review Commission in 2000 to examine the working of the Constitution and suggest changes.[108] However, the political parties sincerely believe that they know more about the problems of the people and need the flexibility to address them without interference from the judiciary. This belief has led to several constitutional amendments and some efforts by the executive to interfere with the independence of the judiciary, most notably during the 1970s when several senior judges were superseded during the appointment of the Chief Justice of India.[109]

[107] http://icj.wpengine.netdna-cdn.com/wp-content/uploads/2012/12/CONGRESS-BOOKLET.pdf, pp. 31–3 (accessed 3 March 2015).

[108] The National Commission to Review the Working of the Constitution was set up in February 2000 by the National Democratic Alliance government, led by the Bharatiya Janata Party (BJP). At the time several concerns were expressed that the constitution of the commission was an effort by the BJP to rewrite portions of the Constitution that it felt were not in accordance with the majoritarian Hindu philosophy. These fears did not turn out to be true in the context of that commission. The commission's report is a valuable document that contains many insights into the functioning of the Constitution. The full report can be found in S. Kashyap, *Constitution Making since 1950: An Overview* (New Delhi: Universal Law Publishing, 2004).

[109] In 1973, following the decision in *Kesavananda*, the three senior most judges of the Supreme Court, Hegde, Shelat, and Grover were superseded and A.N. Ray was appointed as the Chief Justice of India. The primary reason for their supersession was their decision that Parliament could not amend the

The Constitution has seen 100 amendments since 1950. While some of them are operational in nature, several renew the original choices made in the Constitution either by extending the period for which the choices were valid or by introducing new rights and concepts. Several amendments were introduced to negate judicial decisions, for example, the Constitution (First Amendment) Act, 1951, which amended Article 19, introduced Articles 31A and 31B and the Ninth Schedule. The Constitution (Ninety-ninth Amendment) Act, 2014, establishing the judicial appointments commission, was also of a similar nature. This indicates that the political leadership has not shied away from exercising its powers to amend the Constitution to achieve certain goals or correct perceived imbalances due to judicial interpretation and maintain the rule of law.

The political class has also misused its power to amend the Constitution, the most notable instance being the Constitution (Forty-second Amendment) Act, 1976, which was passed when the internal emergency was in force. The said amendment, inter alia, sought to curtail the powers of the judiciary and extend the scope of parliamentary amendment over the Constitution as a whole. The Constitution (Forty-second Amendment) Act, 1976, also sought to negate the protection of the Part III rights to citizens by giving primacy to the Part IV principles. All this was done solely to consolidate power in the hands of one person, the then prime minister, Indira Gandhi. This was done by a parliament that had already finished its five-year tenure and despite boycott by the available opposition (as many opposition leaders had been jailed),[110] clearly a violation of the rule of law.

In practice, the political leadership has not really challenged the understanding of the rule of law as laid down by the Constitution and interpreted by the judiciary, except perhaps in the initial decade after independence. The political class uses the rule of law as a convenient rhetorical phrase

---

Constitution freely and was subject to the basic structure doctrine. Similarly, H.R. Khanna was superseded following his dissenting decision in the *ADM, Jabalpur v Shivakant Shukla* case in 1976. See G. Austin, *Working a Democratic Constitution: The Indian Experience* (New Delhi: Oxford University Press, 1999), pp. 278–89 and 334–44.

[110] Austin, *Working a Democratic Constitution,* pp. 234–53 and 370–88. See also V. Hewitt and S. Rai, 'Parliament', N.G. Jayal and P.B. Mehta (eds), *The Oxford Companion to Politics in India* (New Delhi: Oxford University Press, 2010), pp. 28–42 at p. 35.

without wholly understanding, or desiring to understand, the concept. A prominent leader of a major party once mentioned that most members of Parliament see the Constitution for the first time when they enter the Parliament and take oath on the Constitution.[111] The majority of the political class is ignorant of the basic principles of the Constitution and the important laws of the country. Some political leaders who are also lawyers have tried to bring a more focused approach occasionally, but that has not really helped create any debate about the politician's understanding of the rule of law.[112] Indeed, there has been no serious debate on major Supreme Court rulings that encroach upon legislative powers, or the executive's overreach of its powers in violation of law.[113]

The Parliament and state legislatures have showed a perceptible decline in exercising their primary functions of law-making and holding the executive accountable. Indeed, the Parliament and state legislatures have ceded the primary responsibility of ensuring compliance with the Constitution to the judiciary. While they insisted on the supremacy of the Parliament in matters of constitutional amendments until the *Kesavananda* judgment, they have, thereafter, more or less accepted the basic structure doctrine. There has been no serious challenge to either the basic structure doctrine or the continued expansion of the power of judicial review after the early 1980s. For a long time, the executive did not even fight the judiciary on the Supreme Court's declaration on the appointment of judges to the Supreme Court and high courts. This could be because of the decline in quality of the political leaders over the years and consequent malfunctioning of the Parliament and state legislatures.[114] It could also be because the Court's view of the rule of law has broadly

[111] R. Guha, *India after Gandhi: The History of the World's Largest Democracy* (London: Picador, 2007), p. 660. Guha quotes the late Pramod Mahajan's statement in 2000 when he was a Union Minister.

[112] See for example, Chidambaram's views on the rule of law. P. Chidambaram, 'The Citizen and The rule of law', N.R.M. Menon (ed.), Rule of Law in a Free Society (New Delhi: Oxford University Press, 2008), pp. 10–21 at p. 11.

[113] D. Kapur and P. Mehta, 'The Indian Parliament as an Institution of Accountability', pp. 16–23, available at https://casi.sas.upenn.edu/sites/casi.sas.upenn.edu/files/bio/uploads/The%20Indian%20Parliament.pdf (accessed 8 March 2015).

[114] Kapur and Mehta, 'The Indian Parliament as an Institution of Accountability'. See also Austin, *Working a Democratic Constitution*.

been in compliance with the constitutional scheme, except in the cases of judicial appointments, invocation of the basic structure doctrine and the right to property. Further, the judiciary, despite many broad pronouncements has not been able, in practice, to curtail the powers of the legislature and the executive in any challenging manner.[115]

Further, the internal functioning of political parties does not reflect even a semblance of adherence to the rule of law or democratic principles. This has a direct impact on the functioning of the Parliament and state legislatures, as elected representatives are not even permitted to air their views in a democratic fashion. Bills are passed with little or no discussion, policies are not even presented in the house and are decided by executive fiat, and this when the legislators actually meet, which itself has reduced over time. The inclusion of the Tenth Schedule to the Constitution has curtailed the freedom, responsibility and duty of individual legislators with the threat of disqualification from their posts. With the weapon of the Tenth Schedule in their hands, leaders of political parties get their way on almost all issues without any serious discussion or challenge on the basis of principles and policies. Therefore, no legislator raises a murmur even when policies are made to either pass legislation that dilute some of the fundamental rights of citizens or legalize continuous breach of law in one swoop.[116] The regular use of ordinances to make laws is also a serious challenge to the rule of law.[117]

[115] This is because the political class and the bureaucracy has not imbibed the spirit of the rule of law in the day-to-day functioning and the judiciary is dependent on the bureaucracy for implementing the judgments. For example, despite various rulings of the Supreme Court on treatment of prisoners and undertrials, their lot has not improved. Not a month goes by without some sort of police brutality being reported. Similarly, despite the Court's decisions requiring reasonableness, the government continues to take decisions arbitrarily on a regular basis. This is discussed in greater detail in Chapter 5 of this book.

[116] An example is the Karnataka government's repeated efforts to regularize illegal construction and occupation through the 'Akrama-Sakrama' measure. While this is a clear violation of all rule of law principles, no legislator has opposed the measure. It is left to civil society to challenge these actions in court.

[117] See Austin, *Working a Democratic Constitution*. The use of ordinances is even more widespread at the state level. See D.C. Wadhwa, *Endangered Constitutionalism: Documents of a Supreme Court Case* (Pune: Gokhale Institute

The political mobilization by most political parties in India is on the basis of caste, and other sectarian basis, and is a direct challenge to the spirit of the rule of law embodied in the Constitution. It may be acceptable to claim that despite efforts the constitutional goals of substantive equality and fraternity based on a casteless society have not been achieved because of the long historical legacy and sustaining power of caste. It is deplorable, however, for political parties to actively use caste and religion as the basis of political mobilization, as it directly undermines the rule of law. The mushrooming of religion and caste based parties over the last few decades and their success in different parts of the country reflect that the political understanding, if any, of the rule of law is at times in direct conflict with constitutional values. This also very often translates into governance, laws and regulations and causes enormous strain on society.

As discussed in Chapter 2, the state has a central role in Indian society. This essentially translates into a central role for the political class directly in the form of political parties, and indirectly through the government apparatus, which is influenced by the political class. The political class's poor awareness of the rule of law therefore, not only has long-term implications for society but also causes regular stress in the functioning of the government. Bureaucrats regularly complain of unnecessary political interference in their day-to-day decision making. The problem is magnified in a government apparatus such as the police, which have a citizen facing role and are the most susceptible to political interference.[118] Short term and local political goals play a greater role in the functioning of the government than administrative discipline and the rule of law.

FOUR DOMINANT THEMES

The discourse on rule of law in India has four dominant themes. First, there is no doubt whatsoever that the Constitution has adopted a substantive concept of rule of law. The choices made at the time of drafting

---

of Politics and Economics, 2008), which contains a study of the misuse of ordinances by the State of Bihar and the challenge in the Supreme Court.

[118] The interference in the functioning of the police, in particular, and the need for police reforms in general, has been discussed in detail in *Prakash Singh v Union of India* (2006) 8 SCC 1.

and adopting the Constitution and in its subsequent working clearly show that, initially, the Constituent Assembly and later, successive legislatures and governments have been very clear in their minds that the concept of rule of law is meaningless without the inclusion of substantive social justice and equality. With the judiciary also accepting this narrative, there is no dissenting voice about the substantive nature of the rule of law in India.

Second, the rule of law has been characterized by a constant search for reasonableness. Almost mirroring the Aristotlean search for a society governed by the 'rule of reason', the rule of law discourse in India reflects a constant quest for reasonableness. While the judiciary's declaration that arbitrariness is antithetical to rule of law is par for the course, its insistence that the rule of law also requires all government actions to be reasonable is revolutionary in character. The judiciary has gone beyond the concept of fair hearing and other natural justice principles and suggested that the rule of law in India requires the clear exercise of reason. While there are no indicators of what is reasonable action (only indicators of what is not reasonable action exist), the judiciary's power and inclination to test any state action on the threshold of reasonableness has led to many consequences. Even the basic structure doctrine can be interpreted to be an extension of this demand for reason in all government institutions. And it is not only the judiciary that has imposed its view on what is reasonable. The Parliament has also insisted that the judiciary be reasonable in its exercise of the power of judicial review and has fashioned the unique technique of the Ninth Schedule to save certain actions it considers to be reasonable.

Third, and closely linked to the search of reasonableness, is the desire to fashion a delicate balance between the Part III rights and the Part IV principles. The conflict between Part III and Part IV is at the heart of the rule of law debate between individual rights and substantive societal goals. The Constituent Assembly believed that it had achieved the great balance by including certain substantive goals in Part III itself and leaving the others in Part IV. Subsequent developments show that the balance in the text was not sufficiently clear to many. Therefore, the judiciary has tried to design a new balance and has not been shy about implementing the task it has assigned itself. While the verdict is still awaited on whether a reasonable balance has been achieved, the recognition of the need for such a balance is what makes the rule of law discourse interesting.

Fourth, judicial independence and judicial review have both derived strength from the rule of law principle and in turn added real might to the rule of law. The obsession of the judiciary with its own independence and the general support it has received to maintain its independence, coupled with its desire to effectively exercise the power of judicial review, appears to have upheld and advanced the rule of law, in theory.

The discourse around these four dominant themes has eclipsed the more routine, but equally important aspects of the rule of law. For example, certainty and equality in implementation of the law, two fundamental aspects face serious challenges in India but do not get the attention they deserve. All organs of the state, including the judiciary, are guilty of explaining away some of these challenges by citing 'realities' of the country. In effect, the focus on these dominant themes also explains in a different method, the reasons for the challenges in implementation of the Rule of Law. These issues are discussed in the following chapters.

4

RULE OF LAW AND LAWMAKING

Our legislatures look more like combat arenas, rather than fora that
legislate.... We need a Parliament that debates, discusses and decides.[1]

—Pranab Mukherjee, President of India,
Address to the nation, 14 August 2013

Every single rule in the rule book, every single etiquette is being violated....
If the Honourable members wish the House to become a federation of
anarchists, then it is a different matter.[2]

—Hamid Ansari, Vice President of India and
Chairman of the Rajya Sabha, 13 August 2013

One of the most important features of the modern rule of law is the
involvement of citizens in lawmaking. This has both a theoretical
and practical imperative. The practical imperative is the near universal acceptance of the modern democratic form as the most accepted
method of government. That democracy is a basic and essential feature

---

[1] Quote extracted from A.K. Mehra, 'Indian Parliament and "Cost To
The Country"', in A. Behar, Y. Kumar, and J. Samuel (eds) *Citizens' Report
on Governance and Development, 2013* (New Delhi: National Social Watch,
2013), p. 48, available at http://socialwatchindia.net/images/documents/498/
CRGD- 2013_Full-Report.pdf (available at 20 March 2015).

[2] Mehra, 'Indian Parliament and "Cost To The Country"'. While Vice
President Ansari was talking mainly about the Rajya Sabha, this applies equally
to all elected bodies across the country.

of the rule of law in India is clear from our discussions in Chapters 2 and 3. The theoretical imperative is that a citizen cannot complain about the fairness or reasonableness of laws that he is involved in making.[3] Legislative representation in the new millennium has become more inclusive and broad based than ever before in India.[4] This is part of the larger broadening and deepening of political democracy in India, which has ensured that previously marginalized groups are participating actively in electoral politics. Today, in terms of involvement in politics and participation in the democratic election process, India is doing very well. Following the Constitution (Seventy-third Amendment) Act, 1992, and the Constitution (Seventy-fourth Amendment) Act, 1992, direct elections on the basis of universal adult suffrage are regularly held for all the three tiers of government—union (for the Lok Sabha), states (for the legislative assemblies), and local self-government (municipalities or panchayats).[5] All the elections are not only fiercely contested but see participation by a majority of the people. In the general elections of 2014, out of a registered electorate of 83.41 crore, 55.38 crore people exercised their vote, translating into a voting percentage of 66.4, the highest ever in Indian history.[6] In the elections to various state

[3] Many theorists and philosophers have also argued for this requirement. For example, see R. Unger, *Law in a Modern Society* (New York: The Free Press, 1977).

[4] D. Kapur and P. Mehta, 'The Indian Parliament as an Institution of Accountability', 16–23, available at https://casi.sas.upenn.edu/sites/casi.sas.upenn.edu/files/bio/uploads/The%20Indian%20Parliament.pdf (accessed 8 March 2015). See also Z. Hasan, 'Political Parties', in N.G. Jayal and P.B. Mehta (eds), *The Oxford Companion to Politics in India* (New Delhi: Oxford University Press, 2010), pp. 241–53; V. Hewitt and S. Rai, 'Parliament', in N.G. Jayal and P.B. Mehta (eds), *The Oxford Companion to Politics in India* (New Delhi: Oxford University Press, 2010), pp. 28–42; B.L. Shankar and V. Rodrigues, *The Indian Parliament: A Democracy at Work* (New Delhi: Oxford University Press, 2014).

[5] There have been problems with many state governments not holding elections to the third tier, panchayats and urban local bodies, on time and trying to usurp the powers of the third tier of government. However, this has not completely undermined the political success of the third tier.

[6] The voting percentage has been taken from the data released by the Election Commission of India, which is available at www.eci.nic.in, (last visited on March 12, 2015). The percentage could be higher or lower because of widespread errors in the voter rolls. In any event, the participating percentage compares favourably with most other democratic countries.

legislatures, the percentages vary but generally hover between 60 per cent and 70 per cent. There are about 32 lakh elected representatives in India at all tiers.[7]

This widespread, entrenched, deepened, and vibrant electoral process appears to satisfy the requirement of citizen involvement in theory, as representative democracy works on the assumption that the elected representative of citizens articulate their opinions when laws are enacted by the legislature. In practice, this is a far cry from reality because of the dysfunctional parliamentary system, lack of regular and meaningful democratic interactions between the constituents and their representatives in between elections and lack of democracy within political parties, amongst many other ills that also characterise the Indian democracy. Each of these challenges is discussed separately in the further paragraphs.

THE TENTH SCHEDULE HURDLE

Individual members of legislature do not have the complete freedom to give voice to the views of the people they represent. Instead, they are always bound by party diktat. An individual member cannot vote (or even abstain) against the party line on any matter that comes up in Parliament or legislature except with the prior permission of the party. Failure to do so will result in disqualification from the membership of Parliament or legislature, according to the Tenth Schedule of the Constitution introduced by the Constitution (Fifty-second Amendment) Act, 1985.[8] Members of Parliament or the legislature

---

[7] Mehra, 'Indian Parliament and "Cost To The Country"', p. 20. This number is mentioned in the preface to the report, written by Amitabh Behar.

[8] The Tenth Schedule was introduced to prevent the 'evil of political defections' by elected representatives (lured by money and power rather than principle) resulting in instability of various governments across the country. See statement of objects and reasons when the bill was introduced, available at http://indiacode.nic.in/coiweb/amend/amend52.htm (accessed 22 February 2017). We should note however that the introduction of the Tenth Schedule has not put an end to defections. See M.P. Jain, *Indian Constitutional Law*, edited by S. Pal and R. Pal (Gurgaon: Lexis Nexis, 2014), pp. 45–52 for a concise summary of the law and various cases that have come up before the courts.

therefore vote in all cases in accordance with directions given by the party leadership, irrespective of whether they are in agreement with such decisions (except when at least two-thirds of the members decide to form a separate group or merge with another party). The Tenth Schedule, therefore, directly contradicts the notion that citizens have an indirect role in making laws as their elected representative cannot even vote in accordance with their own wishes. In fact, it is almost impossible to even ascertain the opinions or votes of individual members of Parliament or legislature on specific issues as voting on every issue is not recorded, but passed by voice vote, according to parliamentary procedure. The counter-argument made is that in India, people vote for a party and not an individual, thereby justifying the provisions of the Tenth Schedule which places more importance on the political party rather than an individual member of the house.[9]

The aforesaid theoretical proposition is not borne out by data. In various surveys conducted by the research group DAKSH between 2006 and 2014, a higher percentage of the people surveyed said that the identity of the candidate was a more important factor than the political party in determining their vote in an election.[10] While the party's ideology and its leadership may be relevant factors, the personality of the individual candidate, particularly her accessibility to the constituents and the ability to articulate their concerns, are very important qualities

---

[9] This argument was accepted by the Supreme Court in *Kihoto Hollohan v. Zachilhu* 1992 Supp (2) SCC 651, when it upheld the validity of the Tenth Schedule. Even assuming that people in India vote for political parties, there is nothing preventing political parties from permitting elected representatives to vote as they feel, even against party diktat, except in relation to resolutions that determine the survival of the government.

[10] DAKSH conducts surveys to elicit opinions of people to measure the performance of elected representatives. Their methodology and reports are available at www.dakshindia.org (accessed 22 February 2017). In the survey conducted immediately prior to the general elections in 2014, 37.82 per cent of the 265,000 respondents in more than 500 parliamentary constituencies said that the identity of the candidate was more important than the party. Only 25.64 per cent said that the party was very important, while 20.18 per cent said that the identity of the prime ministerial candidate was very important in making their decision. The author is one of the founding members of DAKSH and was personally involved in conducting the surveys.

in helping people arrive at a decision in exercising their franchise. If individual members of Parliament or legislative assemblies are not allowed to vote according to their opinion, which is supposed to reflect the interest and/or opinion of his constituents, but instead vote according to choices made by party leadership and imposed on them, the fundamental assumption of citizens' involvement in the making of laws ceases to exist. For the citizens, their elected representative is not a mere number adding up the majority for a party in legislature, as the Tenth Schedule assumes.

While it is true that the legislator is not supposed to merely be an aggregator of opinions of her constituents but also bring a nuanced approached to policymaking by considering the interests of the country at large, the current practice of the party leadership controlling the votes on all policy matters more often than not results in a situation where neither the views of the constituents nor the opinion of the individual legislator is relevant. Further, political parties do not clearly communicate their views on various issues during elections. Most parties in fact release their manifestos so late during the campaigning, that electoral debates rarely turn on the promises in the manifesto or issues relevant to the people. Therefore, it is difficult to argue that citizens have participated in policymaking, which is decided by the ruling party's leadership.

PEOPLE AND THEIR REPRESENTATIVES

Lawmaking is clearly the primary role of the elected representative. Interaction between constituents and their elected representative between elections is very important to give substantive meaning to the assumption that the representative conveys the views of his constituents in Parliament or legislative assembly. Such dialogue and discussion needs to focus on the issues facing the constituency, state and country, as well as issues arising in the Parliament or legislative assembly. It has to be a two-way interaction where the representative not only learns about the problems and perceptions of the people he represents but also influences the views in the constituency on various issues. This kind of citizen involvement is very demanding on the elected representative and does not happen in India. Even if it does, it is the exception and not the rule.

Elected representatives do spend a lot of time in their constituency but that time is focused more on delivery of a 'patron-client' service. These services range from simple distribution of money, influencing local government officials to provide essential services on time, attending social and religions functions, participating in government functions, acting as a 'facilitator' for procuring various licences and contracts, influencing transfers of government officials, and generally procuring particular goods for individual constituents.[11] The interaction very rarely involves any discussion on policy issues that affect the constituency, the state or the nation as a whole, and the position that the elected representative should take in the forum that he is elected to. Kapur and Mehta come to a similar conclusion after surveying the existing scholarship on the role of members of Parliament (MPs) and observe,

> The fact that MPs often consider their primary function as a go-between says something about how the functions of representatives are seen in Indian politics. MPs are not often seen as lawmakers; most of their constituents are unaware of the bills they are associated with and they are seldom judged on policy accomplishments. In fact ... about half of the MPs said that they were expected to be in their constituency even when Parliament was in session. To a certain extent, this is inevitable in a party-based parliamentary system, where the role and standing of parties is decisive. However, if MPs internalize the view that they are not principally lawmakers, it will have deleterious effects on parliamentary legislation.[12]

It may not be correct to say that elected representatives should not have any role at all in the distribution of various welfare benefits that the state provides. Citizens often demand intervention from their representatives when the bureaucracy fails to do its job. However, that role

[11] In his study of the work done in the constituency by MPs, A. Surya Prakash documents various activities performed by the MP to please her constituents. Among the more bizarre activities Surya Prakash lists out is the provision of service by a MP from Rajasthan, Girdhari Lal Bhargava to immerse ashes of dead people in the Ganga! See, A. Surya Prakash, *What Ails India's Parliament?* (Gurgaon: Indus, 1995), pp. 37–126. Excerpts of the book are available at http://www.asuryaprakash.com/whatailsIP.html (accessed 22 February).

[12] Kapur and Mehta, 'The Indian Parliament as an Institution of Accountability', p. 19.

should be fulfilled through the exercise of the accountability powers of the legislature as a body over all executive action, and not by individual members becoming brokers between the state and the people at the constituency level.

As most individual members do not treat the proceedings of the house seriously, meaningful accountability of the executive through the legislature does not exist. This means that individual members use their people power at the constituency level by cajoling or demanding action from local bureaucrats. All this consumes much energy, which ensures that the representative has no time to focus on policy issues. Further, it is important to remember that the role of the 'broker' cannot be taken on at the cost of the primary role of ensuring a democratic discussion on policy issues. This lack of, or rather, abandonment of, interaction and discussion on policy issues creates a vital breach in the democratic theory of lawmaking and the assumptions of both the rule of law and democracy.

FUNCTIONING OF THE LEGISLATURE

The manner in which Parliament and the legislatures are functioning exacerbates the already tenuous assumption that citizens are involved in the making of law. Parliament and the legislatures do not spend enough time deliberating and discussing the various laws they enact. The average sittings of the Parliament and the time spent on deliberation has dropped sharply in the last two-and-a half decades. Naturally, the legislative and policy output has also reduced significantly. Tables 4.1 and 4.2[13] show the decline in sittings, deliberation and output of the Parliament over the years.

This dramatic reduction in deliberation and output on legislative and policy matters is attributed to various reasons such as repeated disruptions, walk-outs and boycotts of the proceedings by the opposition. Further, MPs do not have the expertise or support to understand, appreciate and make intelligible comments on the bills. Until the establishment of the independent research organisation Parliamentary

---

[13] The information has been sourced from Kapur and Mehta, 'The Indian Parliament as an Institution of Accountability'; the Citizens Report on Governance and Development, Mehra, 'Indian Parliament and "Cost To The Country"'; and the websites of the Lok Sabha and Rajya Sabha.

Table 4.1   Number of Sittings of Parliament, 1952–2014

Decade	Number of Sittings of Lok Sabha (Annual Average)	Number of Sittings of Rajya Sabha (Annual Average)
1952–61	124.2	90.5
1962–71	116.3	98.5
1972–81	97.9	85.5
1982–91	92.7	79.4
1992–2001	81.0	71.3
2002–14 (15 years)	69.0	69.8

Note: The number of sittings in 2002–14 are an approximation, as accurate data was not available for some years.

Table 4.2   Number of Bills Passed by Parliament Since 1952

Decade	Number of Bills Passed (Annual Average)
1952–61	68.0
1962–71	59.3
1972–81	65.9
1982–91	68.9
1992–2001	49.9
2002–14 (15 years)	40.1

Note: The number of sittings in 2002–14 are an approximation, as accurate data was not available for some years.

Research Service (PRS) in 2006, there was no mechanism for individual members to even get advance copies and summaries of bills to be presented in Parliament. Even ruling party members do not have access to draft bills, since the policy decisions and drafting of bills is controlled by the executive and the political leadership of each government. Bills are generally prepared by the government, with little or no discussion and presented in the house at the last possible moment.[14]

[14] It is only in exceptional cases that there is widespread discussion among interested parties and civil society before a bill is drafted and presented in the

Rajeev Dhavan points out that the discussion even on important constitutional amendments is very poor. Dhavan has studied the deliberations of both the Lok Sabha and the Rajya Sabha in relation to the Constitution (Forty-second Amendment) Act, 1976, which was a master amendment that changed many provisions during the emergency, and the Constitution (Seventy-seventh Amendment) Act, 1995; Constitution (Eighty-third Amendment) Act, 2000; Constitution (Eighty-fifth Amendment) Act, 2001; and Constitution (Ninety-third Amendment) Act, 2005, all relating to reservations that amended Articles 15 and 16. In relation to the Constitution (Forty-second Amendment) Act, 1976, Dhavan notes, 'The debates were abysmal. They would be funny if they were not tragic. Authoritarian majoritarianism stalks through the columns of the debate. A new trend of anti-democratic debates had set in.'[15]

While the Constitution (Forty-second Amendment) Act, 1976, can be argued to be an exception, given that it was one of the various sins of the internal emergency declared by the Indira Gandhi government, Dhavan points out that the tendency of abrupt and arbitrary discussions from that period has continued. Dhavan contrasts the discussions in Parliament prior to the emergency with those during the post-emergency period and argues that the pre-emergency debates are full of rich surprises, reflecting an acute understanding of the principles involved, vested interests and public interest. The post-emergency debates are not convincing and show up the lack of rigour in making laws.[16]

All the reservations related amendments mentioned above pertain to Articles 15 and 16 which, as we discussed in Chapters 2 and 3, are

---

house; one example is the Companies Act, 2013 which was the subject matter of much discussion for several years before it was presented. Generally, it is possible to link this widespread discussion with the presence of specific, influential and interested pressure groups.

[15] R. Dhavan, *Reserved! How Parliament Debated Reservations 1995–2007* (New Delhi: Rupa, 2008), p. 24. Dhavan's study on the 42nd amendment is the subject matter of his earlier book—R. Dhavan, *The Amendment: Conspiracy or Revolution* (Allahabad: Wheeler, 1978).

[16] Dhavan, *Reserved! How Parliament Debated Reservations 1995–2007*, pp. 24–5. Dhavan points out the discussions and deliberations prior to the enactment of the Indian Patents Act, 1971 as an example of the excellent work done by Parliament.

an expression of the substantive equality principle contained in the Constitution. All the amendments were introduced to overrule the Supreme Court's interpretation of the scope, extent and depth of the reservations in jobs and in admissions to educational institutions. These two Articles also reflect the delicate balance that the Constitution seeks to establish between guaranteed individual rights and the larger goal of social justice. Any amendments to these Articles, particularly when they sought to overrule Supreme Court judgments, therefore would need to be considered and deliberated by the Parliament in great and minute detail. However, Dhavan's study of the debates shows that there was, at times, no quorum[17] to pass the amendments. Little or no discussion took place and members who wanted to raise substantial points were shouted down. Members even protested that the amendment bills were introduced without adequate notice and in violation of parliamentary procedure.[18] Generally, rhetoric substituted for reasoned argument and majoritarianism prevailed as no one seriously challenged any of the amendments. Dhavan argues that in effect, Parliament sat in appeal over the Supreme Court's decisions and simply reversed them because it felt the Court was wrong. There were no arguments on whether Parliament could simply reverse the Court, whether it should do so, and even whether the Court was wrong at all. Certainly, there was no debate on whether the delicate balance that the Constituent Assembly wanted to achieve was being disturbed.

Similarly, in the case of the Constitution (Ninety-ninth Amendment) Act, 2014, which established the Judicial Appointments Commission, the bill was introduced and passed with only a three-hour discussion in both houses.[19] There was hardly any debate on the

---

[17] Quorum is generally one-tenth of the total strength of each house. Kapur and Mehta point out that they were unable to obtain data on the number of times Parliament has been adjourned for lack of quorum. They believe that it has become normal parliamentary practice to ignore the quorum requirement. Kapur and Mehta, 'The Indian Parliament as an Institution of Accountability', p. 18.

[18] Dhavan, *Reserved! How Parliament Debated Reservations 1995–2007*, pp. 30–6, 50–62, 76–86, 94–102, 112–38 and 152–71.

[19] The transcript of the proceedings on the Constitution Amendment Bill in the two houses can be found at http://rajyasabha.nic.in/rsnew/bill/ls_bill_debate/Lok%20sabha%20debate.pdf and http://rajyasabha.nic.in/rsnew/bill/rs_bill_debate/RS%20debate%20121%20Bill.pdf (accessed 15 March 2015).

individual clauses of the bill. The few amendments suggested were not pressed and most of the members who spoke only talked about the history of the problem rather than the efficacy of the proposed solution. While there had been a discussion on the topic in the public domain for a long time, the bill itself was different from the many suggestions that had been discussed and supported by a wide section of society. The importance of the bill, clearly most fundamental to the governance of the country, was belied by the number of members present. In the Lok Sabha, only 348 members (the total strength of the Lok Sabha is 545) were present at the time of voting, out of which 33 abstained. In the Rajya Sabha, only 181 members (the total strength of the Rajya Sabha is 250) were present at the time of the voting out of which one voted against the amendment.

Dhavan rightly points out that the power of amending the Constitution is the *Brahmastra* (ultimate weapon) in any democracy and ought not to be invoked casually. Parliament should not invoke the amending power merely because its views are different from that of the judiciary or because it feels that the judiciary is wrong. However, the track record of Parliament on constitutional amendments indicates that the amending power has been invoked lightly and without serious reasoned discussion and debate. The Parliament has abandoned its 'constitutional role to a conspiratorial consensus without real discussion'.[20] Lawmaking, and certainly constitutional amendments, should not be an exercise of majoritarian power, but that is precisely what is happening due to lack of proper deliberation.

The experience in connection with the enactment of ordinary statutes is no different. At least constitutional amendments attract media attention and force the government and members of Parliament to consider them with an element of seriousness. Ordinary legislation are not the subject matter of such attention and are treated with either disdain or indifference by members. In the 15th Lok Sabha (2009–14), 35 per cent of the bills were debated for an hour or less and another 20 per cent of the bills were debated for less than two hours. The Sexual Harassment of Women at the Workplace (Prevention, Prohibition and Redressal)

[20] Dhavan, *Reserved! How Parliament Debated Reservations 1995–2007*, pp. 40.

Bill was passed in 20 minutes.[21] Various other bills have been passed in less than 5 minutes.[22]

There are various reasons for this attitude of MPs. First, mastering parliamentary procedure and understanding policy and legislation is a difficult task given the complexity involved. The staff provided to individual members is incapable of assisting the members on these issues. There is no independent professional help available in this sector. Political parties also do not take the task of training individual members seriously. Generally, at the beginning of each new Lok Sabha or legislative assembly, there is one session for half a day, which is supposed to train new members. However, this kind of ad hoc and superficial training hardly serves the purpose. We can safely say that a majority of the members, particularly first-time MPs, do not even know how to read a bill or understand the intricacies of financial proposals or new laws being proposed.[23] Second, members believe that participating meaningfully in Parliament or the legislative assembly is of no use. They firmly believe that the legislatures have become talk shops and make no difference to their constituents or themselves. They would much rather spend their time providing constituency services. The lack of media attention for good performance in the house is also a factor. The media focuses only on disturbances and bedlam created in the house and not on an informed speech by a well-prepared member. Therefore, even when members are present in the house they would much rather behave in a manner that gets them media exposure the following day![24]

Third, and most unfortunate, the political leadership in each party is happy with having most of its members ignorant of policy issues, as

---

[21] S. Singh, 'Has the 15th Lok Sabha Been the Worst Performing Ever?', 4 February 2014, available at http://www.rediff.com/news/report/has-the-15th-lok-sabha-been-the-worst-performing-ever/20140204.htm (accessed 17 March 2015).

[22] A. Behar, D. Samuel, and Y. Kumar (eds), *Citizens Report on Governance and Development, 2010* (National Social Watch 2010), pp. 29–30, available at http://socialwatchindia.net/images/documents/313/Citizens%20report%202010.pdf (accessed 20 March 2015).

[23] Kapur and Mehta point out that there is a high turnover in Parliament and the percentage of new members in each Lok Sabha is quite high. Kapur and Mehta, 'The Indian Parliament as an Institution of Accountability', pp. 5–6.

[24] Kapur and Mehta, 'The Indian Parliament as an Institution of Accountability', p. 18.

this allows the leadership a free hand and also ensures that there is no challenge to them from within the party. The leadership makes little or no effort to enable their members to learn more about policy and legislation and become better parliamentarians. There is also no encouragement or incentive for individual members to elicit opinions from their constituents on matters that affect them or are of significance.

PARLIAMENTARY COMMITTEES

Parliament has a number of committees, standing and select, which are supposed to deliberate on certain bills so that work can be carried out more efficiently in the house. Until the 10th Lok Sabha, these committees were ad hoc in character. Later, the concept of Department Related Standing Committees (DRSCs) was introduced and the committee system has started functioning better. After the DRSCs were formed, more bills and policy issues are being referred to the committees for detailed discussion. Many feel that this has made the consultative process on legislation more widespread.[25] However, the proceedings of the standing committees are not public and the inner workings and compromises reached by the committees are generally shrouded in mystery. Some of the more active committees do invite the public's views on the bills under consideration and produce reports which are accessible to the public. Most committees, however, are happy to interview bureaucrats and conclude their tasks.

Kapur and Mehta point out that the functioning of the standing committees leaves a lot to be desired. The committees do not have any professional staff and support and rely on the government for expertise and information. Most committees finish reading and reviewing the bills in about two sittings. Further, the committees, according to Kapur and Mehta, rarely come up with new policies and proposals and the political party leadership deliberately ensures that the committees do not get stronger. Recent reports indicate that the committees have also become battlegrounds for partisan politics, particularly in light of the various allegations of corruption against the United Progressive Alliance government between 2009 and 2014.[26] Further, the committees are also

[25] Behar, Samuel, and Kumar, *Citizens Report on Governance and Development*, 2010, 40–5.

[26] Mehra, 'Indian Parliament and "Cost To The Country"', p. 63.

very large, with membership ranging between 15 and 40, for them to be effective policymaking bodies.[27] The National Social Watch studied the functioning of three finance committees and 16 DRSCs during the year 2010–11 and the first half of 2011–12. Seven committees did not meet at all during 2010–11 and four did not meet during the first half of 2011–12. The average meeting time was 75–80 minutes.[28] Attendance in the committee meetings, when committees actually do meet, is very poor, averaging between 40 per cent and 45 per cent. Acceptance of the committees' recommendations is also poor, hovering around 50 per cent or less.[29]

STATE LEGISLATURES

The situation is, unfortunately, similar or even worse at the level of the state legislatures.[30] The author studied the legislative activity of the Karnataka state legislature, both the legislative assembly and the council, for the period 2005–7.[31] No references were made to the standing committees by the legislative assembly in connection with any of the laws passed during the three-year period. In the legislative council, during the same period, only one bill (The Karnataka State Civil Services (Regulation of Transfer of Teachers) Bill, 2007) was referred to a select committee. The select committee took a period of four months to produce a report. The assembly spent, on an aggregate of 66 bills that were passed by it, only a grand total of 21 hours and 43 minutes to debate the bills. During the same period, the council spent 59 hours and

[27] Kapur and Mehta, 'The Indian Parliament as an Institution of Accountability', pp. 12–14.

[28] Mehra, 'Indian Parliament and "Cost To The Country"', p. 62.

[29] Behar, Samuel, and Kumar, *Citizens Report on Governance and Development, 2010*, pp. 40–6.

[30] The Karnataka state legislature, for example, did not even meet for 30 days in a year during the period 2008–13. Even when it did meet, it was repeatedly adjourned and did not function properly. After the elections in May 2013, the legislature has met more often than during the previous assembly.

[31] The study was conducted as part of a report this author prepared in 2008 on the working of the Karnataka state legislature on behalf of DAKSH for PRS. The report has not been published. All the data was obtained from the secretariat of the legislative assembly and the council.

45 minutes to debate the 83 bills it considered. Almost all the bills were passed on the day that they were introduced. The break-up of time spent by the council shows that, on an average, less than an hour was spent in introduction, discussion and passing of the bills. Some bills did not take more than 3 minutes to be approved! The assembly did not provide us the detailed break-up of time spent on each bill.

PROMULGATION OF ORDINANCES

The ineffective functioning of Parliament and the legislatures has meant the regular and continued use of power under Articles 123 (power of the President) and 213 (power of the Governor) to promulgate ordinances. Of course, many a time it is not necessarily the ineffective functioning of Parliament, but a deliberate design by the ruling party that leads to utilisation of ordinances. Since 1952, 646 ordinances have been promulgated by the President.[32] Shubhankar Dam has studied all these ordinances and points out that only one of them in fact merited the urgency required for promulgating an ordinance. Every other ordinance could have been discussed in Parliament in the following (or previous) parliamentary session.[33] Even assuming that Dam is exaggerating the problem, we can safely conclude that a majority of the ordinances could in fact have waited for the following, or passed in the previous, session. More than 200 ordinances were promulgated 15 days prior to a parliamentary session while a similar number were promulgated within 15 days after a parliamentary session had finished.[34]

There are two periods when ordinances were used in abundance, during the 1970s (that is, prior to, and during the, emergency) and during

[32] S. Rukmini and A. Joshua, 'Ordinances have Been a "Handy" Tool since 1952', *The Hindu*, 11 January 2015, available at http://www.thehindu.com/news/national/ordinances-have-been-handy-tool-since-1952/article6775674.ece (accessed 16 March 2015). See also S. Dam, *Presidential Legislation in India: The Law and Practice of Ordinances* (Cambridge: Cambridge University Press, 2013).

[33] J.T. Philip, 'Decoding India's Ordinance System', *Mint*, 10 January 2014, available at http://www.livemint.com/Specials/ZRtVJMBfOLoQ4l9Z0MA2wK/Decoding-Indias-ordinance-system-Shubhankar-Dam.html (accessed 16 March 2015).

[34] Philip, 'Decoding India's Ordinance System'.

the 1990s. The contrast is revealing and educative. During the 1970s, a single party was in power and had a good majority in Parliament, but still chose to promulgate ordinances. In the 1990s, a number of minority governments followed one another, none of them being assured support for every legislative action in Parliament. Dam also points out that until 1991, no ordinance had been re-promulgated at the national level, but between 1991 and 1993, 53 ordinances were re-promulgated, one of them five times.[35] While the use of ordinance once may, potentially, be justified, there is no ground whatsoever to justify re-promulgation! The only reason is that the government of the day does not desire for the bill to be debated in Parliament, since it is not assured of support.

The position in the states is no different. For example, in Bihar, between 1967 and 1981, 256 ordinances were promulgated. All the ordinances were kept alive for periods ranging from one to 14 years by re-promulgating them. Eleven of them were kept alive for more than 10 years, 48 were kept alive between five and six years and 138 were kept alive between one and five years. Five ordinances were re-promulgated more than 30 times.[36] The Supreme Court had to intervene and rule that ordinances cannot be re-promulgated without bringing them before the legislature.[37]

The regular promulgation and re-promulgation of ordinances holds a mirror to the effectiveness of Parliament and the legislatures. It is an exercise of power that violates the spirit of democracy and reeks of majoritarianism. The power to make an ordinance is only to be used in an emergency but it has been exercised to suit the convenience and intentions of the ruling party rather than address emergencies that require immediate attention. Use of this power in a non-emergency situation is a clear violation of the rule of law.

[35] Philip, 'Decoding India's Ordinance System'.

[36] D.C. Wadhwa has studied this re-promulgation activity and written a detailed analysis. See D.C. Wadhwa, *Re-promulgation of Ordinance: A Fraud on the Constitution of India* (Pune: Gokhale Institute of Politics and Economics, 1983). Wadhwa has also written a follow-on book detailing the proceedings before the Supreme Court. See D.C. Wadhwa, *Endangered Constitutionalism: Documents of a Supreme Court Case* (Pune: Gokhale Institute of Politics and Economics, 2008). There are no detailed studies about promulgation of ordinances in other states.

[37] *Dr. D.C. Wadhwa* v *State of Bihar* (1987) 1 SCC 378.

CRIMINALIZATION OF POLITICS

A disturbing but significant feature of the Parliament and state legislatures has been the increasing criminalization of these bodies. People who have serious criminal charges pending against them are regularly being elected to Parliament and the state legislature. The Association for Democratic Reforms (ADR) has analysed the criminal records and asset details of MPs for the last three Lok Sabhas based on the affidavits filed by them at the time of contesting elections.[38] Table 4.3 below has the details.[39]

These percentages are not very different in the state assemblies as well. The Rajya Sabha has a slightly lower percentage of members with criminal records.[41] The data analysed by ADR is based only on the cases disclosed by the candidates when they file their nomination during

Table 4.3   Number of MPs with Criminal Cases

Year	MPs with Criminal Cases		MPs with Serious Criminal Cases[40]	
	Number	Percentage	Number	Percentage
2004	125	24	60	12
2009	158	30	78	15
2014	185	34	119	22

[38] The requirement for filing these affidavits itself was pursuant to an order of the Supreme Court. See *Union of India v Association for Democratic Reforms* (2002) 5 SCC 294.

[39] The table has been created based on the information available on the ADR website, http://myneta.info/ (accessed 20 March 2015).

[40] Any offence where (a) punishment is five years or more, (b) offence is non-bailable, (c) offence pertains to the violation of electoral rules or bribery, (d) offence relates to loss to exchequer, (e) offence relates to assault, murder, kidnap, or rape, (f) offence is mentioned in Section 8 of the Representation of the People Act, (g) offence under the Prevention of Corruption Act, or (h) offence relates to crimes against women, is classifieed as a serious criminal case. See http://adrindia.org/content/criteria-categorization-serious-criminal-cases (accessed 20 March 2015).

[41] See http://www.myneta.info/rajsab09aff/ (accessed 26 March 2015). The website also contains data for each of the state assemblies.

elections. No analysis has been done by anyone to understand the nature and circumstances of the cases against each member.

The large percentage of members with criminal cases against elected representatives has a number of consequences. The most obvious one is the impact on the investigation and decision of the concerned criminal case itself. The investigating officers are unlikely to pursue cases against elected representatives with the same vigour as other cases. Magistrates are more likely to be lenient with the elected representatives during the conduct of the trial. Second, there is a perception problem for democracy. Citizens' faith in the democratic process and the law will diminish if there are a large number of people with criminal charges in the lawmaking body.

Third and most important, it affects the functioning of the Parliament or state legislatures as the case may be. While it is not possible to state with certainty that a person with criminal cases pending against him will not or cannot be an effective representative, the existence of the case will make it more difficult for the person to perform well. Apart from the physical and mental constraints involved, the low credibility of the person while participating in the proceedings of the house or in performing a leader's role in the constituency makes the job difficult and shortchanges the people of his constituency and the country. In the state of Karnataka, during the period 2009–13, there were a number of elected representatives who were incarcerated, but they continued as members of the house. Incarceration means a physical inability of the person to even represent his constituents. This is clearly not an acceptable position, but it happens regularly in India. The effect on the functioning of democracy and the legislature is deleterious.

CONFLICT OF INTEREST

An increasing trend is the direct involvement of businessmen of various hues in electoral politics. Many of them win direct elections to the Lok Sabha and legislative assemblies. Others buy entry into the Rajya Sabha or legislative councils. Some of them become ministers, particularly in the states. Many other individual members are paid consultants for various private organisations. While conflicts of interest of individual members in legislature or various standing committees can potentially be resolved by asking the particular member to absent himself from meetings dealing with the conflicting issues, conflicts of interest of ministers can never be resolved. For example, sugar factory owners end up as ministers responsible for fixing the minimum procurement price for purchase of sugarcane from farmers and individuals who own and run educational institutions are in charge of regulating the same institutions.

The increasing number of individuals with such conflicts of interest compromises the independence of Parliament and government.[42] Even if there is an internal mechanism to address the conflict of interest in a reasonable fashion, the perception of a compromised Parliament causes great harm to the rule of law. The nature of electoral politics leaves it open to the undue influence of certain interest groups, particularly those who are wealthy and can finance electoral politics. However, there has been limited effort in India to even acknowledge the existence of this issue through a formal mechanism. The requirement for members to declare their 'interests' in the Lok Sabha and Rajya Sabha has rarely been followed. Even the existing principle of 'office of profit' which prevents MPs from occupying certain offices is very narrow and is restricted to offices that are essentially funded by the government.[43] No effort has been made by any institution to address the issue of the wider and more harmful effects of conflict of interests of members and ministers' legislative/executive office and their private business interests. ADR's studies have in fact shown that the assets of members increases at the speed of light or more![44]

[42] There are several instances of conflicts of interest that have been detailed and discussed in the media over the last decade. Some examples are B.R. Satish Kumar, 'Conflict of Interest, the Bug Bear?', *The Hindu*, 27 January 2015, available at http://www.thehindu.com/news/national/karnataka/conflict-of-interest-the-bugbear/article6826052.ece (accessed 26 March 2015) and M. Merchant, 'India Needs Institutional Arrangements to Rule of Conflict of Interest amongst Those Holding Public Office', *The Economic Times*, 11 February 2012, available at http://articles.economictimes.indiatimes.com/2012-02-11/news/31050009_1_remunerative-directorships-lok-sabha-mps-bmc (accessed 26 March 2015).

[43] PRS has prepared a useful note titled, 'Conflict of Interest Issues in Parliament', which contains a comparative analysis of the position in different countries, the position taken by the Lok Sabha and Rajya Sabha and disclosures made by various members. See http://www.prsindia.org/administrator/uploads/general/1370583452_Conflict%20of%20Interest.pdf (accessed 26 March 2015).

[44] The information on asset increase of people contesting in various elections is available at http://myneta.info/ (accessed 26 March 2015).

FINANCING OF POLITICAL PARTIES

The financing of political parties and electoral politics is a black hole of gargantuan proportions. Parties do not disclose any meaningful details of their funding, extent, or source. The meagre public disclosure made is clearly not reflective of the actual funds that parties mobilise and spend during elections. Political parties believe that they are not accountable to anyone on this issue. Efforts to bring in more transparency on the funding of political parties have remained on paper, as political parties have resisted any regulation in this area despite much pressure from civil society. In fact, six national political parties in the country have not disclosed their funds and sources of funding despite made by the Central Information Commission under the Right to Information Act, 2005 (RTI).[45]

ADR's study shows more than 75 per cent of even the declared donations is unaccountable and what is declared is generally a very small portion of the total amount that parties mobilize. [46] While the most obvious conclusion is that political parties are operating with contempt towards, and in violation of, various laws of the country, the effect of this unaccounted funding on lawmaking is crippling. Laws made by a group of individuals who deliberately conceal the source of their funds will lack both moral and legal legitimacy. They will also be ineffective as citizens' acceptance, morally and otherwise, of such laws will be in question.

MAJORITARIAN IMPUNITY

Parliament's fundamental character is that of a deliberative and representative body. Elected representatives are expected to advance, discuss and weigh the reasons for approving a policy or statute. Parliamentary debates should convey at least the fundamental rationale of public justification for making laws and policies. Only when such debates occur

---

[45] T. Sastry, 'Defying RTI, Undermining Democracy', *The Hindu*, 25 March 2015, available at http://www.thehindu.com/opinion/lead/defying-rti-undermining-democracy/article7028792.ece (accessed 26 March 2015).

[46] ADR has carried out a detailed analysis of political party funding and expenditure. http://adrindia.org/research-and-report/political-party-watch (accessed 26 March 2015).

in public view, the soundness of such justification is examined and monitored by the people. In a plural society, it is important that parliamentary debates evolve into a reasonable compromise or consensus, resulting in law and policy. The lack or total absence of reasoned debate reflects legislative arbitrariness and majoritarian impunity, which does not have a place in a society governed by the rule of law. Yes, outcomes in legislatures are dependent on majority vote, but the vote should be for good reasons that are recorded.

Parliament and the legislatures are limited only by their lack of imagination and failure to deliberate. Unlike the judiciary or the executive, they are not limited in the choices they can make to achieve different outcomes. They have a wide canvas to act upon, but that wide canvas can be utilised only if each legislator participates fully and freely in the deliberations. Stifling deliberation, either in the name of majoritarianism or prevailing sentiment or a goal set in the past, narrows the canvas available to the legislature. Majoritarianism does not mean a majority community, but the prevailing majoritarian view (this could at times include the ruling party in conjunction with the opposition parties or a ruling party with a large majority in Parliament). The absence of reasoned discourse and deliberation is the hallmark of majoritarianism. The exercise of power without respect for the rule of law, fundamental rights, constitutional and parliamentary propriety and even at times, political and social morality, is also evidence of majoritarianism.

Dhavan has rightly pointed out in the context of the constitutional amendments on reservations that the Parliament has been amending the Constitution without proper discussion due to the existence of a majoritarian consensus.[47] Kannabiran highlights an equally, if not more, worrying trend. Majoritarian impunity has led, in his view, to the enactment of statutes that are in clear breach of the Part III fundamental rights frequently.[48] Citing the examples of the Terrorist and Disruptive Activities (Prevention) Act, 1985 (TADA); the Armed Forces (Special Powers) Act, 1958 (AFSPA); the Andhra Pradesh Preventive Detention Act, 1970; and the Andhra Pradesh Suppression of Disturbances Act, 1967, Kannabiran argues that these enactments are an indication of the

[47] Dhavan, *Reserved! How Parliament Debated Reservations 1995–2007*, p. 40.

[48] K.G. Kannabiran, *The Wages of Impunity* (Hyderabad: Orient Longman, 2004). See in particular pp. 1–12, 30–62, and 91–101.

majoritarian acceptance of 'security of the state' and 'law and order' as the reason for governance. He points out that most of these enactments were passed unanimously by Parliament and the state legislatures without discussion on the rights and liberties being trampled by the enactments. In his view, this is an abuse of power by the legislature.

Kannabiran's logic is difficult to fault. The Parliament and state legislatures have displayed a worrying trend of abandoning their responsibility to protect Part III rights in the name of law and order and security of the state. They have forgotten that the judiciary is not the only institution with the responsibility to protect the Part III rights.

Various other scholars such as Usha Ramanathan and Suhas Chakma support Kannabiran's views. Chakma compares the debates in Parliament when the AFSPA was passed is 1958 and the Prevention of Terrorism Act, 2002 (POTA)[49] was introduced in 2001, and points out that while a number of members took a principled stand against violation of fundamental rights in 1958, there was no such position in 2001, merely token protests.[50] It is, of course, a different matter that the AFSPA, which was enacted as a temporary measure, continues to hold the field and is being implemented in several states.

Ramanathan observes how statutes such as TADA, POTA and the Narcotic Drugs and Psychotropic Substances Act, 1985 (NDPSA) changed the fundamentals of criminal law in violation of various human rights, for example, the right against self-incrimination and right to privacy. She also points out that while the Supreme Court has repeatedly declared that death penalty should only be prescribed in the rarest of rare cases and has held that mandatory death penalty is unconstitutional, the NDPSA mandated the death penalty until an amendment in 2014 removed the provision.[51] Unfortunately, most debates on the civil liberties infringement by these statutes occur outside the legislature. The legislature itself sees token statements of support that swing wildly between extreme positions.

[49] This statute was repealed in 2004.

[50] S. Chakma, 'Do Ends Justify Means?', available at http://www.india-seminar.com/2002/512/512%20suhas%20chakma.htm#top (accessed 26 March 2015).

[51] U. Ramanathan, 'Crime and Punishment', available at http://www.india-seminar.com/2006/557/557%20usha%20ramanathan.htm (accessed 26 March 2015).

The above instances indicate that the legislature is either unaware of its role in protecting the rights of citizens as set out in the Constitution, or it gets swayed by the mass hysteria generated by phrases such as 'law and order' and 'security of the state'. It is a combination of the two alternatives that explains the situation—our legislature is guilty of both. Legislatures cannot, and should not, become cyclical policymakers in relation to the fundamental rights of citizens. When power is exercised with impunity and by ignoring principles and reasoned debate legislatures become trapped by cyclical majoritarian sentiments.

Majoritarianism also leads to the enactment of statutes that are symbolic in nature, either for purely political reasons or for sending a message on the importance of the issue. Symbolic legislations are sometimes useful to set goals, but generally tend to undermine the issues involved, as the law itself may be impossible to implement for a variety of reasons. One of the obvious examples of a meaningful and necessary symbolic legislation is the prohibition of untouchability in Article 17 of the Constitution and various statutes that have been enacted to give teeth to Article 17.[52] A counter-example is the introduction of Article 21A, guaranteeing the right to primary education as a fundamental right, much after the Supreme Court had read the right into Article 21. This introduction has not radically altered the plight of children in the country, as merely conferring a right, without the resources to implement it, is meaningless. Similarly, the enactment of POTA has not reduced terrorism in India, but only raised concerns on civil liberties.

The introduction of symbolic legislation undermines parliamentary power and authority, as it defeats the very purpose of lawmaking and undermines the rule of law. Having a variety of legislations on the statute books when they are not implemented properly or are incapable of implementation challenges the notion that law should guide behaviour and punish those who do not follow the law. The legislature needs to consider this issue at the time of making laws, but do not do so. This is an example of the lack of reasoned debate on lawmaking and the implementation of the laws made. Symbolic legislation permits political parties to possess bragging rights without actually bringing about real change.

---

[52] The Protection of Civil Rights Act, 1955 and The Scheduled Castes and Scheduled Tribes (Prevention of Atrocities) Act, 1989 are examples of laws passed to give effect to Article 17.

MULTITUDE OF LAWS

Bibek Debroy opines that our statutory framework is unsatisfactory and inefficient.[53] Certain areas suffer from too much legislation, while others do not have sufficient legislation. Debroy highlights the labour and employment sector which, in his view, suffers from over legislation that has resulted in confusion and uncertainty. There are at least 45 central legislations that regulate labour rights and welfare measures. There are more at the state level, as labour is an item in the concurrent list of the Seventh Schedule to the Constitution. Debroy notes,

> Do we really need 45 and more statutes? Apart from the constitutional angle of the Seventh Schedule, are special statutes needed for cine workers, dock workers, motor transport workers, sales promotion employees, plantation labour, working journalists and workers in mines? Consider also the time span of the legislation, from the Fatal Accidents Act of 1855 to the Public Liability Insurance Act of 1991. Over a period of time, concepts and definitions have changed. So has the case law, contributing to further confusion. The law does not agree on definitions of adolescent, child, contract labour, wages, employee, workman, factory and industry. The case law only makes it worse. The case law under the Industrial Disputes Act has held almost everything to be an industry—panchayat samitis, state hospitals, real estate companies, running of tubewells, primary health centres, Federation of Indian Chambers of Commerce and Industry, religious institutions, universities and research institutions.[54]

Debroy further points out that many welfare measures belong to the previous century and are not relevant anymore. He gives the example of the Factories Act, 1948 providing for adequate number of spittoons and space for keeping clothing for the benefit of employees.[55]

The example of the labour sector is not an exception. There are too many laws in India that work at cross purposes. The Law Commission has, in 2014, in its 248th, 249th, and 250th reports, identified nearly 250 statutes for wholesale repeal and a number of others for partial repeal. This is not the first time that the Law Commission has considered this

[53] B. Debroy, 'Why We Need Law Reform', 2001, available at http://www.india-seminar.com/2001/497/497%20bibek%20debroy.htm (accessed 26 March 2015).

[54] Debroy, 'Why We Need Law Reform'.

[55] Sections 20 and 43 respectively.

issue. The 96th, 148th, and 159th reports of the Law Commission also recommended repeal of various statutes, some of them enacted before 1947.[56]

In 1998, the P.C. Jain Commission was constituted to review administrative laws and in its report, that commission also suggested the repeal of 1,300 central laws out of a total of 2,500 laws it studied.[57] Clearly, not much has transpired in terms of repealing unnecessary laws and bringing clarity to the applicable law. Debroy points out that it is in fact almost impossible to determine the exact number of statutes across all the states in India, since many of them are sometimes not even published. On the basis of a few assumptions, Debroy estimates that there could be between 25,000 and 30,000 statutes in force in India.[58]

Not surprisingly, the legislature has also been very slow, or been unresponsive, in making new laws. An example is the confusion on the laws applicable to companies that aggregate taxi operators. Following the unfortunate incident of the rape of a female passenger by a taxi driver in Delhi, the union government issued an advisory to all the state governments to ban operations of companies that aggregated taxis if they did not comply with the 'applicable' laws! Following the directive some states issued circulars banning the operations while others claimed that they have banned the operations without actually issuing any official circular or notification.

However, there was no clarity forthcoming on the law that actually applied to these companies, which were really operating as online marketplaces for customers and taxi operators to find each other. It was another matter that these companies had been operating in India for a number of years. It was also a fact that there was no specific law regulating these operations. All the government had to do was to amend the Motor Vehicles Act, 1988, or clarify the applicable provisions if no amendment was needed. Neither action was however forthcoming. Similarly, there are a number of other sectors, particularly in light of

---

[56] All reports of the Law Commission are available at www.lawcommissionofindia.nic.in (accessed 26 March 2015).

[57] *Report of the Commission on Review of Administrative Laws, 1998* https://darpg.gov.in/sites/default/files/Review_Administrative_laws_Vol_1.pdf (accessed 26 March 2015).

[58] Debroy, 'Why We Need Law Reform'.

technology advancements, that are crying out for legal regulation but the legislature has not responded.

The Vidhi Centre for Legal Policy published a report in 2014 suggesting various important amendments to existing laws and identifying areas that urgently need new laws.[59] Some of the suggested areas for legislation are safer clinical trials, internet neutrality, crowdfunding of small businesses and nuclear liability. Even if one does not agree with the list brought out by Vidhi, the report highlights the inadequacy of the legislature in making necessary amendments, repealing useless laws and making new laws. The legislature has failed to respond adequately even in those circumstances where the judiciary has identified the need for a new law and passed directions until such time the law was made. It took the Parliament more than 15 years to enact the Sexual Harassment of Women at Workplace (Prevention, Prohibition and Redressal) Act after the Supreme Court's 1997 judgment in *Vishaka* v *State of Rajasthan*.[60]

BRINGING THE LAWS INTO FORCE

Even after a bill is approved as a statute, in several instances the legislature has delegated the power to bringing the statute into force to the executive. This power generally extends to deciding the date from which the statute, in either in its entirety or in parts, comes into force and also whether it will come into force in all of India at the same time. Sometimes, the effectiveness of the statute is dependent on the establishment of certain institutions by the executive. There are many statutes in India which have been passed by the legislature but have not been brought into force by the executive or have been brought into force but have not been given effect intentionally or otherwise, by the executive.

A few instances are discussed here to illustrate the point. Following the Constitution (Seventy-third Amendment) Act, 1992, and the Constitution (Seventy- fourth Amendment) Act, 1992, to usher in a third tier of government in rural and urban areas, states were required to pass laws giving effect to these constitutional amendments. While most

---

[59] The report is titled *25 Legal Reforms for India*, available at http://www.vidhilegalpolicy.in/FinalVidhiBook.pdf (accessed 26 March 2015).

[60] (1997) 6 SCC 241.

states took steps to give effect to the provisions in rural areas through the creation of panchayats at all levels—district, taluk, and village—similar provisions for in urban areas have never been given effect. While elections are held for municipal corporations, provisions that mandate establishment of ward committees and area sabhas have been ignored. In Bengaluru, only after a direction was issued by the Karnataka High Court in 2013, ward committees were established at great speed within a fortnight. Area sabhas have not seen the light of day yet. Similarly provisions to set up a metropolitan planning committee for the city of Bengaluru was on the statute books since 1994 but not established until 2014, when the Karnataka High Court ordered for rules to be framed and elections to be held.[61]

The Companies Act, 2013, is another great example of executive mismanagement in bringing into force a statute enacted by legislature. The President gave his assent to the bill as passed by Parliament on 29 August 2013 and the act was published in the gazette on 30 August 2013. Except for 98 sections that were brought into force in September 2013, there was no announcement as to when the new act would come into force. Suddenly on 27 March 2014, another 184 sections provisions were notified as coming into force from 1 April 2014. Subsequently, other provisions were brought into force in no particular order or logic over a period of six months. For a statute that took more than 20 years to make, it would have been easy to prepare a timetable for enforcement, given that it is a widely used statute. The enforcement was however mired in confusion and required several 'removal of difficulties' clarifications issued by the Ministry of Company Affairs. The ministry also had to make various rules to give meaning to certain provisions of the statute. While the rules were made, they were not properly notified in the official gazette. Some rules specify the date from which

---

[61] See 'BBMP told to set up ward committees', *The Hindu*, 11 January 2013, available at http://www.thehindu.com/news/cities/bangalore/bbmp-told-to-set-up-ward-committees/article4295537.ece (accessed 22 February 2017). See also 'Metropolitan Planning Committee Issue: Karnataka HC Notice to State Election Commission', *The Times of India*, 29 January 2014, available at http://timesofindia.indiatimes.com/city/bengaluru/Metropolitan-Planning-Committee-issue-Karnataka-HC-notice-to-State-Election-Commission/articleshow/29565446.cms (accessed 22 February 2017).

they will come into effect and others state that they will come into effect when they are published in the official gazette, but nobody is aware of whether they have been published in the official gazette. G.S. Patel J., of the Bombay High Court took judicial notice of this impropriety and observed,

> A final word about the manner in which these rules and sections are purportedly being brought into force. The website of the Ministry of Corporate Affairs has, on its front page, a link to a single scanned PDF file entitled "COMPANIES ACT 2013—STATEMENT OF NOTIFICATION OF RULES". Some 21 rules are listed. They are all said to be effective 1st April 2014. Several of these are not yet gazetted; at least I have not been able to find any gazette. I do not see how any such rules can be made effective on this basis where a ministry simply puts up some scanned document under the signature of one of its officers but sans any publication in the official gazette. That publication is not an idle formality. It has a well-established legal purpose. That purpose is not and cannot be achieved in this ad-hoc manner. Therefore, till such time as these rules are gazetted, or there is some provision made for the dispensation of official gazette notification, none of the rules in the Ministry of Corporate Affairs PDF document that are not yet gazetted can be said to be in force.[62]

These examples illustrate that even in the mechanical task of implementing statutes, in terms of time alone, there is confusion and lack of certainty. Whether there is certainty in the language of the statute and its meaning is another matter altogether.

EXECUTIVE LAWMAKING

Article 73 of the Constitution provides that the Union's executive powers shall extend to all matters with respect to which the Parliament has the power to make laws. Similarly, Article 162 provides similar powers to the executive at the state level. In addition, many statutes empower the executive to make rules and regulations to effectively implement the statutes. Such delegation is circumscribed by the provisions of the statute and the executive cannot exercise rule-making power in violation

[62] Judgment dated 8 May 2014 in 'Company Summons for Direction No. 256 of 2014', available at http://bombayhighcourt.nic.in/generatenewauth. php?auth=cGF0aD0uL2RhdGEvanVkZ2VtZW50cy8yMDE0LyZmbmFtZT T1PU0NTRDQ0NzE0LnBkZiZzbWZsYWc9Tg (accessed 26 March 2015).

of the statute. Certain statutes also provide that the rules made have to be placed before the relevant legislature for approval before they can take effect. Further, the number of laws that exist in the country is significant, and almost all of them delegate some form of authority to the executive to make rules and regulations. This, coupled with the general residuary power under Articles 73 and 162 of the Constitution, empowers the executive to take action in an extremely wide area—in a nearly unlimited and unfettered fashion given the weakness of the legislative and judicial systems in supervising executive action.

The executive issues a large number of regulations, rules, orders, circulars, directions, and guidelines on an almost daily basis. It is impossible for any citizen to keep a track of all executive action. The government itself is not fully aware of all the actions that it has taken. The P.C. Jain Committee noted, and tellingly so, in its report,

> The commission was seriously constrained by the fact that it did not have access to a complete set of subordinate legislation in the form of rules, regulations and administrative instructions, issued under different central Acts, by individual ministries and departments. It appears that the legislative department itself did not have such a complete compilation of rules, regulations and procedures issued by the ministries. The problem is compounded by the fact that in terms of certain laws like the Essential Commodities Act, as many as 13 ministries have issued over 150 orders.... Another handicap was that the central ministries did not have full information about the rules and regulations issued by state governments.[63]

Imagine the plight of the ordinary citizen if a government-appointed commission is lamenting the unavailability of access to laws! The problem of accessibility is only one of the challenges to the rule of law. Most executive orders are made in a tearing hurry—they are poorly drafted, suffer from vagueness and uncertainty, exceed their powers and more often than not are a reaction to one or two specific fact circumstances. And of course, there are too many of them. The executive uses various terms to describe the many pieces of law that it generates from time to time—circulars, notifications, rules, regulations, directions, etc. However, apart from the rules and/or regulations expressly contemplated under statutes, there is no clarity on the hierarchy among these various categories. Further, there are internal administrative guidelines

---

[63] *Report of the Commission on Review of Administrative Laws, 1998*, p. 4.

that are the basis of many a government action, which are not available to the public.

A few examples will illustrate this problem clearly. The Reserve Bank of India (RBI) is one of the more efficient regulatory organisations in India. One of the statutes it administers is the Foreign Exchange Management Act, 1999, (FEMA) that regulates the flow of foreign exchange into and out of the country. The RBI has wide-ranging discretionary powers to make rules and regulations under FEMA. From January 2000 to January 2015, the RBI has issued 26 different types of regulations under FEMA. These 26 types of regulations have been issued or amended 290 times, an average of 20 per year (see Table 4.4). In one year, there were close to 40 notifications. Certain regulations have been amended twice in the same month! The frequency of the notifications is so high that it became impossible to keep track of the regulations, forcing the RBI to publish a master circular for each type of regulation every year for the last few years. Unfortunately, the master circulars do not clearly identify when every amendment was made to the regulation, making the task of tracking amendments even more difficult.

The RBI's regulations are certainly better drafted than those issued by most other government bodies. However, that does not mean they are clear. It can be safely said that there is no single RBI notification on FEMA which is without confusion. As the RBI has no particular period during which it amends these regulations, one has to constantly keep watch for activity by the RBI. While one cannot oppose the need for emergency regulation, given the volatility of the foreign exchange market, there is no logic or reason for the RBI's frequent changes in regulations. In any event, the RBI does not publicly disclose the reasons for all the changes it makes. The RBI also issues circulars to the authorised banks, who then implement additional conditions, on the basis of those circulars, on the citizens transacting with them from time to time. Table 4.4 below contains the details of the frequency of notifications issued by the RBI. In addition to the RBI regulations, the Ministry of Finance and the Ministry of Commerce also issue circulars from time to time.

Another example is the law for regulating taxi services. Under the Motor Vehicles Act, 1988, which is a central statute, each state government has the power to make rules to give effect to the statute. The Motor Vehicles Act creates only one broad category of permits in connection

Table 4.4 FEMA Notification Frequency

	Jan.	Feb.	Mar.	Apr.	May	June	July	Aug.	Sep.	Oct.	Nov.	Dec.	Total
2000	0	0	0	0	25	0	0	2	2	0	2	1	32
2001	1	5	2	0	0	0	0	0	1	0	1	1	11
2002	2	2	5	4	2	3	1	3	1	0	5	0	28
2003	5	0	2	2	1	4	3	2	0	8	0	0	27
2004	2	1	6	0	1	2	2	1	1	1	1	1	19
2005	3	0	3	1	2	0	3	1	0	1	0	2	16
2006	0	1	2	0	0	1	0	1	0	0	0	0	5
2007	1	0	0	0	1	3	0	1	5	5	1	2	19
2008	1	1	0	0	0	0	1	2	1	1	0	0	7
2009	3	4	0	0	1	2	2	0	3	1	2	0	18
2010	0	0	0	2	0	1	1	0	0	0	0	0	4
2011	2	0	0	0	0	1	0	0	0	0	0	0	3
2012	0	0	6	2	3	0	0	0	7	3	3	2	26
2013	3	6	8	2	3	1	3	4	3	4	2	0	39
2014	0	1	5	1	6	3	3	0	5	3	3	4	34
2015	1	1	0	0	0	0	0	0	0	0	0	0	2
													290

with the provision of taxi services, which is the contract carriage permit. Because taxi services may be required across states, to ensure ease of travel for the passenger, the permits within each state may be extended to other regions by the transport authorities of each state. The central government has made rules to enable these interstate services to operate as tourist taxi vehicles.

Under Section 74, the regional transport authority in any state may impose certain conditions while granting a contract carriage permit. Pursuant to Section 75, the central government may frame a scheme for renting of motor cabs, which it has done in 1989.[64] Under Sections 95 and 96, the state governments have the power to make additional rules to regulate contract carriages in certain aspects and to give effect to the provisions of the act. Various states have formulated a scheme called the 'city taxi scheme' to regulate the plying of taxis and fares charged, within a city. The state of Maharashtra introduced this scheme by way of an amendment to the Maharashtra State Motor Vehicles Rules. The scheme permits any taxi with a contract carriage permit to be part of the city taxi scheme as long as the additional conditions are met. Other states, such as Karnataka and Delhi, have also introduced city taxi schemes, but they have done so without amending their respective state Motor Vehicles Rules. Further, their schemes apparently create a new kind of permit, called the 'city taxi permit', although no transport authority in the country actually issues anything called a city taxi permit.

Following the rape of a passenger by a taxi driver in Delhi in December 2014, the transport authorities in cities with the city taxi schemes began to stop taxis without these so-called 'city taxi permits' and impounded them. When an application was made under the RTI, seeking details of the 'city taxi scheme', the Secretary, Department of Transport, Government of Karnataka responded saying that his office neither had a copy of the scheme nor the details of when and how it was brought into force and the application was forwarded to the office of the Transport Commissioner, a subordinate officer. Interestingly, the city taxi scheme was notified by the office of the Secretary, Department of Transport, Government of Karnataka. The Transport Commissioner claimed that the 'city taxi scheme' was formulated pursuant to the

---

[64] The scheme is the Rent-a-Cab Scheme of 1989 which was published in the official gazette on 12 June 1989.

powers in Sections 74 and 93 of the Motor Vehicles Act, although the scheme does not mention it. The Transport Commissioner could not provide us with a gazetted copy of the scheme.

Appendix 4A contains the list of cities in which the city taxi scheme has been formulated, whether the scheme has been made pursuant to an amendment to the relevant state rules and whether the scheme creates an additional kind of permit. The table evidences the divergent approaches and the apparent uncertainty and confusion in the minds of various state governments about the correct process to follow in framing a city taxi scheme. In 2016, Karnataka has framed new rules under the heading of Taxi Aggregators Scheme, again mandating a new license adding to the confusion. A few other states have draft rules, on similar lines, ready for promulgation. The fundamental issue is of course one of arbitrary and improper exercise of power. The executive has to specify the authority under which it is taking certain actions, those actions must be through a legally permissible method and within the powers granted by the enabling statute. Creating a new permit altogether is not within the executive's powers.

Another example that needs to be mentioned is the daily rule-making that the Government of India and the RBI resorted to in the context of demonetization of the 1000 and 500 denomination notes in November and December 2016. The rules were made on the fly with little or no reasoning, lacked clarity and caused enormous amount of confusion. In a period of 50 days between 8 November and 30 December 2016 there were 75 notifications issued.[65]

---

[65] See, H. Narasappa, 'Demonetisation and the Rule of Law', IndiaTogether, 27 November 2016 available at http://indiatogether.org/demonetisation-and-the-rule-of-law-economy (accessed 22 February 2017). See also, N. Wahi, 'Why Demonetisation Notification is Illegal and Violates the Constitution?', *Economic Times*, 11 December 2016, available at http://economictimes.indiatimes.com/news/economy/policy/why-demonetisation-notification-is-illegal-and-violates-the-constitution/articleshow/55916594.cms (accessed 22 February 2017). See also 'Demonetisation: 50 days, 74 notifications', *The Indian Express*, available at http://indianexpress.com/article/business/economy/demonetisation-50-days-74-notifications-central-government-narendra-modi-reserve-bank-of-india-rbi-rules-cash-crunch-ban-4452455/ (accessed 22 February 2017).

The illustrations above are not an exception but reflect the day-to-day functioning of the executive. Rules, schemes, circulars, and other directions are framed without reference to existing law or compliance with proper procedure. Reasons are hardly ever given for making or changing the rules. It is not beyond one's imagination to conceive that a thorough and detailed study of 'laws' made by the executive would render many of them illegal because of improper exercise of power. A proper exercise of power may not lead to substantively and qualitatively different laws, but it would certainly bring order, clarity, and certainty into the executive lawmaking process and help the citizens in better compliance.

LAWMAKING—PROBLEMS FOR THE RULE OF LAW

The discussion so far clearly shows that the making of law, both in terms of process and substantive content, suffers from serious lacunae that undermine the rule of law. Even the basic parameters of the rule of law such as availability of laws, clarity and certainty are lacking most of the time. However, there are more serious conceptual challenges to the rule of law as well. First, the lack of democratic and reasoned deliberation in Parliament and legislatures threatens to undermine all that is good about a democratic society governed by the rule of law. The ideal notion of the legislature as a deliberative body, where all the considerations relevant to legislation are aired and discussed, with outcomes reflecting the weight of stronger arguments, is a far cry from reality in any country. However, in India, the problem is more acute and has worsened in recent years. In the public mind, Parliament and the legislatures are essentially sites for adversarial combat rather than deliberative clarity. Given the record of Parliament and the legislatures, one is left to wonder if they are capable of reasoned choice or if they will continue to function merely as aggregators of majoritarian preferences.

Richard Ekins argues that legislatures cannot be aggregators of preferences, like a voting machine.[66] Such aggregators would fail to exercise legislative authority and would be unlikely to enact reasonable legislation. The legislature is a space for reasoning about what should be done

---

[66] R. Ekins, *The Nature of Legislative Intent* (Oxford: Oxford University Press, 2012), pp. 77–98.

and making decisions. Mere aggregation can be done even by a dictator. The characteristic of a democracy is openness and participation in lawmaking that can only be met through deliberation and reasoning. Even to perform the role of an aggregator of preferences, individual legislators need to be responsive to the preferences and demands coming from their respective constituents.

However, it is unlikely that people have preferences on every issue in respect of which the legislature makes policy. Hence, the legislator also has to perform a role that conceptualises the policy in a manner that safeguards the interests of his constituents. The object of legislative action is not aggregation of individual preferences, but common good in its full scope and complexity. The central purpose of legislative action is to identify one amongst many opportunities to introduce a valuable state of affairs and adopting a plan to that end.[67] Our Parliament and legislatures are failing to do so and are abandoning their power and responsibility. This has enabled an oligarchy of senior political leaders and bureaucracy to take over, almost unassailably, the role of lawmaking and reducing the Parliament to a secondary role.

Second, while our elected bodies show an increased diversity of representation, diversity of opinion is seriously lacking, leading to majoritarian assertion in the house. The legislature is the epitome of institutional reasonableness and deliberation, unlike the other two branches of government. The legislature speaks as one and there is no appeal on legislative action, except on grounds of the action breaching certain rights in the Constitution. It is therefore imperative that the diversity of representation translates into diversity of opinion and expression on the floor of the house. Without this, it is impossible to seek legitimacy and acceptance for the policies and laws being made by the legislature. Modern democratic states require such legitimacy for the rule of law to be effective.

Julius Stone argues that in a democracy it is important to build consent around socio-ethical convictions in society to ensure that law is accepted by everyone.[68] This can only be done by ensuring that diverse opinions are heard and deliberated upon, compromises arrived at in

---

[67] Ekins, *The Nature of Legislative Intent*, p. 98.

[68] J. Stone, *Social Dimensions of Law & Justice* (New Delhi: Universal Law Publishing, 2009), pp. 616–21.

legislatures, and that these compromises are conveyed to the people transparently. The failure of elected representatives to interact with their constituents on matters of policy, lack of diversity of opinions in the legislatures and increasing majoritarian impunity means that it is difficult to claim consent of the vast majority of the people for the laws being made in their name.

Third, our elected representatives not only make laws and policies but also have an important role in interpreting them for the people by action, moral and thought leadership, given the central role of the state and the numerous demands for welfare measures arising from universal adult suffrage. Rajani Kothari observes,

> The political elite constitutes the new priesthood of modern India, partly because of its revolutionary role in bringing about mammoth changes, partly because of the exemplary and saintly or the grand and heroic styles of men like Gandhi and Nehru, and partly because of the overriding importance of the politician in social life and his growing intimacy with society's life processes. One result of this convergence is the expectation of the politician as a moral man, the frequent resort to exhortation and sermonizing, and the pressure to make promises and assurances that almost everyone knows cannot be fulfilled. Indians value the leader's combining the qualities of a man of thought and a man of action: hence the great fascination for men like Nehru.[69]

The failure by political parties and elected leadership to meet even the basic requirements of democratic discourse has a cascading impact on the rule of law as their actions set a benchmark for others to follow. If the political leadership does not meet certain essential requirements and violate the law regularly, the rule of law does not stand a chance. Unfortunately, the political leadership in India has not only failed to properly conduct itself but is also seeking to place itself above the law by resisting regulation of electoral funding, constantly flouting the taxation laws with impunity and violating orders under the RTI. By continuing to regularly field people with a criminal background, the parties are consistently and repeatedly challenging political, societal, and legal morality. The rule of law has very little chance of survival when the people empowered to make laws are seeking to place themselves above the very laws they make.

[69] R. Kothari, *Politics in India* (Hyderabad: Orient Blackswan, 2nd edn, 2012), p. 268.

Fourth, and more as an outcome of all the other aspects discussed above, the Parliament and legislatures are failing to regularly renew the political ideals incorporated in the Constitution. Increasingly, our elected representatives are resorting to token compliance with the ideals in the Constitution—they have shown extreme willingness to compromise on, and abandon in many instances, the fundamental features of liberty, equality, and justice promised by the Constitution.

The people on the other hand have not done too badly when compared to the elected representatives. They have kept their faith in democracy and over the last three decades have been voting out anybody who has not performed, even within the limited options that they have been presented with. They have taken to the streets repeatedly, seeking better performance by the government and delivery on the rights promised by the Constitution. In addition, people's movements and civil society groups have been approaching the courts regularly by way of public interest litigation to reinforce the fundamental rights in the Constitution and human rights, including seeking orders that are in the nature of lawmaking on occasions. Justice Leila Seth terms this 'initiatory democracy'.[70] Even with such active initiatory democracy, the elected representatives have not stepped up in times of necessity.

---

[70] L. Seth, *Talking of Justice: People's Rights in Modern India* (New Delhi: Aleph Book Company, 2014), p. 57.

APPENDIX 4A   TAXI SCHEMES BY STATE/UNION TERRITORY (AS OF FEBRUARY 2016)

State/ Union Territory	Whether City/Radio Taxi Regulations in Place If Yes, (i) Whether Made Part of the State/Union Territory Rules, or (ii) Provision of Law under which such Regulations are Purported to be Made	Whether a City/ Radio Taxi Operator Licence is Mandated	Whether a New Vehicle Permit is Created
Andhra Pradesh and Telangana	'Radio Cab' regulations in place *vide* Rule 176-B of the Andhra Pradesh and Telangana Motor Vehicles Rules (*Grant of permits for motor cabs fitted with tracking devices*). Rule 176-B notified under the powers of Section 96, Motor Vehicles Act.	Yes	No; however, vehicle-level conditions applicable
Chandigarh	Radio Taxi Scheme, 2006. Not part of Union Territory Rules. Provision of law conferring power not mentioned.	Yes	Yes
Gujarat	Circular by the Transport Commissioner makes regulations for 'on-call'/radio taxis, which are made as additional permit conditions under Section 74, Motor Vehicles Act. Not a part of State Rules. Purported to be made under Section 74, Motor Vehicles Act.	Yes	No; however, vehicle-level conditions applicable
Karnataka	Regulations for 'city taxis' are made under the City Taxi Service Scheme, 1998. Not part of the State Rules and not notified in the Official Gazette. The Scheme is purported to be made under Sections 96 and 74 of the Motor Vehicles Act (stated in response to an RTI application).	Yes	Yes

(Cont'd)

Appendix 4A   (*Cont'd*)

	In 2016, the Karnataka On-Demand Transportation Aggregator Rules were notified.		
Kerala	None other than the State Rules, which fix certain conditions for taxis relating to fares and metering.	No	No
Maharashtra	Fleet Taxi Service Scheme, 2006, and Call Taxi Scheme, 2010. Certain provisions for 'fleet taxis' incorporated as Rule 66-A of the State Rules. Provision of law conferring power not mentioned.	Yes	Yes
Delhi, National Capital Region	Radio Taxi Scheme, 2006 (as amended in 2014), and Economy Radio Taxi Scheme, 2010. Not a part of State Rules. Provision of law conferring power not mentioned.	Yes	No; however, vehicle-level conditions applicable
Rajasthan	None other than the State Rules, which fix certain conditions for taxis relating to fares and metering.	No	No
Tamil Nadu	None other than the State Rules, which fix certain conditions for taxis relating to fares and metering.	No	No
Uttar Pradesh	'Radio Cab' regulations in place *vide* Uttar Pradesh Motor Vehicles (Fourteenth Amendment) Rules, 2013. Such amendment notified under the powers of Section 96, clauses (1) and (2)(xxiii) of the Motor Vehicles Act, and Section 21 of the General Clauses Act.	Yes	Yes

5

ENFORCEMENT OF RIGHTS
AND LAWS

There is universal agreement that India has not been able to achieve its constitutional goals. The Constitution Review Commission characterizes India's story since Independence as one of 'lost opportunities'.[1] While India is not exactly a failed state and there has been significant progress in certain areas since 1950, primarily in the establishment of democracy, everyone accepts that more needs to be done particularly in terms of social and economic development.[2] Statistics and debates about poverty and all the problems associated with poverty dominate the social, political, and economic discourse. The failure of the state to eradicate poverty, discriminations of all kind, the crippling

---

[1] Paragraph 2.3.7 of the *Report of the National Commission to Review the Working of the Constitution*. The full report is available in S. Kashyap, *Constitution Making since 1950: An Overview* (New Delhi: Universal Law Publishing, 2004), pp. 243–520.

[2] The historian Ramachandra Guha has surveyed and examined India's progress in all its facets since independence and very often uses the phrase 'fifty-fifty' to describe India's democratic progress. See R. Guha, *India after Gandhi: The History of the World's Largest Democracy* (London: Picador, 2007) and R. Guha, 'A Fifty-Fifty Democracy: Seven Threats to Freedom of Expression', *The Telegraph*, 24 January 2015, available at http://www.telegraphindia.com/1150124/jsp/opinion/story_9857.jsp#.VSoYbvmUdOE (accessed 10 April 2015).

corruption, slow pace of development, lack of accountability of public institutions, and regular violation of fundamental rights by the state are the subject matter of serious works by academics and intellectuals,[3] and daily reporting in the news media.

Devesh Kapur and Pratap Bhanu Mehta point out that there are three dominant explanations for the Indian state's poor development record. One view suggests that the reason is an ideologically driven policy choice, another suggests that the reason for failure is the capture of state institutions by social forces, bringing with them all the divisions and attitudes prevalent in society, crippling the institutions. The third argues that the reason is the rapid rate of social mobilization, which has outpaced the capacities of institutions to manage the mobilization. Kapur and Mehta argue that a critical factor in India's limited record in governance and development is the limited effectiveness of its public institutions.[4]

While academic works focus on the institutional design and rights framework, the day-to-day debate on these issues reveals a mystifying blame game. The ordinary citizens always complain that the 'system' is immune to their rights, needs, and aspirations; it does not respond, correctly and in a timely fashion, to their problems and demands. The language of the people in power indicates that although they are relentlessly striving to achieve the constitutional goals of equality, justice, liberty, and fraternity, they are almost always thwarted by the 'system'. The political parties and elected representatives also blame the 'system'—the bureaucracy, mainly, and the judiciary occasionally— for erecting unnecessary barriers in the path of achieving the promised goals. The bureaucracy blames political parties for not allowing it to

[3] There are many scholarly works in this area. A few of them are J. Drèze and A. Sen, *An Uncertain Glory: India and Its Contradictions* (London: Allen Lane, 2015); N.G. Jayal (ed.), *Democracy in India* (New Delhi: Oxford University Press, 2007); N.G. Jayal and P.B. Mehta (eds), *The Oxford Companion to Politics in India* (New Delhi: Oxford University Press, 2010); G. Austin, *Working a Democratic Constitution: The Indian Experience* (New Delhi: Oxford University Press, 1999); and A. Panagariya, *India: The Emerging Giant* (New Delhi: Oxford University Press, 2008).

[4] D. Kapur and P.B. Mehta (eds), *Public Institutions in India* (New Delhi: Oxford University Press, 4th Impression, 2011). The comments made by Kapur and Mehta are in the Introduction to this volume.

work the 'system', which is preventing its proper functioning. The judiciary also blames the 'system', everyone except itself, as the reason for constant deviation from the constitutional mandates.

It is of course, never clear as to who or what comprises this all-pervasive obstructionist 'system' that is preventing everyone from achieving the constitutional goals, if the judiciary, legislature, and the bureaucracy consider themselves to be outside the troublesome system! The answer, of course, is that each of the legislature, including political parties and elected representatives, the bureaucracy and the judiciary are part of the system. The fact that each one of them claims that every-body else is obstructionist is revealing in itself, as it indicates that each believes it is doing its job properly but nobody else is doing theirs.

The achievement of constitutional goals is dependent on the enforce-ment of the rights guaranteed by the Constitution, and the laws that have been made to facilitate the implementation of those rights. The enforcement of rights and laws requires the proper functioning of all the three branches of government, the legislature, executive, and the judi-ciary. Chapter 4 focused on performance of the legislature. This chapter evaluates how the executive and the judiciary have performed in enforc-ing the rights of the people and the laws that guarantee those rights.

THE INDIAN EXECUTIVE—A SOVEREIGN IN ITSELF?

The citizen mainly deals with the executive branch of government in the conduct of his daily affairs. It is the executive's functioning that has the maximum impact on the rights of citizens. By executive, we mean the political executive consisting of the prime minister (or the chief minister in the states), the council of ministers and the permanent executive consisting of the bureaucracy including the civil administra-tion, the police and any other functionary of the state, excluding the judiciary and legislature, at all levels. The executive has wide-ranging powers, as discussed in Chapter 4, and its actions affect every minute aspect of life in India. The executive and its functioning has been studied in detail by various government committees and commissions,[5]

---

[5] The government of India appointed two administrative reform commis-sions, the first in 1966 and the second in 2005 to study public administration and suggest recommendations. The P.C. Jain Commission was established in

academics,[6] civil society groups,[7] and scholars.[8] Many retired bureaucrats[9] and politicians[10] have also opined on the positives and negatives of the manner in which the executive functions. T.S.R. Subramanian, the former cabinet secretary, distils the following four laws that the executive almost always follows:

1. Administration is conducted for the benefit of administrators.
2. In a conflict between private interests and public interest, the former shall prevail.
3. The country belongs to the haves, and the have-nots do not exist.
4. A public servant's work output and rewards, are inversely related.[11]

1998 to study administrative laws. Apart from these, the Constitution Review Commission and the Law Commission have also studied the functioning of the executive in some detail.

[6] One of the more interesting academic studies is by Subrata K. Mitra. See S.K. Mitra, *The Puzzle of India's Governance: Culture, Context and Comparative Theory* (Oxford: Routledge, 2006).

[7] The National Social Watch publishes with regular reports on governance. Their reports are available at http://socialwatchindia.net/ (accessed 10 April 2015). Various other NGO's publish annual sector-specific reports.

[8] Some examples are Kapur and Mehta, *Public Institutions in India*; Austin, *Working a Democratic Constitution*; and B. Jalan, *The Future of India: Politics, Economics & Governance* (New Delhi: Penguin, 2006).

[9] There are many books published by retired bureaucrats mainly in the form of memoirs. Some of them are T.S. Krishnamurthy, *The Miracle of Democracy* (Noida: HarperCollins, 2008); A. Sinha, *India: Democracy & Well-being* (New Delhi: Rupa, 2005), V. Rai, *Not Just an Accountant: The Diary of the Nation's Conscience Keeper* (New Delhi: Rupa, 2014); and T.S.R. Subramanian, *Journeys through Babudom and Netaland: Governance in India* (New Delhi: Rupa, 2004).

[10] Many politicians have written about the functioning of the executive. One of the best descriptive analysis is by Arun Shourie. See, A. Shourie, *Governance and the Sclerosis That Has Set In* (New Delhi: Rupa, 2004).

[11] Subramanian, *Journeys through Babudom and Netaland*. An extract of the book containing the quote is available at http://atiwb.gov.in/index_htm_files/Readings%20in%20Public%20Administration%20Part-2.pdf, pp. 84–5 (accessed 10 April 2015).

These four laws are clearly in violation of all principles known to the Constitution and the rule of law, but unfortunately reflect the reality that people face while dealing with the executive.

This chapter does not discuss the various problems with the executive's functioning which scholars have already identified, but instead reviews some major reasons for its malfunctioning to analyse the impact of the executive's functioning on the enforcement of rights and laws.

CORRUPTION

Corruption is all-pervasive and affects all levels of the executive.[12] From obtaining birth certificates to death certificates, filing a complaint with the police, registering oneself for welfare benefits, changing revenue records following the death of a parent, claiming refund of tax paid to obtaining a driving license or a voters' photo identity card, there is no interaction with a government official that does not involve an illicit exchange of money. Every act of corruption, however minor, is an assault on the rule of law, and is not just a poorly paid official making some quick money. The official is acting in violation of the law that prohibits him from seeking any favour for doing his job. Each such action tramples upon citizens' rights with impunity.

Corruption is not limited to simple administrative actions, but also extends to decisions where an officer is exercising discretion in choosing the beneficiaries of government welfare measures, making policies that could decide the future of millions of people, awarding government contracts, granting approvals for large projects, utilization of natural resources, using the power of eminent domain to acquire land, changing planning regulations, etc. Corruption in these circumstances essentially convert rights and laws into tradable commodities sold to the highest bidder, or to multiple bidders.[13] The rationale for the exercise of power

[12] N. Vittal, 'Corruption and the Rule of Law', in N.R.M. Menon (ed.), *Rule of Law in a Free Society* (New Delhi: Oxford University Press, 2008), pp. 131–46.

[13] This argument has been advanced by this author in an unpublished paper, 'India's Governance: The Challenge of Commodification', presented at the Fourth Annual Conference on Public Policy and Management in August 2009 at the Indian Institute of Management, Bangalore.

as mandated by the Constitution and the laws empowering the executive to make those decisions are completely ignored. Transparency in decision-making, which is one of the basic tenets of the rule of law, is the direct victim of corruption of this type.

Corruption does not only indicate monetary benefits. It also evidences abuse of power and the establishment of a social relationship based on patronization and quid pro quo between the governance machinery and the governed. This is qualitatively different from the relationship that ought to exist between the administrative machinery and citizens in a democratic society—a relationship based on the primacy of people with the administrative machinery only being a mechanism established for achieving the recognized goals of society.

Granville Austin claims that two important concepts add to corruption in India: (i) survival society syndrome, and (ii) personalization of governance. Austin believes that India is a survival society from those at its top to those at the bottom of its vast disparity. This leads to each man being directly responsible for his own family and its security. Every man has been taught this so firmly that he disregards the state of those outside his immediate family; he is not disturbed if they go hungry while he has plenty. This orientation produces an indifference to the well-being of others and to the condition of society as a whole. Austin quotes P.N. Haksar, one of India's respected civil servants who says, 'our civil services are first of all committed to themselves and their nuclear family ... making secure the future of our sons and daughters and, if possible ... the members of our sub-caste, caste, community and region'.[14]

For most above the poorest, nearly every aspect of life outside the home is 'politicized', sought to be based on kinship and 'connections'. Personalization is the attitude of 'me-first-and-not-the-country'. The rampant corruption in India can also be understood in terms of the personalization of governance—of the scriptural injunction to help one's own even when it is a clear threat to the credibility of governance. Our bureaucrats work the system for their own sake. Indeed, there is a degree of approval—or at least of understanding—granted to minor corruption, because of one's responsibility for helping relations.

However, Austin and others that he relies upon ignore the fact that, every act of corruption is also an act of violence by the state and its

---

[14] Austin, *Working a Democratic Constitution*, pp. 637–45.

officials against the citizens. It may not be physical violence, but it has all the other characteristics of violence. The victim of corruption feels a sense of humiliation, helplessness, and disempowerment, similar to an instance of physical violence. Her rights are violated and the people tasked to protect her are the ones perpetrating the violation. Such abuse of power is synonymous with violence.[15] Victims of corruption are also very often pushed into the vicious circle of illegality in routine matters, as the cost of legality becomes expensive due to corruption. Most acts of corruption go unpunished. With every act of corruption that goes unpunished, there is further erosion of the rule of law. Complaining against corruption can be a traumatic experience for the complainant. In an extreme case, a man who went to the police station was himself arrested and subjected to violence, resulting in death.[16] The act of corruption and the failure to punish the act reinforces the superiority of the state and its officials in comparison to ordinary citizens. It also creates an atmosphere of lawlessness, impunity, and arbitrariness, all of which are the antithesis of the rule of law.

LACK OF INTERNALIZATION OF THE RULE OF LAW

The judiciary has passed, and continues to pass regularly, a number of orders that mandate the executive to act with reasonableness and not arbitrarily, that it should follow the principles of natural justice, record reasons for decisions and make decisions within the four corners of the law as laid down by the legislature. Apart from these general principles, the judiciary has laid down specific principles in nearly all areas in which the executive exercises its powers, ranging from regulation of education institutions to award of tenders. Nevertheless, nearly each government action of significance is challenged in a court on the grounds of violation of well-established principles. Yes, some of the challenges in court do fail, but the depth, width, and breadth of lack of compliance with law during the exercise of executive power is astonishing.[17]

[15] K.G. Kannabiran, *The Wages of Impunity* (Hyderabad: Orient Longman, 2004), p. 1.

[16] *State of Uttar Pradesh* v *Ram Sagar Yadav* AIR 1985 SC 416.

[17] See M.P. Jain, *Indian Constitutional Law*, edited by S. Pal and R. Pal (Gurgaon: Lexis Nexis, 2014), pp. 441–59 for a discussion on the nature of mandamus and certiorari writs that come up before various high courts.

Transparency is replaced by opaqueness, reasonableness with arbitrariness, and principles of natural justice with personal prejudices or directions of political masters. One only has to attend the proceedings before a judge hearing writ petitions in any high court in the country on any day to get an understanding of the scale of executive non-compliance. The only conclusion that one can draw is that the executive has failed to understand and internalize the concept of compliance with law. It has also failed to internalize the goals of the Constitution and the rule of law. Many trace this failure to the colonial administration, particularly so in the case of the police, as it was established to rule the people and not serve the people. As independent India retained the bureaucratic framework of colonial India, many believe that the post-Independence bureaucracy is also of the firm opinion that it is entitled to rule the country rather than serve the country. While it may be true that this was the case in the first few decades after Independence, it is extremely unlikely that such a genealogy is correct today as we have had more than 60 years of our own bureaucracy which has to a large extent shed its elitist character and is representative of the various classes of people. We are giving too much credit to the colonial administration's 'spirit' and failing to recognize the sheer impunity and lawlessness of the post-Independence bureaucracy.

We should not understand lack of internalization of the rule of law as a failure to internalize the procedure that comes with legalism. If anything, there is too much emphasis on formalistic legal procedure and many complain that the state is very procedure oriented with no emphasis on outcomes,[18] that the procedures are too cumbersome and archaic and need revision. We should instead refer to the goals of the Constitution and the spirit of the Constitution. There is no internalization of the fundamental rights that citizens have and the manner in which they should be treated. However, the bureaucracy is fully aware of its own rights under the Constitution. We only need to look at the numerous cases regarding promotions and other service conditions that are filed regularly by individual members of the bureaucracy against the state. This dichotomy is ironical, but is lost on the bureaucracy. There is a possible explanation for this in Upendra Baxi's observation—the rich

---

[18]   A. Shourie, *Courts and Their Judgments* (New Delhi: Rupa, 2001), p. 9.

and powerful in India do not follow the law because they feel they are above the law and that it does not apply to them.[19]

The bureaucracy is very powerful in India and ordinary citizens treat any government official with deference and respect even when they know that the person is corrupt or unreasonable. Even the person occupying the lowest level of the bureaucracy believes that he is powerful and it is his right to exercise that power against people who are not part of government, even at the cost of trampling upon the rights of the people. It is this attitude that is at the heart of the failure to internalize the spirit of the Constitution. Education is clearly the way forward to correct this fundamental error,[20] but suitable and effective punishment of erring officials is also necessary. In that, the bureaucracy has failed miserably.

RHETORIC VERSUS ACTION

Austin highlights the rhetoric or the empty promise syndrome as one of the reasons affecting India's governance system.[21] This syndrome, Austin claims, cannot be equated to mere hypocrisy or cynicism, but has deep cultural sources. Austin cites examples of promises made and not kept, but more importantly are repeatedly renewed. This rhetoric from the housetops and its non-implementation seem to come from a disjunction between word and deed, or from treating them as synonymous. The word is treated as equivalent to action and repetition of the promise is treated as fulfilment. Closely related to the word-equals-deed phenomenon is that of initiation-equals-completion: a programme is started, an institution established, but follow-up and functioning are ignored. A building is constructed, but not maintained. Whatever the reasons, equating the word and deed gives a make-believe air to public policy and adversely affects governance. Arun Shourie observes that the bureaucratic structure is best described as 'kargozari, the show of work, not work. There is at all times much activity, but at most little movement'.[22]

A flagrant contradiction between what we say and what we do has become our way of life. This also reflects the lack of accountability in

---

[19] U. Baxi, *The Crisis of the Indian Legal System* (New Delhi: Vikas Publishing, 1982), pp. 4–6.

[20] Kannabiran, *The Wages of Impunity*, pp. 23–4.

[21] Austin, *Working a Democratic Constitution*, pp. 643–7.

[22] Shourie, *Courts and Their Judgments*.

governance, and more critically, that the people responsible for governance do not believe that accountability is an issue. When there is no accountability in reality or in perception, the commodification of governance becomes easy. In fact, the lack of accountability and the rhetoric syndrome, act as incentives for commodification, as the leaders need to be incentivized for converting statements into actions and initiation into completion. It also means that the executive—both the political leadership and the bureaucracy—can continue mouthing good governance while undermining such governance through corruption and commodification.

This equation of rhetoric with action is also the reason for the perception that India is a country that has a working system compliant with the rule of law. This is because, on paper, we have all the institutions that are necessary to make the rule of law work, but unfortunately, they do not work. For example, the state of Karnataka has constituted a human rights commission which has significant powers, but there has been no full-time chairperson for more than four years.[23] In Gujarat, the Lokayukta was not appointed for many years.[24] Similarly, in Karnataka, the state had not constituted the Police Complaints Authority for more than three years. When it was finally constituted, it was only given power to recommend punishments rather than the power to punish.[25] These are important institutions from a rule of law perspective as they perform functions that are vital for the accountability of government institutions and promote constitutional goals. Yet, they are deliberately ignored or disempowered in practice, even while they continue to exist on paper.

[23] On 2 January 2018, the Government of Karnataka has announced that it has recommended the appointment of Justice D.H. Waghela as the new chairperson, a post that had been lying vacant since the retirement of Justice S.R. Nayak in early 2012.

[24] No lokayukta had been appointed for seven years between 2004 and 2011. When the governor, in August 2011, appointed a lokayukta on the recommendation of the Chief Justice of the Gujarat High Court without consulting with the executive, the response of the then BJP government was to bring in a new law removing the powers of the governor to appoint the lokayukta.

[25] B. Khanna, 'Police Watchdog Authority Grows a Head, but No Teeth', Citizen Matters, 21 October 2013, available at http://bangalore.citizenmatters.in/articles/police-complaint-authority-no-staff-functional-pca (accessed 10 April 2015).

VIOLENCE

Kannabiran points out that the Indian state is extremely violent and has been so regularly since the late 1960s. Kannabiran argues that the state equates state perpetrated violence with exercise of legitimate power. There is an overwhelming play of violence as power and power as violence, sometimes in breach of the law and sometimes for the enforcement of law. This is because, in Kannabiran's view, maintenance of law and order has become the *raison d'être* of governance in India. This is not permissible in a constitutional democratic society governed by the rule of law. Kannabiran observes,

> Expressions like 'law and order', 'public order' and 'state scrutiny', enable the state to employ violence against the people without a corresponding obligation to exercise discretion. Any scrutiny of this exercise of power by the state is only possible after the damage has been done. An assembly of protestors, for instance, brings to life the exercise of free speech and the citizens' right to association and assembly. It also involves the freedom of movement of the citizens constituting the assembly. There are constitutional safeguards that protect these rights. Very briefly, in maintaining public tranquillity, the assembly of protesting persons may be declared unlawful; they may be dispersed and their leaders taken into custody. If the assembly does not disperse, force may be employed to disperse it, but orders to open fire must only be issued in the presence and with the authorisation of a magistrate. These safeguards, however, have never been complied with, from Jallianwala Bagh and the Hunter Committee report during colonial times to the present day... The constant promulgation of Section 144 of the Criminal Procedure Code, prohibiting assembly of more than five persons without police permission, points to the looming threat of violence legitimised by law. The promulgation itself is violence, because the rights to free speech, assembly and movement stand withdrawn. Ironically, the government brings this provision into operation around Parliament and the Legislative Assemblies when they are in session, thereby protecting elected representatives from the citizens who elected them. Violence under cover of law manages to remain unaccountable.[26]

Unfortunately, Kannabiran's examples in the above passage only reflect the mildest form of violence by the state. Almost all interaction between the police and the ordinary citizenry carries a threat of

[26] Kannabiran, *The Wages of Impunity*, pp. 2–4.

violence. Reports of illegal arrests, use of violence during interrogations and to disperse crowds do not shock people anymore as it has become a part of their daily life. Custodial torture, rape and deaths, and encounter deaths generate outrage, but are forgotten in a maze of departmental and judicial inquiries. The use of violence against ordinary citizens in the name of law and order is repeated too often by governments across the country. The identity of the ruling party has not mattered much when it comes to the holy grail of law and order. Shourie argues that often political parties sponsor violence while the state merely watches.[27]

While the government machinery appears eager to perpetrate violence at the cost of the citizens' liberties, it is not so effective in redressing victims of violence. Independent India's history is replete with examples of mass violence where the victims have silently suffered as the state has not been able to either identify the perpetrators or punish them effectively when they are actually identified. A group of researchers has published its study into four different incidents of mass violence— Nellie 1983, Delhi 1984, Bhagalpur 1989, and Gujarat 2002—in which they evaluate the response of the criminal justice system, accountability of officers of the state and the rehabilitation, resettlement and compensation measures for victims.[28] In their conclusion the authors' note:

1. Victims of mass violence have been severely let down by the criminal justice system. Flawed recording of first information reports led to poor investigation leading to high—eight to ten times higher than normal—summary closure rates. Gross negligence by the police was followed by poor prosecution. Rates of acquittal were so high as to suggest that the judiciary at the trial court level has been passive to the point of being complicit in subverting fair, credible trials.

2. People in senior government positions and high political offices have rarely faced trial. Rather than the courtroom, government functionaries are more likely to have faced commissions of inquiry. Very often such commissions of inquiry are appointed to provide muted findings.

[27] Shourie, *Courts and Their Judgments*, p. 6.

[28] S. Chopra and P. Jha (eds), *On Their Watch: Mass Violence and State Apathy in India: Examining the Record* (Gurgaon: Three Essays Collective, 2014).

3. Governments have been more willing to provide monetary compensation to victims. However, this compensation does not restore the victims to their original position. There are no binding norms on compensation and it is left to the discretion of the people in office to decide on the appropriate compensation.[29]

Equally worrying is the increasing instances of particular organized groups seeking to limit freedom of speech and expression of individuals on the ground that it offends them. Some of these organized groups resort to violence regularly in the name of culture and custom. Neither this violence nor private censorship has been addressed by the government with any seriousness. In fact, the civil administration or the police, and increasingly, the judiciary, take it upon themselves to make peace between the protagonists in the name of law and order, and more often than not, free speech and expression ends up on the losing side. The 'voluntary death' of the author Perumal Murugan; the censorship of the works of M.F. Hussain, A.K. Ramanujan, and Rohinton Mistry; the destruction of the Bhandarkar Institute in Pune; the assault on Prashant Bhushan following his views on the Armed Forces Special Provisions Act in Kashmir; the drama of forced marriages every year on 14 February; the enforced cuts in the movie Jolly LLB 2, at the suggestion of a court appointed lawyers' committee, after the censor board had cleared it; and the shocking attacks on young women in a pub in Mangalore in 2011–12, reveal the regular violence on freedom of speech and expression by private groups that have explicit or tacit support of political parties. The executive has done little or nothing to support freedom of speech in all these cases.

The state of course, is not far behind in its willingness to censor works that may not be convenient to the party in power or that affect 'law and order' or 'security of the state'. The regular use of filing criminal defamation cases against citizens is another illustration of a chilling effect on the freedom of speech and expression.[30] Guha notes that the

[29] Chopra and Jha, *On Their Watch*, pp. 334–6.

[30] C.R. Irani, member of the Constitution Review Commission in his note to the Commission's Report illustrates five examples of powerful politicians, state, and business houses filing criminal defamation action to prevent people from criticising them on flimsy grounds. Kashyap, *Constitution Making since 1950*, pp. 517–19.

police are always eager to supress freedom of expression, pusillanimous politicians never come out openly in support, and archaic colonial laws are pressed into action at momentary notice, adding to the constant threat to freedom of expression.[31]

The threat to the rule of law arises from such failure or refusal of the executive to recognize and protect these rights in the first instance. The executive in most cases appears to assume that rights do not inhere automatically in citizens. It appears that the executive feels most of the rights are only entitlements of citizens granted by the state, which is the subject matter of the executive's discretion and can be negotiated in each case. A right becomes available only when, through litigation, an order is obtained from the court allowing the citizens to speak, express, write, assemble, and move as an assembly, and stating that the objectionable activity is actually inherent in the citizen. Of course, in most cases it is too late by the time the court is able to decide on the matter given the enormous judicial delays in the country.

RIGHTS VERSUS ENTITLEMENTS

The failure of the executive to differentiate between rights and entitlements is part of the larger misunderstanding of the nature of rights by all organs of the state. The Constitution is a document that the people of India gave themselves, and it reflects their political aspirations, as discussed in Chapter 2 of this book. The Constitution is a document through which the people of India created the state and its machinery. The Constitution also contains limitations on the exercise of state power, most importantly in the form of the fundamental rights in Part III. Part III regulates state power when individual freedoms and state action intersect with each other and provides for certain state actions to be considered legitimate in such interactions. It is a fallacy to argue that the rights in Part III are bestowed by the Constitution on the citizens and can be extinguished or modified, at will, by any organ of the state. To accept such an argument would mean that citizens do not have any rights, but instead have only entitlements. The difference of course, is that rights inherently reside in people, irrespective of the Constitution or its provisions. Without these rights of equality, liberty, fraternity, and

---

[31] Guha, 'A Fifty-Fifty Democracy'.

justice, the people of India could not have created and given to themselves the Constitution. Entitlements on the other hand are created by the legal regime and does not inherently reside in people. Entitlements can be taken away by law, rights cannot be so taken away.

Kannabiran correctly opines that the fundamental reason for the state's inability to deal with rights is that even after the Constitution came into force, the emphasis did not shift from the exercise of power by the state to the inviolability, and entrenchment, of rights. The executive believes that it can exercise its powers to change illegality to legality and bestow or deprive rights at will. Kannabiran further points out that the failure to recognize the preamble and every expression used therein, the rights enumerated in Part III, and the fundamental governance obligations in Part IV as primarily political concepts has reduced the rights discourse to a debate on legalities, dwelling instead on the assumption that rights were granted by law, thereby becoming entitlements, and therefore could be withdrawn at will. This misconception has displaced 'we the people' or the grantors, to the status of 'we the other people' or subjects, rather than citizens in our own democracy. The misconception persists because of the continuation of the colonial structure in most of our penal laws, particularly the Indian Penal Code (IPC). Kannabiran notes the irony of independent India continuing to enforce the provisions of the IPC and other penal laws which were originally enacted to keep a subject population under control and to suppress any demands for independence.[32] Particularly offensive to the idea of rights are, inter alia, sections 124A (sedition), 377 (sodomy), 295A (deliberate and malicious acts intended to outrage religious feelings), 298 (uttering, words, etc., with deliberate intent to wound the religious feelings of any person), and sections 499 and 501 (criminal defamation) of the IPC.

The rights versus entitlements debate acquires even greater significance in the context of deprived sections of society and the exercise of their rights. Partha Chatterjee critically analyses the manner in which the state regulates population groups such as street vendors, illegal squatters, and others, whose habitation or livelihood verges on the margins of legality. They only have entitlements, and not rights, which are the subject matter of constant political negotiation. Consequently, government agencies always treat any benefits given to these groups as exceptions to

---

[32] Kannabiran, *The Wages of Impunity*, pp. 68–9.

the rule. Illegal squatters may be given water supply or electricity connections, but on exceptional grounds so as not to club them with regular
customers who secure legal titles to their property; street vendors may
be allowed to trade under specific conditions that distinguish them from
regular shops and businesses which comply with the laws and pay taxes.[33]
The fact that the Supreme Court has recognized a right to livelihood or
that every citizen has a right to drinking water is conveniently forgotten.

The rule of law is violated at every stage of this interaction between
the state and the people. The state takes either a passive attitude or
plays an abetting role when these groups entrench themselves 'illegally'
in violation of existing laws. However, the passive attitude is only on
paper, as rampant corruption is involved at this stage with local officials
and politicians being paid off, even for these illegal settlements. Once
the settlements are in place, the law is violated on an everyday basis,
as the settlers are provided basic services and facilities in breach of the
law, as Chatterjee points out. And finally, when the situation reaches
a tipping point, because they cannot be provided services as entitlements anymore and the 'illegality' needs to be removed or converted
into 'legality', the state ends up making regulations that violate all the
regular norms of lawmaking.

Of course, the rights of those people who have during all this time
complied with the law and are likely to be adversely affected by the
conversion of 'illegality' into 'legality' are also ignored as a result of
the uncertainty created by the actions of the executive.[34] Given the
identity of the people involved— generally those who are struggling
to make a decent life for themselves—hard questions about the state's
responsibility to improve their lot arise, particularly so because our
state is, theoretically, a welfare state.

[33] P. Chatterjee, 'The State', in N.G. Jayal and P.B. Mehta (eds), *The Oxford Companion to Politics in India* (New Delhi: Oxford University Press, 2010), pp. 3–14 at pp. 9–14. Chatterjee identifies such groups living on the verge of illegality as 'political society' as against 'civil society', that is groups which are generally compliant with the law, consisting largely of the urban middle classes.

[34] In his descriptive work on life in Mumbai, Suketu Mehta narrates many instances of this transformation from illegality to legality as well as the regular travails of people who live on the margins of society. S. Mehta, *Maximum City: Bombay Lost & Found* (New Delhi: Viking, 2004).

LEGALITY VERSUS ILLEGALITY

There is no such difficult choice to be made in the case of wilful defaulters of the law who do not face a livelihood issue. An example is the widespread non-compliance with planning, zoning, and building by-laws in urban areas. In a rapidly growing city such as Bengaluru, almost every other building being constructed is in breach of by-laws. The lack of coordination amongst various authorities responsible for granting permissions, the opaqueness in granting such permissions, the complicity of the officers in ignoring violations, the law that allows 'permissible deviations' and the lack of fear about strict enforcement of laws have contributed to this widespread illegality. At the time of construction, the authorities who grant permission are either actively complicit in this illegality or look the other way. However, when illegality becomes the norm leading to environmental and civic issues and when this illegality needs to be dealt with the state comes out with an ad hoc plan to regularize this illegality, with no idea whatsoever to deal with similar future illegalities.

The creation, and use, of the power to regularize illegalities[35] is an unreasonable and arbitrary exercise of power without understanding either the rights of citizens who have complied with the law or the irretrievable damage caused to the rule of law by such an action. It is nothing but an effort to give lawlessness a colour of legality and respectability. However, governments across the country have made regular efforts to this precise end and claim that it is 'considered necessary and expedient in the public interest'.[36] The only explanation is that massive corruption and vested interests drive the enactment of these laws and their implementation, both of which require the exercise of discretionary power. The example of Karnataka, which made an effort to push through an Akrama-Sakrama scheme[37] to regularize illegal buildings despite the

---

[35] Section 76FF of the Karnataka Town and Country Planning Act, 1961, introduced by way of an amendment in 2007, was notified in 2013 and again amended in 2014. It empowers the planning authority to regularize violations committed prior to 19 October 2013, subject to payment of a fee and if the violations are permitted to be regularised according to the rules notified in this regard.

[36] These words are used in the preamble of the Karnataka Act No. 1 of 2007 that introduces Section 76FF into the statute books.

[37] The Akrama-Sakrama scheme's details are available at http://bbmp.gov.in/akrama-sakrama (accessed 10 April 2015). For an analysis of the issues,

judiciary having expressed serious reservations, is illustrative of this vicious circle of legality and illegality. This easy interchange of legality and illegality contributes to the pervasive lawlessness, reduces the legitimacy of lawmaking and implementation, and deals a body blow to the rule of law.

EQUALITY—A RIGHT OR AN ENTITLEMENT—THE CASE OF SCHEDULED CASTES AND TRIBES

The rights and entitlements misconception is also evident in the debates around the equality right as applicable to the scheduled castes and tribes. There are two aspects to this equality right: (i) as enshrined in Articles 17 and 15(2), which not only recognize political and social equality of status for the scheduled castes and tribes, but also to promote the fraternity of all individuals and (ii) special provisions that the state can make pursuant to the prescriptions in Articles 15(4), 15(5), and 16(4A). Much of the debate has focused on the second aspect, due to the regular challenges to various reservations made in employment in the government and its affiliated organizations and admissions to educational institutions. Unfortunately, not much has been said about the continued violation of the rights in Articles 17 and 15(2). Even after six decades, reports of inhuman abuses of scheduled castes and tribes by other castes are common—feeding of human faeces and urine, rape, torture, public stripping, maiming, and beating have continued even in 2016.[38] This is a blot on our collective conscience, Constitution and the rule of law.

---

see M. Akshatha, 'Will Akrama-Sakrama Scheme Create Yet Another Mess?' Citizen Matters, 4 March 2015, available at http://bangalore.citizenmatters. in/articles/akrama-sakrama-implementation-problems-bangalore (accessed 10 April 2015). See also, 'All That You Need To Know About Akrama Sakrama', Bangalore Mirror, 4 March 2015, available at http://www.bangaloremirror. com/bangalore/civic/All-that-you-need-to-know-about-Akrama-Sakrama/ articleshow/46448039.cms (accessed 10 April 2015).

[38] See, for example, 'Dalit Man's Nose Chopped Off for Having Food with Upper Castes in UP', India Today, 19 February 2015, available at http:// indiatoday.intoday.in/story/dalit-lower-caste-up-violence-nose-chopped-off/1/419703.html (accessed 5 April 2015). Every year there are reports of many such incidents across India. See also, A. Namala, 'Violence against Dalits: There is a Discernible Pattern to this Madness', The Indian Express,

In 1989, after four decades of independence, the Parliament passed the Scheduled Castes and Scheduled Tribes (Prevention of Atrocities) Act. Section 3 of the Act enumerates 22 categories of atrocities which it then makes punishable. Among them are:

1. Forcing a member of a scheduled caste or a scheduled tribe to drink or eat any inedible or obnoxious substance.
2. Acts with intent to cause injury, insult or annoyance to any member of a scheduled caste or a scheduled tribe by dumping excreta, waste matter, carcasses or any other obnoxious substance in their premises or neighbourhood.
3. Forcibly removing clothes from the person of a member of a scheduled caste or a scheduled tribe or parading them naked or with painted face or body or committing any similar act which is derogatory to human dignity.
4. Wrongfully occupying or cultivating any land owned by, or allotted, to a member of a scheduled caste or a scheduled tribe.
5. Wrongfully dispossessing a member of a Scheduled Caste or Tribe from their land or premises or interfering with enjoyment of their rights over any land, premises, or water.
6. Intentionally insulting or intimidating with intent to humiliate a member of a scheduled caste or a scheduled tribe in any place within public view.
7. Corrupting or fouling the water of any spring, reservoir, or any other source ordinarily used by members of the scheduled caste or scheduled tribe so as to render it less fit for the purpose for which it is ordinarily used.
8. Denying a member of a scheduled caste or scheduled tribe any customary right to passage to a place of public resort or obstructing such member so as to prevent them from using or having access to a place of public resort to which other members of the public or any section thereof have a right to use or access.

---

available at http://indianexpress.com/article/blogs/dalit-violence-gujarat-gau-rakshaks-2930876/ (accessed 24 February 2017); A.K. Jha, 'The Dalits: Still Untouchable', *India Today*, 3 February 2016, available at http://india-today.intoday.in/story/dalits-untouchable-rohith-vemula-caste-discrimination/1/587100.html (accessed 24 February 2017).

9. Forcing or causing a member of a scheduled caste or a scheduled tribe to leave their house, village, or other place of residence.

It is both shocking and heart-rending to read the list of activities that have been classified as offences in a statute. Clearly, Parliament believed that these inhuman actions existed even after four decades of independence, otherwise there would have been no need to enact such a law. While the occurrence of an incident or two does not mean that society has completely failed to accept the equality of status to all individuals including members of the scheduled castes and tribes, the repeated occurrence of these incidents across the country shows that there is precisely such a lack of acceptance. Unfortunately, the executive's reaction such instances is unsatisfactory—generally, compensation is announced for the victims or their families and commissions of enquiries are constituted and forgotten until the next incident. Until and unless these atrocities are viewed as a breach of fundamental rights and not just offences under a statute against entitlements that society has bestowed upon the scheduled castes and scheduled tribes, the constitutional promises will not be met.[39] Unfortunately, the debate on reservations and the negative impression in certain sections of society regarding the 'unending quotas' in favour of scheduled castes and scheduled tribes create a division in society, which translates into neglect of the seriousness of challenges to equality of status of the scheduled castes and scheduled tribes.

JUDICIAL ENFORCEMENT OF RIGHTS

As discussed in Chapter 4, the legislature has generally failed to properly supervise executive performance.[40] This failure has shifted the entire

[39] Kannabiran points out that dealing with Dalits has always been a matter of charity or compassion and never matter of reform or correction. Kannabiran, *The Wages of Impunity*, pp. 186–203. See also, S. R. Sankaran, 'Social Exclusion and Criminal Law', in K. Kannabiran and R. Singh (eds), *Challenging the Rule(s) of Law: Colonialism, Criminology and Human Rights in India* (New Delhi: SAGE, 2009), pp. 121–41.

[40] For a discussion on the Parliament's failure as an institution of account-ability, see D. Kapur and P.B. Mehta, 'The Indian Parliament as an Institution

burden of protecting the rights of the citizens and holding the executive accountable on to the judiciary. The judiciary today deals with a wide range of matters in relation to executive action by exercising its powers under Articles 32 and 226 of the Constitution. While the judiciary has not shied away from invalidating executive action if it is in breach of the Part III rights or where executive action has not complied with various statutory provisions or principles of natural justice, the judiciary has its own set of problems that make the enforcement of citizens' rights uncertain and allows the executive to continue with its impunity unhindered.[41]

JUDICIAL DELAY

Justice Leila Seth observes, 'Delayed justice is today perhaps the biggest bane of judicial administration in India. What use is a divorce decree when one is too old to remarry, or the return of a house when the owner is dead?'[42] As of 30 June 2016, there were 28,125,304 cases pending in the lower judiciary, 3,945,158 cases in the high courts and 62,646 cases in the Supreme Court.[43] The number of cases pending in the courts

---

of Accountability', pp. 16–23, available at https://casi.sas.upenn.edu/sites/casi.sas.upenn.edu/files/bio/uploads/The%20Indian%20Parliament.pdf (accessed 8 March 2015).

[41] There are various scholarly works that address this topic. Some of them are P.B. Mehta, 'India's Judiciary: The Promise of Uncertainty', in D. Kapur and P.B. Mehta (eds), *Public Institutions in India* (New Delhi: Oxford University Press, 4th Impression, 2011), pp. 158–93; Baxi, *The Crisis of the Indian Legal System*; U. Baxi, 'The Avatars of Indian Judicial Activism: Explorations in the Geographies of [In]Justice', in S.K. Verma and Kusum (eds), *Fifty Years of the Supreme Court of India: Its Grasp and Reach* (New Delhi: Oxford University Press, 2003), pp. 156–209 at p. 156; and F.S. Nariman, *India's Legal System: Can It Be Saved?* (New Delhi: Penguin, 2006).

[42] L. Seth, *Talking of Justice: People's Rights in Modern India* (New Delhi: Aleph Book Company, 2014), pp. 162–3.

[43] This information is available on the website of the Supreme Court of India, http://supremecourtofindia.nic.in/courtnews/2016_issue_2.pdf (accessed 24 February 2017). However, the National Judicial Data Grid website mentions the number of cases pending in the subordinate courts on 27 February 2017 as 23,492,390. See http://njdg.ecourts.gov.in/njdg_public/main.php (accessed 27 February 2017).

has grown at more than 30 per cent over the last two decades. Various reasons are given for this massive backlog of cases including inadequate number of judges, lack of infrastructure, complex procedural laws and inefficiency of lawyers and judges. Irrespective of the reasons the time taken for each case to navigate the judicial system takes decades. While no detailed study has been done to measure the average life cycle of a case from institution to final disposal, the law reports reveal that often the Supreme Court and high courts are rendering judgments in cases that were filed in the lower courts nearly two decades earlier.

The non-governmental research organisation DAKSH has recently started building a database of all pending cases in the high courts to analyse in detail the pendency problem.[44] In the 29 high courts (including benches of various high courts)[45] from where DAKSH has started collecting data, the average pendency is 1,296 days for the cases currently pending.[46] There are matters from the 1950s still pending in some courts. The oldest matter on record has been pending since 1958. Data has also been obtained from 3,000 lower courts across the country and the average pendency in those courts is 2,155 days. In the Supreme Court, the average pendency of cases pending is 1,148 days.

The huge backlog of cases is not just a time-related problem as most observers believe. There is no doubt that delayed justice is equivalent to denial of justice in many cases. However, this glosses over the equally serious 'quality of justice' problem that is a direct consequence of the severe backlog. Judges are required to hear nearly 100 matters a day on a daily basis. While some may be minor procedural matters and cannot be compared to a substantial hearing, expecting a human being, even a highly skilled and trained one, to take 100 decisions in a period of five

[44] See www.dakshlegal.in.

[45] The database is available at http://dakshindia.org/statistics-and-reports/ (accessed 4 March 2017). See also H. Narasappa and S. Vidyasagar (eds), *State of the Indian Judiciary: A Report by DAKSH* (Bengaluru: DAKSH, 2016).

[46] The DAKSH database has been created by collecting the data from the cause lists published by each court every day for the benefit of lawyers and litigants. On the assumption that every pending case is listed at least once in a calendar year, if data is collected for a year we will be building a database of nearly all the cases pending in these courts. The average pendency is determined based on the date filed in each case and the duration it has been pending before the high court. The average varies each day as more cases are added to the database.

hours, to be fair and reasonable, and to ensure justice, is an impossibility. The sheer volume of cases that a judge has to hear each day affects the quality of his/her behaviour in court, orders and judgments. Judges just do not have the time to give each matter the time it deserves, reflect upon it, review existing precedents and then pass a considered order.

Law reports contain a number of cases where judges have made fundamental errors that cannot be pardoned.[47] Judges also end up writing judgments that are nothing more than a collation of quotes from past cases making it impossible even for experienced lawyers to decipher the judgment.[48] The length of these judgments and the difficulty in unravelling the ratio of the case are daunting obstacles, which discourage any attempt at effective communication of the law laid down to the public. Poor quality of justice and indecipherable judgments also increase the number of appeals, resulting in more cases and further delays. This means that the appellate courts are dealing mostly with cases more than a decade old, and which are not necessarily the most important current issues facing society.

Pratap Bhanu Mehta argues that judicial administration, including docket management, has never been taken seriously by the judiciary. Mehta observes,

---

[47] A couple of examples will suffice to illustrate this point. In Bengaluru, a magistrate accepted a complaint of harassment and issued notice, when the relief sought was to parade the accused naked on the streets, garland them with slippers and force feed them with human faeces. In a case reported from Gujarat, a magistrate had issued bailable arrest warrants against the President, the Chief Justice of India (CJI) and other high functionaries without even scrutinising the complaint once. The incident was reported widely in the press. See 'Warrants against President, CJI Quashed', *The Hindu*, 28 April 2004, available at http://www.thehindu.com/2004/04/28/stories/200404280080 1500.htm (accessed 10 April 2015).

[48] Many scholars have written about the oceans of ink and mountains of paper used by judges to write their judgments. In the Kesavananda case, there is no unanimity about what the judgment says even today. See, T.R. Andhyarujina, *The Kesavananda Bharati Case* (New Delhi: Universal Law Publishing, 2011). See also, S. Parathasarathy, 'Critical Judgment: How Vague Prose Can Muddle the Rulings of Our Highest Courts', *The Caravan*, 1 April 2015, available at http://www.caravanmagazine.in/perspectives/critical-judgment-courts-vague-prose (accessed 10 April 2015).

As an institution, almost all levels of the judiciary exhibit what can only be described as administered chaos. There is unanimity in the view that the court system is administratively inefficient. Judges are excessively passive in an adversarial legal system, excessive party control allows respondents to delay cases with impunity and there are few alternatives for dispute resolution other than an ill-managed trial. The administrative infrastructure of most courts is woefully inadequate. Records of filings are mostly kept by hand, documents are difficult to trace, judges orally summarize testimony for court recorders, judges are moved around from bench to bench faster than depositions are filed. Judges seem to seldom exercise the power to impose costs for frivolous litigation; interim injunctive relief and adjournments are routinely granted; and the number of possible appeals while a case is still on is large enough to effectively fracture the trial or stay it.[49]

The inefficiency of the judicial system directly contributes to the increasing lawlessness in the country. The system has become so oppressively slow that it is incapable of protecting the rights of citizens and has resulted in the executive acting with utter impunity. The Law Commission in its 120th report observed that one of the costs of judicial delay was an 'all-declining respect for the rule of law'.[50] In fact, members of the judiciary themselves have shown a lack of faith in the rule of law due to the massive judicial delays. The most shocking example in recent times is a sessions judge in Mumbai seeking the help of an underworld don to settle his affairs.[51]

In 1986, Bhagwati J, in his law day address observed,

The judiciary is on the verge of collapse. The backlog of cases, the inordinate delay in deciding matters before the courts, and the inevitable collapse of evidence in the time that it takes to reach trial and judgment has led to a decline in credibility. The corruption among the police, the prison system and the judicial process has done little to shore up the reputation of the system.[52]

[49] Mehta, 'India's Judiciary: The Promise of Uncertainty', pp. 181–2.

[50] Paragraph 13 at page 4 of the Report. See http://lawcommissionofindia.nic.in/101-169/report120.pdf (accessed 10 April 2015).

[51] R.K. Sen, , A. Dasgupta and M.K. Dasgupta (eds), *Crime and Corruption in Indian Economy* (New Delhi: Deep and Deep Publications, 2001), p. 209.

[52] The quote is extracted from U. Ramanathan, 'Crime and Punishment', available at http://www.india-seminar.com/2006/557/557%20usha%20ramanathan.htm (accessed 26 March 2015).

The position has only worsened after nearly 30 years. There has been very little effort to study this problem in minute detail. There are many reports by the Law Commission on the issue of judicial delay and multiple suggestions have been made by the Commission with almost no implementation by the executive and the judiciary. However, even the Law Commission acknowledges that the problem cannot be studied properly in the absence of properly maintained data by the courts. In its 245th report, the Commission observed that there is no scientific collection and maintenance of data by the high courts to even begin to study the backlog problem in detail.[53] As a result, most suggestions are based on surmises and anecdotal evidence.

At the chief justices' conference in April 2015, the then Chief Justice of India (CJI) set a target of five years for the disposal of each case at the trial court stage.[54] The five-year period may sound great for people who are used to trials going on for decades. However, from a rights' perspective, this reflects a severe lack of ambition in setting targets that make real change to the life of litigants. Five years in the trial court means that final disposal in the highest court may not happen for a minimum of 10–15 years after institution of a case.

ACCESS TO JUSTICE

It is not certain that India is an extremely litigious country as the severe backlog and delays suggest. To the contrary, many argue, it is an under-litigated country with persistent access to justice problems.[55] Some initial data available from DAKSH's research gives credence to this argument. As an example, let us look at the number of writ petitions filed in 2014

---

[53] Last para, page 1 of the report, available at http://lawcommissionofindia.nic.in/reports/Report_No.245.pdf (accessed 27 December 2017).

[54] The then CJI H.L. Dattu's comments can be seen in 'Nearly Three Crore Cases Pending, CJI Says Trial to End within 5 years', *The Indian Express*, 5 April 2015, available at http://indianexpress.com/article/india/india-others/nearly-three-crore-cases-pending-cji-says-trial-to-end-within-5-years/ (accessed 10 April 2015).

[55] The former CJI, M.N. Venkatachaliah, has consistently maintained this view. He made this point to the author and the DAKSH team in an interview on judicial delays, available at http://blog.dakshindia.org/2015/03/an-evening-with-justice-mn.html (accessed 10 April 2015).

in Karnataka. The population of Karnataka is around 6.4 crore, according to the 2011 census. In 2014, 69,994 writ petitions (out of a total of 120,370 matters) were filed in the high court, amounting to just over one per cent of the population filing writs, assuming that each writ has been filed by a separate individual, which is generally not the case. Given the enormous dissatisfaction of society with executive action and inaction, this is an incredibly small number of writs. However, writ petitions in fact constitute nearly 60 per cent of the total number of cases filed in the Karnataka High Court, which also clearly indicates that the biggest cause of litigation, at least in the superior courts, is the state in its many avatars.

In Gujarat, there were 29,265 writ petitions out of a total of 85,559 matters filed. In Jharkhand, there were 6,717 writ petitions out of a total of 29,320 matters filed. In both Gujarat and Jharkhand, writ petitions are filed by less than 0.5 per cent of the population. Apart from writ petitions, many categories of cases are directly between the citizens and the state, such as tax cases and land acquisition matters. However, as a percentage of the population dealing with an all-pervasive state, the overall number of writ petitions is quite low. This relatively low number is also reflective of citizens' reluctance and fear in approaching a system where any meaningful remedy takes several years and comes at very high cost. This reluctance is understandably greater among the poorer sections of society, as they do not have access to good quality legal advice. While there is a legal services authority that provides legal aid to deserving people, the quality of legal aid has not only been very poor but also only a myth most times.[56]

The judiciary has tried to innovate through the concept of public interest litigations (PILs) and lok adalats. Lok adalats, however, have been reduced to a mechanism for achieving disposal rates by the judiciary. Unfortunately, it is the poor who are often forced to settle their

---

[56] Many scholars have written repeatedly about this issue. For example, see N.R.M. Menon, 'Serving the Justice Needs of the Poor', *The Hindu*, 3 December 2013, available at http://www.thehindu.com/opinion/lead/serving-the-justice-needs-of-the-poor/article5415018.ece (accessed 10 April 2015). The data on writ petitions filed in Karnataka, Gujarat, and Jharkhand have been obtained from the DAKSH database and the websites of the high courts. See www.karnatakajudiciary.kar.nic.in; www.gujarathighcourt.nic.in; and www.jharkhandhighcourt.nic.in (accessed 4 March 2017).

cases through lok adalats, as they do not have the luxury of financing a long-drawn litigation and hoping for a favourable result at its end. For all their perceived success in reducing backlogs, the overall number of cases have not reduced because of lok adalats. Kannabiran argues that the fact that lok adalats are so vociferously promoted itself highlights the problem with the justice system.[57] At best, lok adalats are an inequitable form of mediation for the poor and at worst, they are a fraud on the justice system, as the poor are being forced to settle matters because of the inability of the judiciary to provide remedies for breach of their rights.

PUBLIC INTEREST LITIGATION

One of the celebrated innovations of the Indian judiciary is the development of public, or social, interest litigation (or PIL) in the higher courts, as discussed in Chapter 3. Much has been written about the history, success and limitations of PILs.[58] In this section, the focus is on the problems in rights enforcement that PILs hide, rather than their success in certain areas or the various other jurisprudential questions they raise. As counter-intuitive as it sounds, PILs, like lok adalats, are a direct consequence of the general inability of the executive and the judiciary to provide justice to individuals who are adversely impacted by the actions or inactions that become the subject matter of PILs. Therefore, while we should celebrate the judiciary's innovation in relaxing locus standi requirements for complaining against rights' violations, several PILs do not attest to the existence of the rule of law. To the contrary, they hide the inability of the system to provide an effective rights enforcement mechanism. A system based on rights has to provide meaningful

[57] Kannabiran, *The Wages of Impunity*, p. 208.

[58] See A. Bhuwania, *Courting the People: Public Interest Litigation in Post-Emergency India* (Cambridge: Cambridge University Press, 2017). See also Baxi, 'The Avatars of Indian Judicial Activism'; U. Baxi, 'The (Im)possibility of Constitutional Justice', in Z. Hasan, E. Sridharan and R. Sudarshan (eds), *India's Living Constitution: Ideas, Practices, Controversies* (New Delhi: Permanent Black, 2006), pp. 31–63 at p. 55; L. Rajamani and A. Sengupta, 'The Supreme Court', in N.G. Jayal and P.B. Mehta (eds), *The Oxford Companion to Politics in India* (New Delhi: Oxford University Press, 2010), pp. 80–97.

remedies for their violation. These remedies should necessarily contain two aspects: first, the person suffering the violation should either be restored to his original situation or suitably compensated, and second, the person causing the violation should be made to pay, either monetarily or otherwise. PILs have generally not been able to rectify the inability of the legal system to do either. While there are instances where victims have received succour through judicial orders in PILs, there are very few cases where the violator has been punished. The absence of punishment ensures the continuance of the practice that caused the rights violation in the first place.

Let us take the case of treatment of undertrial prisoners. The Supreme Court ordered in 1980 that such prisoners should not be handcuffed, as it is a prima facie violation of their human rights.[59] However, this practice has not stopped and it is common to see the accused handcuffed, even in court premises where lawyers and magistrates are present. Similarly, the courts have on numerous occasions ruled that undertrials should be released if they have served as much or more time than the prescribed punishment for the offence they have been accused of.[60] However, very often, civil society groups have to approach the judiciary for implementation of the same order—there is no continuous compliance without further intervention by civil society. Even today, many undertrials continue to languish in jails across the country after 30 years of the Supreme Court's order. In 2013, a study showed that more than 75 per cent of prisoners in India are undertrials. Given that the conviction rate in India is very low, the long incarceration of undertrials is in itself a violation of rights.[61]

PILs have also resulted in grand and eloquent pronouncements on the law, human rights, and state of affairs of the country. However, scholars and activists complain that the implementation of these pronouncements happens only occasionally as the judiciary does little to ensure

---

[59] *Prem Shankar* v *Delhi Administration* (1980) 3 SCC 526. The point was reiterated in *Citizens for Democracy* v *State of Assam* (1995) 3 SCC 743.

[60] *Hussainara Khatoon* v *Home Secretary, State of Bihar* AIR 1979 SC 1369.

[61] A. Behar, D. Samuel, and Y. Kumar, eds., *Citizens' Report on Governance and Development, 2013* (National Social Watch 2013), p. 102, available at http://socialwatchindia.net/images/documents/498/CRGD-2013_Full-Report.pdf (accessed 10 April 2015).

implementation of its orders. Shourie narrates the case of the bonded labourers in mines and quarries in Delhi and Haryana and the nearly decade-long PIL fought by various activists and groups. The Supreme Court pronounced a very 'grandiloquent order' initially, but did not suitably enforce when a contempt petition was filed for its breach.[62] In the original PIL, Bhagwati J, had observed,

> The system is totally incompatible with the new egalitarian socio-economic order which we have promised to build, and it is not only an affront to basic human dignity but also constitutes gross and revolting violation of constitutional values. The appalling conditions in which bonded labourers live.... They are non-beings, exiles of civilisation, living a life worse than that of animals, for the animals are at least free to roam about as they like.[63]

On 16 December 1983, the Court went on to order that 21 specific actions were to be taken, and certain activities had to be stopped within six weeks of its order. Shourie narrates the sequence of events that occurred over the next eight years—blatant violations of the Court's order by the executive, appointment of different sets of commissioners, contempt petitions, the ebb and flow of the Court's interest and enthusiasm, pleas by prominent citizens asking the Supreme Court to at least implement its own order, change in benches, rumours of a retiring chief justice who did not pass a final order in the hope of becoming a nominee for the post of vice president—all of which resulted in a final order only in 1991. And the final order merely observed that the persons identified as bonded labourers should be rehabilitated in accordance with the scheme prepared by the union government.[64]

Shourie notes that one of the consequences of grand orders in PILs is that they cannot be enforced. He observes, '[It] requires little imagination that if orders are of such sweep that they cannot be implemented, or if no one seriously follows them up to ensure that they are implemented, the orders will boomerang on those who give them.'[65]

---

[62] Shourie, *Courts and Their Judgments*, pp. 18–25. The case is *Bandhua Mukti Morcha* v *Union of India* AIR 1984 SC 802. There are various orders in the same case reported in later years.

[63] Shourie, *Courts and Their Judgments*, p. 17.

[64] Shourie, *Courts and Their Judgments*, pp. 17–25.

[65] Shourie, *Courts and Their Judgments*, p. 147.

There is a sweet irony in this as far as the executive is concerned; the judiciary is dependent on the executive to enforce its orders, but also needs to be critical of, and correct the executive's action on a daily basis. While we cannot hold the judiciary fully responsible for lack of executive support in implementing judicial orders, it is certainly the judiciary's problem that it is taking the cover of grand pronouncements instead of enforcing individual rights. Kannabiran points out that the executive's intransigence regarding judicial orders also arises because of the tactic of 'gentle persuasion' adopted by the judiciary. The judiciary fails to uphold rights in a decisive manner in most cases, and instead appeals to the executive to do the right thing. Kannabiran observes,

> The courts have always acted as if the government and its men should not be dealt with harshly, that they should be treated as slow learners. But then, in implementing the constitutional scheme, pious homilies have no therapeutic value. They merely tend to make the executive more and more arbitrary. None of the courts' gentle admonitions have had any effect. The abuse of law has continued at every level. In the case of liberty, lawlessness on the part of government agents subjects persons to physical pain, indignity and humiliation and therefore needs urgent attention.[66]

Very often, successful litigants in civil cases have to resort to filing execution petitions, even where the order is directly against an organ of the state, as they are otherwise unable to enforce judgments in their favour. This is more so in the case of PILs, where the judiciary makes grand policy pronouncements, as against specific orders, which cannot be meaningfully implemented. Shourie agrees with Kannabiran and points out that the judiciary has been left to demand action only by expressing indignation and pain in writing. Such pious demands make no difference to the executive or even to lower courts which routinely ignore the orders by the higher courts.[67]

As the number of PILs have increased, it has become difficult to predict the courts' approach to different PILs. There is an inconsistency in the judiciary's approach that can only be explained by judges' personal preferences. Admission or rejection of PILs and the nature of orders granted depend on the individual judges hearing the matter. After the halcyon days of 1980s, when the judiciary's PIL innovation generated

---

[66] Kannabiran, *The Wages of Impunity*, p. 74.
[67] Shourie, *Courts and Their Judgments*, pp. 370–96.

much excitement as the harbinger of a rights revolution, it is today a mixed bag as PILs are also seen as undemocratic tools of oppression against the very poor people which the PILs originally intended to protect. Anuj Bhuwania takes the example of the Delhi vehicular pollution case before the Supreme Court and the slum demolition case before the Delhi High Court to argue that the judiciary did not even pay lip service to the rights of those adversely affected by its orders, something that was unlikely to have happened in a regular adversarial process. Bhuwania further argues that PILs have permitted judges to wilfully initiate roving enquiries into complex issues that affect millions, pass orders, and force implementation through chosen individuals, with handpicked lawyers (in the form of amicus curiae, or otherwise) deciding the course of the petition and not hearing parties affected by the decisions.[68]

Upendra Baxi argues that the initial enthusiasm has today degenerated into chaos and disenchantment because of the judiciary's inconsistent approach to PILs, its failure to address issues that address larger 'macro-structures' of power in the Indian state, and its inability to convince the executive to enforce many orders in true spirit.[69] PIL courts, it is argued, have essentially become panchayats or medieval durbars with unrestrained power vested in the judges and committees or amicus curiae appointed by the judges.[70] This unrestrained power has led to some serious rights violations. Here is an example of the exercise of such power from the recent national anthem case:

51A. Fundamental duties—It shall be the duty of every citizen of India–
(a) to abide by the Constitution and respect its ideals and institutions, the National Flag and the National Anthem.

From the aforesaid, it is clear as crystal that it is the sacred obligation of every citizen to abide by the ideals engrafted in the Constitution. And one such ideal is to show respect for the National Anthem and the National Flag. Be it stated, a time has come, the citizens of the country must realize that they live in a nation and are duty bound to show respect to National Anthem which is the symbol of the Constitutional Patriotism and inherent

[68] Bhuwania, *Courting the People*, pp. 52–75 and 80–106. As Bhuwania's work was published after this book was completed, I have not had a chance to review his work in fuller detail.

[69] Kapur and Mehta, 'The Indian Parliament as an Institution of Accountability'.

[70] Bhuwania, *Courting the People*, pp. 51–2 and 117–29.

national quality. It does not allow any different notion or the perception of individual rights, that have individually thought of have no space. The idea is constitutionally impermissible.[71]

In a case where the petitioner was complaining about incidents of disrespect to the national anthem, Dipak Misra J, relied on this flawed logic above to direct, in an interim order, that the national anthem has to be played before the screening of every movie across the country. Apart from the many wrong things with this order highlighted by many,[72] what is appalling is the complete lack of legal reasoning and the underlying impunity of the judges passing the order. Essentially, a bench decided to pass an order which was not even pleaded for by the petitioner just because a judge (or two) felt the urge to do so.

The order is clearly unsustainable because it places fundamental duties a notch above fundamental rights, and is therefore ultra vires the Constitution. Equally evident is the total lack of judicial discipline both in the contents of the order (in that it does not refer to a single earlier case of the Supreme Court itself, including the celebrated judgment in *Bijoe Emmanuel*[73]) and the failure to hear parties that are likely to be affected by this order or even consider the likely consequences of the order. Following this order there have already been instances of people beating up other citizens who, in their view, disrespected the national anthem when it was played in a movie theatre.[74]

[71] *Shyam Narayan Chouksey* v *Union of India*, WP 855/2016, order dated 30 November 2016, available at http://supremecourtofindia.nic.in/FileServer/2016-11-30_1480502585.pdf (accessed 24 February 2017).

[72] See, A.P. Kumar, 'Supreme Court's National Anthem Order Mocks Judicial Process, Constitution', FirstPost, 1 December 2016, available at http://www.firstpost.com/india/supreme-courts-national-anthem-order-mocks-judicial-process-constitution-3134204.html (accessed 23 February 2017). See also, G. Bhatia, 'The Illegality of the Supreme Court's National Anthem Order', blog entry in *Indian Constitutional Law and Philosophy*, available at https://indconlawphil.wordpress.com/2016/11/30/the-illegality-of-the-supreme-courts-national-anthem-order/ (accessed 23 February 2017).

[73] *Bijoe Emmanuel* v *State of Kerala* AIR 1987 SC 748. The Court in this case, in a reasoned judgment, held that a citizen has the right not to sing the national anthem. Misra, J., did not even refer to this case in his order.

[74] See K.V. Lakshmana 'Chennai: Students Attacked for not Standing During National Anthem in Theatre', *Hindustan Times*, 11 January 2017, available at

The general delay in judicial process has also affected PILs. And when petitioners have urged the judiciary to progress the matter swiftly, it has drawn a venomous response, at times. In *Sheela Barse* v *Union of India*,[75] a committed social worker mentioned that she would withdraw her petition if the Court was unable to finally hear her matter even after three years. The Court responded by saying that it would not allow her to withdraw the petition, observing, 'We refuse to withdraw the petition. You will get out. You have no right to continue. You were given a privilege. We are withdrawing that privilege…. The Court is the protector of the children, and not Sheela Barse. If you assume roles not entitled to you, you are wrong. The case can go on without you.'[76]

The Court later passed an order removing Ms Barse as petitioner and substituting in her place the Supreme Court Legal Aid Society. Seervai has criticised the judgment by the Court as containing a confused account of PIL and noting that the right under Article 32 was no privilege. Seervai notes,

> It may be added that in the course of the discussion between the Bench and Ms. Barse, she added that the Sup. Ct. [Supreme Court] had become 'dysfunctional', that is to say, that it had ceased to fulfil the purpose for which it was created, namely to dispose of matters brought before it with all practicable speed and not postpone the disposal for an indefinite period of time. In my submission Ms. Barse was right when she said that the Sup. Ct. had become dysfunctional…. Consider the conduct of the two judges in respect of admittedly illegal detention of undertrial and convicted juveniles in jail: 25 adjournments were granted in the space of nearly 3 years; eight final hearings were fixed, but no final hearing took place; and yet the two judges refused Ms. Barse's request to fix a firm date for final hearing and hear the petition on that day.[77]

---

http://www.hindustantimes.com/india-news/chennai-four-detained-for-not-standing-up-during-national-anthem-before-movie/story-HMoQNbO-jNnOOGQg6wpjk4N.html (accessed 23 February 2017); See also http://indiatoday.intoday.in/video/wheelchair-bound-national-anthem-movie-theatre/1/791032.html (accessed 23 February 2017).

[75] AIR 1988 SC 2221.

[76] The words are those of Ranganath Misra, J. and have been reproduced in H.M. Seervai, *Constitutional Law of India*, Volume 2 (New Delhi: Universal Book Traders, 4th edn, 2002), pp. ix–x.

[77] Seervai, *Constitutional Law of India*. The final order removing Sheela Barse was made by M.N. Venkatachaliah, J.

Unfortunately, the Sheela Barse case is not an exception. Increasingly, the judiciary treats petitioners in PILs with suspicion. While there have been instances of PILs being used to pursue private interests, this by itself is not an excuse for the judges to tar all petitioners with the same brush. Even when the Court has not replaced the petitioners, it has proceeded to appoint amicus curiae (generally, a senior advocate) and asked the petitioners to make all submissions to the amicus who becomes the arbiter of whether the petitioner's arguments are worth mentioning before the Court.[78] Further, the judiciary's assumption that it is the protector of all rights and that the petitioners are only exercising a privilege granted to them by the judiciary is an affront to the rule of law and the Constitution. While the judiciary is an integral part of the rule of law, it certainly does not have the right or the power to claim ownership or monopoly over protection of rights.

CORRUPTION

The proper administration of justice is dependent foremost on a fearless and honest judiciary. While there are not too many reported cases of judicial corruption, the few that are reported indicate that the malaise runs deeper than most people assume. Reporting of judicial corruption is generally low because of the difficulty in investigating and prosecuting corrupt judges, particularly in the high courts and the Supreme Court, where removal of judges is only possible by impeachment in Parliament. Even in the few instances where corruption is reported, there is not even a preliminary inquiry or investigation. The examples of K.G. Balakrishnan, P.D. Dinakaran, Soumitra Sen, and C.S.K. Prasad, all of whom faced or are facing allegations are fresh in our memories. In those cases where the judiciary did take steps to investigate the matter and prima facie verify the allegations, no meaningful punishment was initiated because of the burdensome process required for removal of the tainted judges. Some of them resigned, while others completed their term and also got post-retirement positions. Since Independence, no judge of the Supreme Court or any high court has ever been successfully impeached. The Supreme Court has refused to order any investigation in response to an interview (first) and later affidavits filed by

[78] Bhuwania, *Courting the People*, pp. 40–4.

Shanti Bhushan and Prashant Bhushan in 2010 that eight out of the previous 16 CJIs were corrupt. The Court in fact initiated contempt proceedings against Prashant Bhushan for the interview and demanded an apology. The proceedings are still pending after the affidavits were filed and a sealed cover with the names of the 'corrupt eight' former CJIs was submitted. The fact that two well-respected senior advocates, one of them a former law minister, were making these allegations and were willing to file affidavits to that effect is itself an indicator of the sad state of affairs. The judiciary's refusal to apply to itself the same standards of transparency, as it has demanded from other organs of government, only increases the suspicion that the higher judiciary considers itself above the law. Even if the allegations were exaggerated, it is necessary for the 'conscience keeper' of the Constitution to ensure that there is a mechanism in place to examine and decide on them.

Judges in the subordinate judiciary have been punished occasionally on charges of corruption and misuse of office. The case of the former cabinet minister of Karnataka, Janardhana Reddy, and his associates bribing a trial judge to secure bail is both shocking (because of the amount of money involved, that is Rs 60 crore, and the number of sitting and retired judges involved) and unsurprising (because of the general perception that the lower judiciary is corrupt). Apart from the judge who decided the matter, a retired judge who acted as the intermediary and two other sitting judges who tried to act as intermediaries, were arrested. Also in the mix were criminals with long records, ministers, and lawyers.[79] The case is worrying because of the number of judges involved and the ease with which criminals appear to have approached many judges without fear of rejection or prosecution. It opens a window into the worrying and murky world of corruption in criminal cases in the lower judiciary and indicates the widespread prevalence of corruption.

It is not merely monetary corruption that afflicts the judiciary. Judges are more often bribed by their ambitions and loyalty than by money. Many believe that the decision of the Constitutional Bench of the Supreme Court in the *Habeas Corpus* case[80] during the emergency, with only H.R. Khanna J, dissenting, is a case in point as the judges

---

[79] Behar, Samuel, and Kumar, *Citizens' Report on Governance and Development*, p. 105.

[80] *ADM, Jabalpur* v *Shivakant Shukla* (1976) 2 SCC 521.

constituting the majority decided in favour of the government of the day.[81] Recently, the same kind of ambition has raised questions about the former CJI, P. Sathasivam, who was appointed as the governor of a state. There are many allegations that Supreme Court judges have ruled in favour of those in power with a view to seek appointments by the government following their retirement. Yet another aspect of judicial corruption is the 'uncle judges' syndrome, where the kith and kin of many sitting judges practise in the same court and get favourable orders from other judges whom they interact with socially.[82]

Scholars and lawyers have expressed concerns about the increase in corruption and fall in values in the judiciary in recent times. This is not surprising given the general fall in integrity among people who hold public offices. Leila Seth emphasises this point by quoting two well-known legal figures, Lord Devlin, the former law lord, and H.M. Seervai. Lord Devlin had observed, 'Judges are not now, neither have they been in the past, much better or much worse than other public servants.'[83] Seervai, in his Setalvad lecture of 1970, had observed,

> No constitutional safeguards can secure an incorruptible judiciary unless the men who appoint judges, and the men who are appointed judges, are imbued with the high standards of public administration on which those safeguards rest. It is necessary to remind ordinary citizens that an incorruptible judiciary, which they may take for granted and to which they confidently turn for the protection of their rights, whether against the state or against individuals cannot survive if they do not demand and secure integrity in public life.[84]

The increasing allegations of corruption, the lack of punishment even in the few cases where judges have been found guilty, the judiciary's obstinate refusal to permit any transparent scrutiny of judges' affairs in the name of judicial independence and its eagerness in slapping contempt proceedings against people alleging corruption as well as honest critics of judicial conduct has not only taken the shine off judicial armour, but also landed a severe blow to the rule of law. The

---

[81] Mehta, 'India's Judiciary: The Promise of Uncertainty', p. 187.

[82] Behar, Samuel, and Kumar, *Citizens' Report on Governance and Development*, pp. 105–6.

[83] Seth, *Talking of Justice*, p. 187.

[84] Seth, *Talking of Justice*, p. 188.

judiciary cannot place itself above public scrutiny merely on the ground that it is protecting the rights of people.

STATE AS A LITIGANT

The government is the largest litigant in the country. That statistic is not surprising given its central role in society and the general arbitrariness of executive action. However, it is the government's attitude towards litigation that makes it a large contributor to both judicial delays and chaos in the legal system. The government does not shy away from regularly appealing every order that goes against it, without pausing to consider if the matter is worth appealing. This is because of the state's extreme adherence to procedure. Shourie gives examples of states filing appeals all the way to the Supreme Court when there is no more than Rs 15,000 or Rs 20,000 at stake. Courts have observed on innumerable occasions that the government should not file appeals automatically, but examine if there is a serious issue that needs resolution, rather than because of adamant behaviour, cantankerous attitudes, or egos of the officers involved.[85]

Litigation between two different arms of the same government is also very common and is generally persisted with even after courts have observed many times that two arms of government should not fight in court by spending money on counsels' and court fees and procedural expenses, and by wasting public time.[86]

Shourie asserts that litigation between the state and its employees is one of the largest block of cases in which the government is involved.[87] These cases often take 15 or 20 years to be decided, even when the issue relates to study leave, sanction for prosecution of officers, suspensions, dismissals, and other implementation of service conditions. Shourie narrates details of the day-to-day movement of a few of these cases, highlighting a potent combination of extreme procedural orientation and litigious attitude of the government and its employees, the inefficiency of the courts and the triviality of the issues involved leading to years of litigation without any concrete outcome.[88]

---

[85] Shourie, *Courts and Their Judgments*, pp. 370–4.
[86] Shourie, *Courts and Their Judgments*, pp. 370–96.
[87] Shourie, *Courts and Their Judgments*, p. 10.
[88] Shourie, *Courts and Their Judgments*, pp. 319–69.

RIGHTS

Kannabiran argues that the judiciary is also guilty of not understanding the rights philosophy in the Constitution. The judiciary has too often converted the debate about the rights of citizens into a debate on the power of the state against its own people. This has been the case right from independence and only a few judges have correctly emphasized the rights discourse as against the discussion on power. Vivian Bose J, is one example when he observed,

> Brush aside for a moment the pettifogging of the law & forget for the nonce [sic] all the learned disputations about this & that, & 'and' or 'or', or 'may' & 'must'. Look past the mere verbiage of the words & penetrate deep into the heart & spirit of the Constitution. What sort of State are we intended to be? Have we not here been given a way of life, the right to individual freedom, the utmost the State can confer in that respect consistent with its own safety? Is not the sanctity of the individual recognised & emphasised again & again? Is not our Constitution in violent contrast to those of States where the State is everything & the individual but a slave or a serf to serve the will of those who for the time being wield almost absolute power? I have no doubt on this score.[89]

Justice Khanna is another example when he observed in his famous dissenting opinion in the infamous *Habeas Corpus* case,

> I am of the opinion that Article 21 cannot be the sole repository of the right to life and personal liberty. The right to life and personal liberty is the most precious of human rights in civilised societies governed by the rule of law.... Even in the absence of Article 21 in the Constitution, the State has got no power to deprive a person of his life or liberty without the authority of law. This is the essential postulate and basic assumption of the rule of law and not of men in all civilised nations. The principle that no one shall be deprived of his right to life and personal liberty without the authority of law is rooted in the consideration that life and personal liberty are priceless possessions which cannot be made the plaything of individual whim and caprice and that any act which has the effect of tampering with life and liberty must receive sustenance from and sanction of the laws of the land.[90]

---

[89] S. *Krishnan* v *State of Madras* AIR 1951 SC 301.

[90] *ADM Jabalpur* v *Shivakant Shukla* (1976) 2 SCC 521, pp. 747–50.

In the post-emergency height of judicial activism, a number of judges made an effort to change the discourse from one focusing on the power of the state to one focusing on rights. Bhagwati J, and Krishna Iyer J, are the two leading lights of this period, writing between them a number of judgments that increased the scope of the judiciary's powers and the Part III rights, particularly Article 21. However, their approach was focused on grand pronouncements that at times proved incapable of enforcement. Moreover, there was much inconsistency in their approach, particularly Bhagwati J, who has been accused of swaying with the political winds. The inconsistency of approach is not limited to just one judge over time, although that is quite deplorable, but different judges concurrently, given that the high courts and the Supreme Court sit in benches of different judges. The latter can be explained by way of personal preferences of individual judges, but if that is indeed correct, it is a clear violation of the rule of law and makes judicial decisions on rights no different from political or administrative decisions, as Unger has argued. The emphasis on reason by the Supreme Court time and again disappears when we study the inconsistent approaches of the various judges. The inconsistency can only be explained by accepting that there is a lack of internalization of the primacy of rights by the judiciary.

Mehta argues that the courts have not been devoted to a civil liberties rights-based discourse. Rather, the courts have legitimized their interventions in the rights arena largely based on the idea that government ought to be forced to intervene in certain areas to achieve 'substantial goals' whose content is largely defined through the Part IV framework.[91] Formulating the basic structure doctrine to limit the ability of Parliament to amend the Constitution, reading various rights into Article 21, making policy prescriptions, and widening judicial review have all given the impression that the judiciary is protecting the rights of the citizens. However, this may not necessarily be true given the judiciary's own patchy record in enforcing rights. The judiciary's surrender in respect of the right to property, its unwillingness to go the full mile in respect of civil liberties and its mixed approach to social welfare rights show that its impact is far less than it should be.

The ever-widening of the power of judicial review and connected activism is in fact seen as a political exercise of power by the

---

[91] Mehta, 'India's Judiciary: The Promise of Uncertainty', p. 165.

judiciary rather than one dictated by the philosophy of rights and the Constitution. Most of the times, it is merely stepping into the vacuum created by an ineffective legislature and executive. And in a small number of cases, such as the national anthem case discussed earlier, it is nothing but an improper exercise of political power in the knowledge that there is no superior power to invalidate such exercise. This jurisprudence has been criticised as one of 'helplessness'[92] or 'impunity' rather than one motivated by the need to protect rights. Mehta observes,

> The [Supreme] court's concern for its own authority has meant a reading of the political tea leaves as it were; the judicialization of politics and the politicization of the judiciary have turned out to be two sides of the same coin. It is not an accident that the Indian constitutional law has been relatively unstable, or that the same courts can appear strong and assertive in some areas and not in others. It may be the case that Indian courts have acquired much legitimacy and power not because of the clarity and consistency of an underlying constitutional vision but because of the opposite. One could interpret all of the courts' decisions as modus vivendi, between competing group values and aspirations which is sufficiently indeterminate and open ended to keep the players motivated enough to play it. In a way the court's legitimacy rests precisely on the fact that in its attempt at providing a modus vivendi, it has given a sufficient number of parties enough partial victories to give them an incentive to keep on playing the game.[93]

While this kind of activism by the judiciary can possibly give relief in the short term, it is hurtful to the cause of rights and the rule of law in the long term, as the other institutions are quite happy not to do anything and pass the buck to a willing judiciary. It also results in the weakening of other institutions rather than strengthening them.

The rights jurisprudence is undermined by two further aspects. First is the tendency of the judiciary to apply its rulings only prospectively on grounds of 'practical considerations and difficulties' in undoing the effects of illegal actions.[94] The judiciary resorts to this prospective overruling approach often. The effect of prospective overruling is protection

[92] Mehta, 'India's Judiciary: The Promise of Uncertainty', p. 165.
[93] Mehta, 'India's Judiciary: The Promise of Uncertainty', p. 171.
[94] The prospective overruling concept has been used in the context of constitutional amendments, validity of statutes and executive actions. For a brief discussion on the topic, See, Jain, *Indian Constitutional Law*, pp. 1636–8.

to the beneficiaries of illegal actions, and it does not meaningfully compensate the victims of illegal actions. The beneficiaries of illegal action and the executive are so used to prospective overruling by the judiciary that they do not hesitate to take action even when they are aware of its illegality. On the few occasions when the judiciary has refused to permit the effect of illegal actions to continue, it has resulted in a massive protest about judicial overreach! The protests following the cancellation of the 2G telecom licences pursuant to the Supreme Court's finding that the allotment of the licences was illegal[95] is an example of the confidence the executive has in the concept of prospective overruling. While it may appear to be a minor issue, prospective overruling and the resulting protection of the fruits of illegality is a major factor in executive decision-making and is based on the assumption that the rights discourse is only about exercise of state power, which the judiciary has made legitimate.

Leila Seth highlights the second aspect by pointing out that many judges appear to be oblivious of the existence of rights itself and are more influenced by personal, class and societal prejudices. Seth cites the example of the decision by the District and Sessions Court, Jaipur in the *Bhanwari Devi* rape case and observes,

> What is historic, however, is the view taken by the judge that the accused, by virtue of their age and social standing, were necessarily incapable of a crime like rape. The judgment suggests that rapists are usually teenagers. This may or may not be statistically true, but extending that to mean that all those who are not teenagers cannot rape is ludicrous. If this were to be accepted, all cases of rape should be dropped the moment it is established that the accused have crossed their teens. Equally astonishing is the claim that since the alleged rapists were middle-aged they must necessarily be 'respectable', a contention supported neither by statistics nor by elementary logic. The most astounding reason given for acquittal, however, was that the accused (one of whom was a Brahmin) were fairly highly placed in the caste hierarchy, and that this ruled them out as possible rapists of a lower-caste woman. Such caste characterization of crime, apart from being morally objectionable, betrays an entirely ahistorical perspective. And this perspective, while insidious in society at large, is even more abhorrent within the judiciary.[96]

---

[95] *Centre for Public Interest Litigation v Union of India* (2012) 3 SCC 1.

[96] Seth, *Talking of Justice*, p. 21.

Unfortunately, this is not an isolated incident.[97] Other high profile examples of the judiciary being oblivious to the rights of people include the national anthem case discussed above and the *Naz Foundation* case where the Supreme Court derisively described the LGBT community as 'a miniscule fraction of the country's population' as if numerical strength makes a difference to rights.[98]

A CHAOTIC CRUMBLING SYSTEM

The executive and the judicial systems responsible for enforcement of rights and laws are crumbling and on their last legs. It is a hollow, moth-eaten system, being destroyed both from within and outside. While different problems afflict the executive and the judiciary, the end result is the same—an ineffective system incapable of performing the primary tasks for which it has been established. The only certainty that both the executive and judiciary guarantee the citizens today is uncertainty. Citizens cannot rely on either the executive or the judiciary for enforcement of their rights in a timely and effective manner. This uncertain system is the antithesis of a society that claims to be governed by the rule of law. It is an indicator of the widespread lawlessness in society. While the law may exist, it appears to be hanging limp, considering when, and whether, to act with the full force it has at its command.

The uncertainty is accompanied by instability in jurisprudence as well as enforcement. This instability arises out of an increasingly unsettled position of the courts faced with repeated attacks on rights of citizens. The judiciary's response to the repeated attacks is inconsistent, political and suffers from a lack of commitment to the rights of individuals. A political exercise of judicial power only increases the instability and undermines the rule of law. Where there is clarity on the

---

[97] See Bhuwania, *Courting the People*, pp. 112–29, for some more examples of personal prejudices of judges. See also M. Satish, *Discretion, Discrimination and the Rule of Law* (Cambridge: Cambridge University Press, 2017), pp. 38–50 and 148 where he discusses the lack of knowledge of victim rights, personal prejudices of judges and lack of consistent reasoning in the context of rape conviction and sentencing. Satish's work was published after the author completed writing this book and it has not been discussed in detail.

[98] *Suresh Kumar Kaushal* v *Naz Foundation* (2014) 1 SCC 1.

rights, enforcement is poor or non-existent. The judiciary is often left to plead helplessness and put itself at the mercy of the executive to enforce its orders at least to some extent. Its refusal to come down heavily on the executive, even in contempt proceedings, for lack of enforcement adds to the instability.

The failure to recognize, implement, and sustain a culture of rights means that the discourse in India continues to be one of entitlements which the executive in its discretion bestows on people, raising the question if India is still a 'subject' society. While the success of electoral democracy ensures that claims of India being a 'subject' remain muted, the everyday impunity of the executive makes the case for bringing these muted voices to the surface. Judicial impunity, lack of consistent reasoning while exercising judicial discretion and judicial delay have added to the desperation of citizens, who have no one to turn to for effective enforcement of laws, contributing to the sense of lawlessness.

The rule of law hangs in the balance.

6

QUEST FOR REASON

A FAILING ENDEAVOUR?

Chapters 2 and 3 helped in identifying the salient features of the rule of law in India. The three broad principles of the Indian rule of law are:

1. The rule of law was part of the revolutionary changes that the Constitution heralded. The Indian rule of law goes beyond the substantive theories espoused by Western theorists and charts its own path. There is a strong emphasis on the realization of substantive rights and socio-economic goals which are sought to be included within the law.
2. The rule of law in India is accompanied by a constant search for reasonableness to achieve the balance between the need for discretion required to achieve constitutional goals and the propensity of the state to misuse its powers. This is an important facet of the rule of law in India given the state's central role in India society.
3. The power of judicial review, and its rapid growth since the adoption of the Constitution, has given might to the rule of law. Judicial review has primarily focused on bringing an element of reasonableness into the decision-making powers of the state. Reason (or at least the evidence of having applied reason) has become a mandatory requirement of every decision taken by the state.

THE FUNDAMENTAL ROLE OF REASON

The fulfilment of the hope that accompanied India's independence and the political goals enshrined in the Constitution required governance driven by rule of law. The rule of law that the Constituent Assembly consciously chose was different from that understood by Western liberal theorists. This choice was not driven purely by socialist considerations. It was a unique blend that did not have many parallels at the time. The state was to be at the centre of independent India and it was given vast powers to lead the country—politically, legally, socially, and morally. The state's powers were not to be limited by the theoretical restrictions imposed by Western theorists such as Dicey and Hayek. At the same time, the state could not be an entity of limitless powers that trampled upon or ignored the rights of the citizens.

The state would endeavour to achieve the political goals of the Constitution by utilizing its powers in an enlightened and visionary fashion, at the same time be restricted by the delicate balance of rights and powers in the Constitution. Perhaps it was the idealism of the time—or in fact, a pragmatism about the challenges to the rule of law in a discriminatory political, economic, and social structure of Indian society—that determined the powerful central role of the state. For the Constitution to work, the state not only had to follow the rule of law but also had to play a central and guiding role in leading society to follow the rule of law. This dual role of an all-pervasive state with enormous discretion and the responsibility of achieving justice and equality in a society, deeply unjust and unequal, demanded the understanding and practice of that elusive quality that many philosophers have strived to identify and promote—'reason', without the influence of individual passion or desire.

Reason was the tool that would enable India to break out of the shackles imposed by centuries of oppression, dogma, and inequality. Reason was to underpin the actions of the state in reforming the society and propel India to its desired destiny. The Constituent Assembly had argued, reasoned, and compromised for two years to achieve a delicate balance in the Constitution. Unlike Aristotle's reasoned judges, India expected every institution in the rule of law system—legislature, executive, and judiciary—to be filled with reasonable individuals who would then act reasonably in the service of the country and society. It was a huge leap of faith by the Constituent Assembly, but it was a conscious one made at a time when not making such a choice would have denied legitimacy to the Constitution.

The Constituent Assembly was certainly aware of the risks involved in its choice as discussed in Chapter III. Quite apart from the thin theory requisites of certainty, stability, generality, and predictability, the political choices made at the time of independence required the consistent application of reason for the rule of law to survive and establish deep roots in India. An arbitrary exercise of power in the pursuit of substantive goals would render the rule of law meaningless even if the thin theory formalities were met. Instead, reason was to be the hallmark of public political and legal discourse and guide institutional and individual decision-making. This reasoned decision-making was to be guided by the political ideals of the Constitution and not by majoritarianism, social and religious dogmas, or arbitrariness. Failure to do so would necessarily mean the failure of the rule of law.

Based on the discussions in Chapters 4 and 5, we can conclude that this burden of reason has largely not been met. The story of the rule of law in India is one of failure to consistently utilize reason in the making, implementation and interpretation of the law. This chapter examines this failure to utilize reason in greater detail, drawing upon the discussions in earlier chapters. The factors that have replaced reason are also identified and discussed.

LACK OF LEGALISM

Three decades ago, Upendra Baxi argued that legalism as a value had not been internalized in India. Baxi observed,

> But what is truly striking about India is the lack of respect for rules of law, not just by the people but also by those who make and enforce them. Legalism in the sense of a moral or ethical attitude prescribing that the legal rules ought to be followed because they are rules of conduct is not a dominant characteristic of Indian behaviour and culture. It is not that the Indian people, as distinct from their governors, are unable to develop a strong commitment to legalism. It is rather that both the rulers and the ruled collectively feel that most legal rules do not set any genuine moral constraints to behaviour motivated by strong personal or group interests. Rather, for the most part rules are seen to provide occasions for discretionary manipulation in

a complex process of social interaction which is genuinely instrumental or result oriented. Individual or group self-interest predominates over the value of following rules.[1]

Baxi further argues that nobody in India willingly follows the law. The privileged believe that they are above the law and the poor follow it only because they do not have a choice as the law is only enforced against them.[2] Baxi's arguments hold good even today, as the situation has changed, if at all, only for the worse. However, Baxi does not clearly distinguish between formal legalism and substantive legalism. By formal legalism, we mean procedures and rules that govern the decision-making process of the government, whether legislature, executive or judiciary. It is the existence of excessive formal legalism, coupled with the lack of substantive legalism that allows corruption and manipulation to flourish. Most challenges against legislative and executive action before the judiciary are also for violation of formal legalism.

There are innumerable cases in the law reports that evidence the judiciary's intervention in instances of non-compliance with formal legalism. The discussions in Chapter 3 show that the judiciary, through its intervention over the years, has tried to build in an element of reason and fairness into all formal decision-making procedures and has succeeded to some extent. The manipulation of discretion however continues unabated, and is at the root of most corruption. The lacunae of formal legalism can be addressed if the officers violating the rules and the people seeking exemption from the rules through corruption and manipulation are punished effectively and quickly. The ineffectiveness of the government in doing so has meant that the sense of lawlessness in society has heightened.

A simple example is the enforcement of traffic rules. Most Indian roads are experiments in chaos, with almost every single traffic rule being violated continuously. Violators are however not punished sufficiently to discourage further violations. Breach of traffic rules only results in a minor monetary fine, and even that can be avoided by bribing the police officer. There is no fear of penalty for breaching the

---

[1] U. Baxi, *The Crisis of the Indian Legal System* (New Delhi: Vikas Publishing, 1982), p. 5.

[2] Baxi, *The Crisis of the Indian Legal System*, pp. 6–8.

rules, thereby encouraging almost everyone to commit a breach. People who do follow the rules find no real benefit in terms of ease of movement or courtesy from other drivers on the street. It is a classic case of no reward for following the rules and no punishment for violating the rules. Consequently, violation of traffic rules has become the norm, creating an environment of lawlessness in addition to the chaos. This is an example of the law just sitting by limply, while those who defy it go free and those who seek its protection lose hope.[3]

The lack of respect for substantive legalism is the bigger problem. Substantive legalism refers to the rights, obligations and duties that are at the heart of any law. As discussed in Chapters 4 and 5, there is a serious lack of internalization of the rights philosophy in the Constitution by all the arms of the government. Kannabiran argues that the primary reason for the lack of substantive legalism is the failure to realize the fundamental difference between colonial rule and the rule of law in independent India. He observes,

> What resulted was a mere transfer of subjecthood to elected representatives and to the very courts entrusted with the task of protecting citizens' rights through the interpretation of the law in consonance with the spirit of the Constitution. This was a direct consequence of the fact that the institutions retained after attaining independence were not restructured with the vision necessary to discharge the trust bestowed on them by the people. All the laws passed by colonial rulers were retained, specifically the penal laws that had been devised to suppress the movement for independence. Thus, a legal structure designed to buttress colonial rule now became the legal structure of independent India.[4]

We examined in Chapter 5 the manner in which the rights discourse has turned into a discourse on exercise of power and discretion by the state and its officers, whether legislature, executive, or judiciary. Such reasoning about the exercise of power and discretion

---

[3] This is a modification of the statement of Judge Curtis Leigh who originally said, 'The law should not be seen to sit by limply, while those who defy it go free and those who seek its protection lose hope', cited in L. Seth, *Talking of Justice: People's Rights in Modern India* (New Delhi: Aleph Book Company, 2014), p. 190.

[4] K.G. Kannabiran, *The Wages of Impunity* (Hyderabad: Orient Longman, 2004), p. 65.

is nothing but reasoning mainly about formal legalism and not true substantive legalism, although at times it gives the impression of being a discourse about substantive legalism. Let us take the example of the debate on judicial independence in India. There is no doubt that judicial independence is an essential feature of the rule of law and the Constitution, because of the need to ensure the existence of an independent body to act as a check against the violation of citizens' rights by the executive and legislature. However, the debate on judicial independence has turned into a discourse primarily about the appointment of judges and misconduct of judges. The innovation of the collegium structure has meant that the appointment of judges is one of the best kept secrets in the country.[5] The very standards that the judiciary has demanded from other organs of government regarding appointments and exercise of power and discretion have miraculously ceased to apply in the matter of appointment of judges and in the monitoring of their conduct.[6] The reasoning used to justify judicial independence has turned into an exercise of increasing the power of a few judges at a certain point in time and not about the use of judicial independence to adjudicate disputes and deliver justice.

The incredible power usurped by the judiciary in the name of judicial independence is not being used for the enforcement of rights in a manner mandated by the Constitution as discussed in Chapter 5.

For substantive legalism to entrench itself in society, citizens' rights in day-to-day affairs need to be protected and enforced. Relief and succour has to be provided to a person who is the victim of a crime or is wrongfully arrested by the police; an unpaid vendor must be given the support of law to recover money due to him; a poor citizen running from pillar to post for minor social benefits ought to be relieved of that burden; an officer who misuses his office has to be punished when found guilty; and a person whose property has been encroached upon restored his possession with the full force of law. Only when these actions are taken

---

[5] The statement is attributed to Justice Ruma Pal, cited in Seth, *Talking of Justice*, p. 173.

[6] The most recent instance of this conduct is in relation to a former judge of the Karnataka High Court, K.L. Manjunath. Details are available at http://www.thehindu.com/multimedia/archive/02380/Justice_Manjunath__2380239a.pdf (accessed 24 April 2015).

successfully and continuously will substantive legalism entrench and sustain itself in society.

The failure of institutions to ensure substantive legalism is the principal reason for lack of internalization of legalism in society. Given the central role of the state in the Indian society, the failure of the institutions to reason and internalize substantive legalism has a ripple effect in society. This is further exacerbated by India's famed diversity and plurality, where there are always competing interests difficult to regulate even by an extremely efficient legal system. The failure to ensure substantive legalism encourages a culture of lawlessness and creates a vacuum which other organized groups such as the mafia,[7] unregulated panchayats, and various religious and caste institutions occupy, further threatening the rule of law. It is the failure to apply reason and ensure substantive legalism that is resulting in a culture of lawlessness and not vice versa as Baxi apparently suggests.

RULE OF LIFE VERSUS RULE OF LAW

Baxi's argument about the law being viewed in India as instrumental and result-oriented is correct. There is broad agreement in India that the rule of law needs to follow the rule of life in that the law needs to address the problems in society. As discussed in Chapters 2 and 3, politicians and judges have argued for this. Nehru said on various occasions that the rule of law and Constitution should not be rigid and should follow the rule of life. In the course of his speech on the Constitution (First Amendment) Bill, 1951, on 2 June 1951 Nehru said:

> A Constitution which is unchanging and static, it does not matter how good it is, but as a Constitution it is past its use. It is in its old age already and gradually approaching its death. A Constitution to be living must be growing; must be adaptable; must be flexible; must be changeable.... Therefore, it is a desirable and a good thing for people to realize that this very fine Constitution that we have fashioned after years of labour, is good in so far as it goes, but as society changes as conditions change, we amend it in the

---

[7] Suketu Mehta narrates an interview with a member of a local gang that specialises in 'settling' disputes which the judiciary cannot because of the severe delays that plague the judicial system. See S. Mehta, *Maximum City: Bombay Lost & Found* (New Delhi: Viking, 2004), pp. 190–2.

proper way. It is not like the unalterable law of the Medes and Persians that it cannot be changed, although the world around may change.[8]

Nehru's views are reflective of the broad political sentiment that changing situations demand change in laws and the Constitution, if required. However, the discussions in Chapter 4 show that the legislature has been unable to enact necessary laws from time to time. In respect of the Constitution, as of December 2015, there have been 99 successful amendments. Many other proposals have not succeeded or are still pending. For the instrumental view of law including the Constitution, to work, two conditions must always be met. First, any amendment must be supported by reasoned debate in the legislature. Failure to meaningfully engage in discussion and reasoning is nothing but majoritarianism and has no place in a democracy governed by the rule of law. The discussions in Chapter 4 clearly indicate that reason has gone missing from legislative action. This failure to reason is surprising because no political grouping in India has really challenged the constitutional goals, except for the concept of secularism by the Bharatiya Janata Party. Reasoning and discussions are therefore really only in respect of the methodology to achieve those goals and should not be avoided. India may as well be a society under a dictatorship if such reasoned debate does not necessarily precede any new law or an amendment to an existing law including the Constitution.

Second, no new law or amendment to an existing law or the Constitution should be able to undermine the political goals of the Constitution. The Constitution was made in pursuit of certain political goals enshrined in the preamble and cannot be turned into a document which violates those goals. This is the essence of the rule of law as a political ideal. The goals in the preamble are civilized society's unchanged goals from times immemorial. While it is theoretically possible that mankind may evolve into a different society where these goals are no longer required, on evidence so far, that seems unlikely. Amending the political goals constantly will undermine the rule of law, as citizens' rights are an integral part of the political goals of equality, liberty, fraternity, and justice.

[8] The quote is cited from paragraph 1.4.4 of the Report of the National Commission to Review the Working of the Constitution. The full report is available in S. Kashyap, *Constitution Making since 1950: An Overview* (New Delhi: Universal Law Publishing, 2004), pp. 243–520.

It is important to understand that this second condition is different from the basic structure doctrine developed by the Supreme Court. The basic structure doctrine states that certain essential features of the Constitution can never be amended by Parliament. The judiciary has the right to identify these essential features from time to time. The doctrine was necessitated because the judiciary took the fundamentally wrong position, in the author's view, that citizens only had those rights which were conferred on them by the Constitution. No rights were found to reside in the citizens outside of the Constitution. This necessarily meant that if the Constitution were amended to remove certain rights, citizens would not have those rights. Faced with this position canvassed by the Court itself in the initial decades after 1950 and a Parliament that went on a constitutional amendment spree, the Court, probably, had no choice but to come up with the basic structure principle in order to protect some of the fundamental goals of the Constitution.

If the Supreme Court had instead started on the basis that the Part III rights were merely a restriction on the state and not an exhaustive compendium of citizen's rights, there would perhaps be no need for the basic structure doctrine, as the arguments would then have turned on the nature of rights that citizens possessed in themselves as individuals and as constituents of the society from which the Constitution draws legitimacy. It was this reasoning that Justice Khanna relied upon in his dissent in the *Habeas Corpus* case even after the basic structure doctrine had been enunciated. Khanna's reasoning draws strength from the 'respect for the supreme value of human personality',[9] the rule of law and the political goals of society in enacting the Constitution rather than the mere language of the Constitution. The failure of the Court to consistently use this reasoning to derive, substantiate, and entrench the rights philosophy has meant that the Constitution has unwittingly emerged as a document that restricts the rights of citizens rather than enhance them. It has also created a conflict between the rule of law and the rule of life, whereas the Constitution wanted to harmonize the two using reason, with the goal of transforming India into a modern civilized society.

[9] These words were used by Justice Khanna in *ADM Jabalpur v Shivakant Shukla* (1976) 2 SCC 521 at pp. 747–50.

CONVERGENCE OF LEGALITY AND ILLEGALITY

As discussed in Chapter 5, the line between legality and illegality is very often blurred in India, giving the impression that there is no difference between them. There are two points of relevance in this context. First, the exercise of power and discretion by officials, combined with all-pervasive corruption, ensures that authorities treat both legal and illegal acts in the same manner. To get necessary permissions from the state, one has to pay the authorities irrespective of whether the underlying action is legal or illegal. Of course, the extent of payment may vary, but this is only a matter of degree rather than a conceptual difference. Consequently, there is no great benefit in an action being legal or illegal from the perspective of the citizen. Illegality is created or encouraged by the very persons entrusted with maintaining legality.

Second, enforcing the penalty for illegality and successfully protecting legality takes so long to achieve that it becomes incon-sequential in the short to medium term. While it is possible that illegality will be punished, more often than not it is a case of too little too late, thereby converting it into a semi-legal act. The practice by the legislature and executive of retrospectively converting illegality into legality (and sometimes changing the nature of legality itself) and the application of the prospective overruling principle to acts of illegality by the judiciary add to the convergence between the two. The argument here is not that there is no conceptual differ-ence between legality and illegality; on the contrary, all laws spell out this difference clearly. However, there is enough discretion pro-vided to the executive to make the difference irrelevant in practice. Legality and illegality therefore become only a state of mind rather than real actions that have consequences in the form of reward or punishment.

EQUALITY IN APPLICATION OF LAW

One of the fundamental requirements of the rule of law is that the law should apply equally to all citizens including the lawmakers, officers of the state, and the judiciary. The discussions in Chapters 4 and 5 show that this is not the case in India and, in practice, the law does not apply equally. Justice Krishna Iyer narrates the problem and consequences of this inequality in the application of law,

The greatest trauma of our times, for a developing country of urgent yet tantalising imperatives, is the dismal, yet die-hard, poverty of the masses and the democratic, yet graft-riven, way of life of power-wielders. Together they blend to produce gross abuse geared to personal aggrandisement, suppression of exposure and a host of other horrendous, yet hidden, crimes by the summit executives, pro tem, the para-political manipulators and the abetting bureaucrats. And the rule of law hangs limp or barks but never bites. An anonymous poet sardonically projected the social dimension of this systemic deficiency:

> The law locks up both man and woman
> Who steals the goose from off the common
> But lets the greater felon loose
> Who steals the common from the goose.[10]

Justice Iyer adds,

Leisurely justice, years after the long-drawn out commission proceedings, hardly carries conviction when man's memories would have forgotten the grave crimes, if any, committed and men's confidence in the rule of law would have been wholly demolished by seeing the top brass continuing to hold such offices despite credible charges of gross crimes of misuse. The common people watch the fortunes of these favoured species when they violate the norms of the criminal law and, if they are not punished forthwith, lose faith in the system itself. The cynicism about 'equal justice under the law' sours into 'show me the man and I will show you the law'.[11]

This inability to enforce the law against those in power not only undermines the rule of law and increases lawlessness, but also brings into question the legitimacy of the constitutional mechanism itself. It also furthers the impunity of people exercising power.

FAILURE TO REASON

The failure to reason appropriately within the framework of each institution—legislature, executive, and judiciary—has meant the differentiation envisaged by the Constitution between the legislature, executive and the judiciary has shrunk into a very narrow space. The major dialogue in each of these institutions is essentially about the scope, extent, and depth of its powers in contrast to the others.

---

[10] *In Re: Special Courts Bill 1978* (1979) 1 SCC 380, p. 440.
[11] *In Re: Special Courts Bill 1978*, at p. 442.

All the three institutions have either abandoned or become ineffective in performing their primary roles, as discussed in Chapters 4 and 5. While the legislators are unsuccessfully trying to perform the roles of the executive and judiciary in their constituencies, the executive and the judiciary are trying to perform the role of the legislature. The judiciary has formalized this in its recent order where it has invited comments from the public in connection with the reformation of the collegium's functioning.[12] None of them is equipped for these new roles. Further, the arbitrariness of one institution being replaced by the arbitrariness of another is no solution and results in chaos. It is important to take a hard look at the fundamental process of reasoning followed by each institution and its total lack of respect for the rule of law.[13] Course correction can only occur when along with the inter-institutional relationship, which is critical for the rule of law, the ethos and reasoning of each institution is examined and recalibrated.

VIOLENCE REPLACING REASON

The failure to apply public reasoning in decision-making has led to violence substituting reason in public discourse. Violence is inherent in the social, political, economic, and legal structures in India. This structural violence takes many forms and is most highly visible through corruption, police brutality, exploitation of the poor, lack of enforcement of welfare measures, regular financial frauds on the poor, continuance of untouchability, child labour, manual scavenging, and other inhuman practices, as well as the attack on free speech and expression in the form of moral policing. The list is endless. It appears that the state has accepted violence as the primary instrument of governance and public discourse. Not only has the state failed to successfully supress violence by private actors as is evident in the persistent practice of untouchability, child labour, and moral policing, the state and its instrumentalities themselves unleash violence in the form of police abuse and massive corruption.

[12] *Supreme Court Advocates on Record Association* v *Union of India* (2016) 6 SCC 1.

[13] G.E. Vahanvati, 'Rule of Law: The Seiges Within', in N.R.M. Menon (ed.), *Rule of Law in a Free Society* (New Delhi: Oxford University Press, 2008), pp. 22–31 at p. 31.

Violence is antithetical to the rule of law. Its presence means that the rule of law is absent.

WHERE DOES INDIA STAND?

These discussions, and those in Chapters 4 and 5, show that India fares very poorly even in terms of the thin theory rule of law requirements of stability, certainty, generality, and equality. The limited normative goals of thin theories, such as preventing arbitrariness in governmental actions, enhancing predictability of the law to enable citizens to plan their affairs and ensuring stability in society have not been consistently sustained in India to claim success in achieving them. The failure to do so means that India's legal structure has not fully entrenched itself to the exclusion of certain iniquitous social and economic structures that the Constitution specifically aspired to replace. India's societal and legal structure appears to fit squarely into the duality which Unger identifies.

If we examine the rule of law from a 1950's aspirational viewpoint, India has certainly achieved a great deal and against many hurdles and obstacles. Our electoral democracy has functioned, there have been no persistent attempts to replace democracy, and institutions of governance exist on paper. There is no denying the fact that the institutions do properly perform their role occasionally, renewing hope for the future. Considerable success has been seen in the area of social and economic development, although much more could have been achieved. However, 1950 is an invalid benchmark for measuring the rule of law. Anything that we have done since 1950 will always be considered a success given that 1950 was day zero for India as discussed in Chapter 2. The evaluation has to therefore be done on the basis of reasoned discourse in terms of institutional performance and the entrenchment of citizens' rights. Lawyers, political scientists, economists, sociologists, politicians, bureaucrats, and judges, irrespective of their ideological background, all agree that there is a crisis in India's rule of law.[14] They differ only in their state of mind—whether they show hope or despair!

[14] The views of Upendra Baxi, Arun Shourie, K.G. Kannabiran and Pratap Bhanu Mehta have been discussed in detail in the earlier chapters. They represent the ideological spectrum to the full extent. We can add to this list various other illustrious lawyers and judges who take similar positions. There is no view which asserts that we have a good and functioning rule of law mechanism.

But where does India really stand in its quest for reason and the rule of law? Ramachandra Guha claims India is a 'fifty-fifty' state.[15] The former cabinet minister P. Chidambaram observes, 'We have the choice to call ourselves a functional anarchy or a dysfunctional democracy. Of one thing, I am certain, we have miles to go before we can call ourselves a civil society under the Rule of Law.'[16]

Our discussions show that we indeed have miles to go. We are only hanging on to the rule of law dream by the tiniest of edges of our fingertips. We have to lift ourselves up and stand before we can begin walking the miles towards civil society.

[15] R. Guha, 'A Fifty-Fifty Democracy: Seven Threats to Freedom of Expression', *The Telegraph*, 24 January 2015, available at http://www.tele-graphindia.com/1150124/jsp/opinion/story_9857.jsp#.VSoYbvmUdOE (accessed 10 April 2015).

[16] P. Chidambaram, 'The Citizen and the Rule of Law', in N.R.M. Menon (ed.), *Rule of Law in a Free Society* (New Delhi: Oxford University Press, 2008), pp. 10–21 at p. 21.

INDEX

Note: *n* denotes footnote number, *t* table, and *f* figure.

ABOUT THE AUTHOR

Harish Byrasandra Narasappa is a lawyer based out of Bengaluru. He is the co-founder of Samvad Partners, a pan-Indian law firm. Narasappa's practice encompasses corporate law, mergers and acquisitions, dispute resolution, and social interest litigation. He is also the co-founder of DAKSH, a non-profit organization working towards accountability of state institutions.

Narasappa has a PhD and BA, LLB (Hons) from the National Law School of India University, Bangalore, India and a BCL from the University of Oxford, UK. He has co-edited the *State of the Indian Judiciary: A Report by DAKSH* and *Approaches to Justice: A Report by DAKSH*.